# Maximizing Benefits from IT Project Management

*From Requirements to Value Delivery*

# Advanced and Emerging Communications Technologies Series

## Series Editor-in-Chief: Saba Zamir

---

# Maximizing Benefits from IT Project Management

*From Requirements to Value Delivery*

José López Soriano

CRC Press
Taylor & Francis Group
Boca Raton London New York

CRC Press is an imprint of the
Taylor & Francis Group, an **informa** business

AN AUERBACH BOOK

CRC Press
Taylor & Francis Group
6000 Broken Sound Parkway NW, Suite 300
Boca Raton, FL 33487-2742

First issued in paperback 2019

© 2012 by Taylor & Francis Group, LLC
CRC Press is an imprint of Taylor & Francis Group, an Informa business

No claim to original U.S. Government works

ISBN-13: 978-1-4398-4156-3 (hbk)
ISBN-13: 978-1-138-38204-6 (pbk)

| Library of Congress Cataloging-in-Publication Data |
| --- |

Soriano, Jose Lopez.
  Maximizing benefits from IT project management : from requirements to value delivery / Jose Lopez Soriano.
    p. cm.
  Includes bibliographical references and index.
  ISBN 978-1-4398-4156-3 (alk. paper)
  1. Information technology--Management. 2. Information technology projects. 3. Project management. I. Title.

  HD30.2.S674 2012
  004.068'4--dc23                                                    2011041486

**Visit the Taylor & Francis Web site at**
**http://www.taylorandfrancis.com**

**and the CRC Press Web site at**
**http://www.crcpress.com**

# Contents

# Acknowledgment

The author acknowledges with thanks the invaluable editorial assistance and contributions of Gerald Hill to this book. Jerry is the principal of the Hill Consulting Group, and the author of *The Complete Project Management Office Handbook*, now in its second edition, and *The Complete Project Management Methodology and Tooklit*, both published by Auerbach Publications.

# Preface

For the last 30 years, indeed, since the beginning of my working life, I have been developing information systems for customers belonging to all markets and sectors of economic activity. Since 1979, I have worked in many different positions according to my level of experience and skills, from programmer to manager or principal of a business unit. I have worked on the creation of programs, applications, and information systems for public entities, private organizations, and government institutions in different fields and types of organizations.

My work has taken me from local industries to national enterprises, and even some international corporations. I have been involved with foundations and nonprofit organizations. I have also worked in banks, assurance companies, and financial institutions, as well as industries from quite diverse areas (cement, chemical, construction, food, infrastructure management, publishing, and automotive). My clients include manufacturers, distributors, and trade dealers. Throughout all the experiences in which I have participated, I have been involved in many projects, playing different roles. I have worked in the analysis of organizational problems, designed relevant solutions, and have developed, implemented, and maintained those solutions in operation over periods of years.

In these 30 years, I have seen the technological waves from the front line, in such a direct manner that I feel I have personally participated as one of the actors in this evolving story. I have seen the way information systems have been introduced across a wide variety of business entities. In the long period of my involvement, I have watched as the profession has changed, while the clients and their problems did the same. I participated with clients in adapting solutions to new and emerging requirements. I have also had the opportunity to identify and evaluate these changes and trends in information technology over time through an introspective exercise of auto criticism.

I have watched as the profession has evolved, as have the needs of customers, and I have worked with the technology, equipment, and tools at our disposal over this time to build the solutions demanded by these customers.

Today's perspective has little to do with the outlook I had when I was a young man trying to launch a career in this world in 1979. The outlook I have today has become much more complex, intricate and in some ways difficult, to the point that I think it is worth making a brief review of how this evolution has occurred as a means to better understand where we are and what future developments will look like in the coming years. This review is presented, to a large extent, in the introductory chapters of the *Concepts Section* (Chapter 1).

Despite the sustained changes and transformation generally experienced in the world of technology, professional services associated with information technology have generally remained unchanged and constant over time. Therefore, the technical practices surrounding the introduction of computer systems, the creation of associated programs and applications, and the development and deployment of business solutions are factors that also will be considered in this publication.

All in all, the purpose of this manuscript is to examine precisely a systematic and simplified approach to devising and implementing the practices needed for selecting and evaluating IT projects in organizations. We want to consider ways of ensuring that these projects meet their established goals and objectives. Furthermore, we need to manage our approach to using the project management life cycle, keeping in mind important processes for things like evaluating alternatives, specifying and managing project scope, dealing properly with project scope and technical changes, and defining what is included and what is excluded in each project in order to reconcile the forecast and final results of the project.

In the course of this manuscript, we will examine these facets of information technology work, as we also consider the appropriateness and use of project management methods and system development life-cycle steps.

*Chapter 1*

# Reflections on the Current State of IT Project Management

There have been a number of changes in our society in recent years, and it is appropriate to mention a few because they could become determining factors in changing our business landscape, thereby affecting information technology and important information systems operations. We must be aware of changes such as progressive globalization; the consequent elimination of barriers for commerce and international movements of people, capital and products; the increased competition between companies from different world regions; and an accelerated technological innovation that is pushing up productivity and competition in all industries and economic sectors. These are factors that contribute to an environment of growing business complexity and extraordinary difficulties in the management of today's enterprises.

## Investing in Information Technology

The emergence of a small number of companies as prominent, but unsuspected leaders in their respective markets, as well as the disclosure and dissemination of some of their practices that were key to achieving this success, have prompted admiration in other companies that have recognized the clarity of their vision and strategy. In the process of building new business empires, it appears that the key factors of successful emerging companies include a firm commitment to information systems.

1

Accordingly, investments in today's businesses are focused on the design, development, implementation, and maintenance of information systems, in an attempt to replicate and emulate the success of leading companies. These investments are growing every year and are reaching astronomical figures, without showing any indication of a definite limit.

The consulting firms, technology companies, and providers of services that are needed for the ongoing spread of information technology are becoming larger, year on year, and many have become international in scale. In some cases, their investments have resulted in the creation of global companies with economic results that are the envy of many organizations from all economic sectors around the world. However, in too many cases, this increase in revenue and benefits is not always matched by a similar trend in technical credibility, corporate reputation, and professional recognition. On the contrary, the confidence and respect that have been held by these companies in the past are deteriorating rapidly and continuously as a result of their failed and poor performances on various projects.

It is clear, therefore, that investment in information technology should include investment in an improvement in project performance in implementing information technology solutions.

## Examining IT Project Performance

There are a variety of reasons for this deterioration in the public image of such companies, as well as in the technology sector as a whole. One reason lies in corporate mergers carried out from a myopic perspective, without any consideration about clients or employees. Another reason may be found in far-reaching mistakes in marketing strategies or policies that have sent confusing and contradictory messages to the market. However, above any other consideration we can highlight, there is one prominent, basic reason that should be considered—the fact that there are a significant number of projects that, despite the money, time, and resources spent on them, have failed to reach a successful conclusion.

It is important that we make clear from the beginning that any project could face difficulties that threaten the goal it is attempting to achieve. In fact, most professionals agree that all projects will experience some level of difficulty that could interfere with the project's progress or outcome. For example, sooner or later, projects will need some particular resource that is unavailable, encounter unexpected budget restrictions or increasing project costs, or have the project scope slide away from what was originally intended. However, the simple fact that projects will face such difficulties is not the primary concern. What does matter is how project managers and their teams react to project difficulties—how they respond to each situation that threatens the progress and successful outcome of their project.

The difference between those companies that are successful in project management and those that are not can be seen in how they have positioned their project teams to react to specific project difficulties or to a project that has generally become a problem. These circumstances provide the chance for corporate values, principles, and culture to play a decisive role in the resolution of project difficulties. It is an opportunity for the organization to show that the "beautiful words" they use, such as *commitment, team, respect,* and *support,* are principles that are fully embedded in the corporate culture, and not just words used in marketing speeches and advertising campaigns.

The number of projects terminated before reaching their goals, either because of cancellation, abandonment, or otherwise by executive decision, is an increasingly important consideration, as is the amount of money invested in them. However, the prematurely closed or incomplete project is just the visible tip of a huge iceberg that lurks beneath the surface (Figure 1.1). These "unsuccessful" projects are the visible portions of a much larger problem that lies beyond a superficial glance. The larger problem is that unsuccessful projects are undermining the credibility of a key sector of the current economy and are affecting the development of our businesses, institutions, and even society in general.

There are also an increasing number of so-called "successful" projects that are being delivered with changes that modify or even nullify intended project outcomes in terms of deadlines, budget, and scope when compared with the original planning. The effects of such changes might be considered acceptable, but in certain markets they are simply overwhelming.

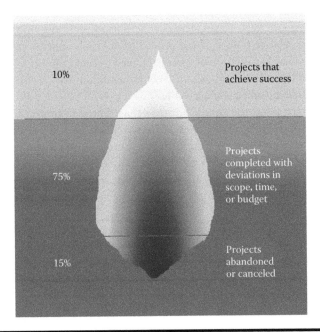

**Figure 1.1  The iceberg of project results.**

Some estimates from independent organizations dedicated to the education and certification of professionals in project management indicate a very low project success rate. For example, the APM Group reflects on this in their introduction to their course for PRINCE2 certification. They present figures that suggest that as many as 90% of projects can be labeled as unsuccessful. That means that only 10% of projects are finishing successfully.

## Dealing with IT Project Performance Outcomes

Suppliers and customers have a common interest in finding a formula that will achieve some semblance of project success. They need to find solutions for achieving specified project goals and objectives as prominent indicators of project success. They also need to develop the means to conclude each project with some dignity as a way to save organizational credibility and maintain personal professionalism within their respective organizations.

Projects that are deemed unsuccessful can usually be analyzed to identify the underlying causes. Circumstances such as underutilizing established standard procedures, dismissing the process for managing scope expansion, or avoiding necessary restatements of the project's objectives are often found to be contributing factors. At the same time, however, we often see attempts made to save the reputations of the executives and project managers responsible to the client organization. This situation can sometimes seriously damage the organization's capability in project management. When managers take actions to avoid the embarrassment of recognizing the relative failure of any project under their control, they essentially deny the analysis and evaluation of what happened to cause project failure. In turn, they are unable to make a diagnosis and recommendation to prevent the repetition of the cited problems on future occasions.

When this happens, the conditions that contributed to project failure remain concealed and hidden from the eyes of management and key decision makers, and continue to spread adversity on subsequent projects and throughout the project management environment. Unfortunately, the frequency with which these conditions occur is prone to increasing, making some customers and suppliers consider this condition to be simply inevitable when starting an information systems project.

There is also another type of project failure to consider. This relates to projects that, although completed within established deadlines, within the established budget and within the established functional scope, do not meet the expectations placed on them by the client organization. When client expectations are not satisfied, the client often sees its investment as one that does not provide the intended benefits. The client therefore perceives the project to be a failure accompanied by a significant dose of deception and frustration as a natural consequence.

This type of project failure appears to represent a large majority of the "failed" projects that can be observed in many companies and organizations and across industries. Some career IT professionals will naturally oppose the client's perception of project failure (based on client expectations) and attempt to provide explanations to sway the client's viewpoint.

However, if we listen to explanations from those professionals, we can appreciate that such statements are usually based on the consideration of two simple parameters: time and budget. These two parameters are project dimensions that are defined and measured for virtually all projects, and they do contribute to evaluating the success or failure of a technology project. However, this puts aside other considerations such as added value and benefits that the client expects to receive with the completion of the project. For the client, these considerations are the very reason that the necessary investment has been made. IT professionals need to consider these factors in the ongoing process of project management.

## Selecting IT Projects

All entities, public or private, select their IT projects for a particular reason, and do so with the hope that the introduction of new information systems will enable their organization to implement a desired change, such as transforming its structures, working procedures, and ways of doing business other than those currently in play. With this change, the organization seeks to respond to the challenges that are expected to arise in the future.

Although the project selection process may sound ethereal and vague, we can be sure that it is not. In essence, the reasons why an organization begins a project can be reduced to two basic and elementary reasons. The first is to provide opportunities for increased revenue associated with IT system implementation. This includes

- Improving financial returns on IT investments in the organization
- Placing products in new markets
- Improving customer assessment of their products
- Increasing the number of clients
- Selling more, selling at a better price, or just achieving better sales recognition
- Achieving a better image by current and potential customers

The second reason is to provide opportunities for reducing costs associated with IT system implementation. This includes

- Identifying and evaluating overall project costs to ascertain where cost reductions can be made in the investment without being detrimental to the project (including costs associated with project materials)
- Reviewing time and schedule constraints to ensure adequate and appropriate durations have been associated with each specified project activity and task

- Examining resource needs against project performance requirements to ensure properly qualified personnel are devoted to the operation (and to avoid the use of overqualified or underqualified team members that affect estimated costs)
- Managing the allocated amount and timing for the dispersal of funds that will be committed to the project effort as a means of managing cash flow

Unfortunately, in too many cases, the project team does not consider these factors when reviewing projects goals and objectives and when preparing project plans. This may be due to the use of methodologies and project management tools that were conceived and designed using a very different paradigm than experienced by the current business environment.

## Reviewing the Evolution of Project Management Practices

Many early project management processes and tools were created by organizations serving the defense industry, which produced new computing systems as required, unique military vehicles and equipment, and strategic and tactical weapon systems. These products were needed, for example, as a means to stay ahead in the arms race between Western and Soviet blocs during most of the second half of the twentieth century. In those times, project deadlines were particularly critical, as projects represented vital competition. It was important to arrive first at every project milestone as a means to maintain the capability to contain threats to the territorial domain, provide strategic superiority, and, ultimately, assure world peace. To a large extent, the need to produce relevant defense systems and equipment in a timely manner was more important than the cost incurred.

Subsequently, the use of these tools and techniques evolved and entered the world of private enterprise. In this new project management environment, business rules differed significantly from those in the public sector, with the motivation changed to consider overall project performance and its impact on business (and no longer just the vital order of milestone accomplishment); companies, finding themselves subject to economic vicissitudes, developed a growing concern about the cost and more believable objectification of project management success.

In contrast, concern for customer benefits has been addressed only recently, probably linked to a number of reasons connected with the history of project management. In the early years, when project management appeared as a management discipline, the purpose and benefits were so apparent to all that customer benefits were not addressed to a greater extent. After all, having a new submarine could mean the difference between the enemy daring to start an armed conflict or not, so all other considerations were somewhat superfluous.

In today's business environment, the paradigm is changing. For example, the difference between the computing capacity required to meet the needs of customers and the capacity actually available within cost constraints is prompting the examination of broader considerations for the successful delivery of information system projects. The objective fact is that today we face a new reality that has surprised many IT professionals. Some of the roles and relationships between different project participants and the customer have changed, and are becoming much more demanding and critical of the consultants used for system design and development. Customers today are asking to receive a real contribution, sometimes a contribution that is valued in excess of the price paid for external services.

## Understanding the Emerging Role of Information Technology

The role of information systems is changing. Just a few years ago, information technologies were only part of the enterprise infrastructure, generally providing a resource available to management to help them oversee personnel costs and respond more quickly to business transactions. Information technology was far from being considered a competitive weapon or a strategic management tool. The information that was managed was primarily an element of control over the production process, and management would simply capture key data points to assist them in their management efforts.

Today, the scope of information management has changed dramatically, and information technology is probably one of the major strategic weapons used by companies to achieve and maintain a competitive or even a leadership position in the market. With the proper use of information technology, there is more comprehensive support for business management and associated transactions and data management. In addition, information technology contributes to the ways in which the business itself develops. This results from having the information and knowledge that these technologies offer relative to managing operations, customers, and the market. All in all, information technology influences the business environments to which it is introduced.

This trend is becoming more significant and will continue to develop increasingly in the coming years. The progress in integrating products and attributes of information will change the markets and how they do business.

## Finding New Solutions to Ongoing Issues and Problems

There are a number of aging issues and practices that need to be examined and updated to address today's technical processes and associated project and business interests. Consider the following:

■ The methodologies, tools, and techniques available for managing projects on information technology were designed 20, 30, and 40 years ago, and are simply obsolete for delivering the value demanded by clients today. In a sense, many practises have completed their life cycle. They have helped solve many management problems in a wide range of organizations and issues, but now they are inefficient or at least insufficient to address the new problems that arise today.

■ There is a general trend to increase the size of projects until they reach the scale of "megaprojects," which are similar to the massive effort used when constructing the pyramids. Responsible project leaders should consider ways to divide larger projects into subprojects that have sufficient size and complexity to be considered as projects in themselves. This makes the work efforts more specific and more manageable, and, as a result, project outcomes will become more predictable.

■ There is an increasing trend to define global frameworks in which contracted projects have their dimensions progressively extended and their scope expanded as a means to present the total project solution at early stages in planning, without fully defining the problems to be solved and identifying the specific work to be performed. Methods for this type of project planning should be reviewed openly as soon as possible, and better processes should be developed and implemented with total solution planning.

■ Practices for project selection in organizations need to be reviewed and updated to ensure that project and business management interests are considered in a comprehensive manner. In particular, the project definition development process should be sufficiently robust as to ascertain the success or failure of pending projects with some certainty. Processes that provide for an adequate review of the project definition (including the questioning of critical assumptions and constraints contained in the project definition) should be formulated and used before closing the definition stage of every project.

■ Project management practitioners must retrieve and incorporate principles generally accepted and used by business organizations in the management of problems. In particular, every project should be examined to determine if it can be broken down into more simple efforts, as a means to facilitate the provision of higher value-added solutions for organizations.

Thus, the purpose of this book is precisely to provide a systematic and simple approach to this way of selecting and evaluating projects to ensure that these meet the established goals and to make extensive this approach to the whole project life cycle, always keeping in mind the analysis of costs and benefits when identifying and evaluating alternatives, considering changes, or determining the scope and defining what is included and what is excluded in order to reconcile the forecast and the final result.

*Chapter 2*

# The Evolution and Influence of Knowledge Management

Any examination of information technology warrants consideration of factors that have contributed to the evolution of the information systems that we use today. Prominent among those factors is the consideration of the emerging discipline of knowledge management. This discipline provides for some important peripheral processes that are readily used in conjunction with information systems that have been implemented across industries.

We will introduce this discussion by first reviewing the societal influences on the evolution of information systems. Then we will examine topics related to pertinent aspects of knowledge management.

## Getting to the Era of Knowledge Management

Human development relative to individuals and as a society has been a continuous process and really exciting for those with interest in the stages of human development. However, the contributing economic and social developments of our civilization have been severely constrained by the type and nature of the resources used to exert influence on its progress. That is to say, it is the mindset of people having social influence that determines how much and what type of progress is made.

To that end, we can talk about the early agricultural or industrial society, where dominance was attributed to the ownership of land and animals or the availability of equipment and facilities, along with the capital needed to operate them. These signs of our riches and the value we placed on them have been stated over time and throughout history. Historically, we can verify that for centuries the possession and control over land, cattle, or natural resources of any type is more or less what has determined the wealth and power of a man, a family, a social group, or even one nation over another.

The so-called agricultural age was replaced with the advent of the industrial society, when the advantage of holding such possessions was no longer important. Rather, in the industrial age, it became more important to hold capital, either as a quantity of money or the holding of financial value taken in the form of credit, in the ownership of production facilities and machinery, or simply in the use of a process or industrial patent that provided a personal or business advantage for the individual or group that owned it.

This transition to new value factors within society is sometimes referred to as the industrial revolution. This period led to the radical transformation of society and to the emergence of important migrations, worldwide, in which people fled the countryside to come to cities seeking industrial and manufacturing jobs that allowed them to improve their living conditions and increase income from their work.

Then we saw the rise of the post–industrial age and the emergence of a knowledge society. When we speak of a knowledge society, we are referring to a modern society. We are assuming that the differential and dominant factor required for business success in a modern organization, or for individual success from a personal perspective, is the ability to generate, establish, and disseminate knowledge that will effectively differentiate and support the professional progress of the organization or the individual.

However, if we try to specify when this new knowledge society started and determine a date for its beginning, we cannot clearly identify a specific period in which that "knowledge revolution" happened. It is difficult to identify specific dates for the transition from one era to another, from one paradigm to another, but we may be able to explain the changes in several ways:

- One possible explanation lies in the intrinsic difficulty of clearly defining historical periods until after that period passes or sufficiently advances to allow us to gain some historical perspective. In turn, we can then study the changes that occurred in a slow and subtle manner. This explanation would be a first choice, and it is one that allows us to assume we are fully engaged in a knowledge revolution.
- Another possible explanation is that the current era is not actually a knowledge revolution, but rather a superposition of one social progress model over another, which enhances rather than replaces that which existed and continues to coexist thereafter.

- Finally, it may be considered that the much acclaimed knowledge society we identified is not as real as we thought. It is possible that we were having an illusion that our mind had built for us, a virtual world such as those sometimes depicted in films.

This new social model known as the knowledge society is probably just the expression of an aspiration shared by a large majority of professionals in our society who are looking for a new model to recognize their use of knowledge management across the variety of technical disciplines that they represent.

## Three Components of Knowledge Management

An examination of knowledge management concepts inherently begins with the identification of its three primary components: data, information, and knowledge. These three components are closely and intimately related, and they are often used interchangeably as synonyms; however, they are not. Rather, they are distinct components that should never be confused, because they represent different stages of development of the same raw material, with the different stages having their own distinct utilities and values.

We define the concepts of data, information, and knowledge as three different states that are progressive and cumulative in their production, their differences, their relationships to one another, and their intended applications. These component differences can be examined in Figure 2.1.

## Using Data

We will begin our examination of knowledge management components at the most basic level of this pyramid, with the stuff that creates the other levels—data. Data are merely the symbolic representations of an attribute or a measurable characteristic of an entity, person, or thing. Data are often represented by numerical values, alphabetical descriptions, or algorithms.

Data alone have no semantic value and no sense. Data are a fundamental form of information used to carry out calculations in arithmetic or logic operations. The results from those calculations allow decisions to be made. This use of data is the basis of any information system and is essential in any scientific discipline.

So, if we take any object, say a geometric figure such as a cube, data are used to describe the different characteristics that define that figure. The color, the lengths of the sides, and the material it is made of are examples of data associated with the figure. In turn, we can operate on the data using an algorithm or formula to derive additional data or even to obtain information such as the volume of the cube. To calculate this information, we will apply relevant data (e.g., the lengths of the

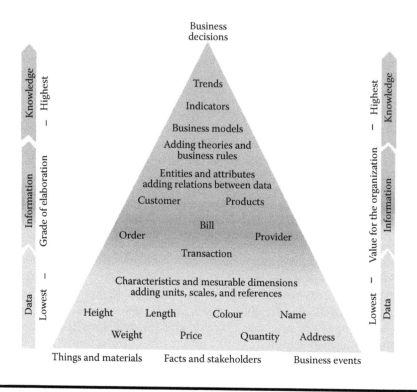

**Figure 2.1 Data, information, and knowledge.**

sides of this cube) to a geometric algorithm that calculates cube volume. In this instance, when we consider a regular parallelepiped, we can obtain its volume by multiplying the measures of its dimensions (height, length, and width) using a geometry axiom that tells us that a cube is a regular parallelepiped with dimensions of length, width, and height that are equal.

## Using Information

The resulting information represents a related data set that describes the form of a unique figure with its own meaning. In other words, the data are integrated and processed in a way that generates the information necessary to facilitate decisions and adopt the best course of action required by our everyday reality, and to ultimately produce knowledge.

In general, information is a very common and elementary asset. Information is also sometimes an intangible and very volatile asset. Its utility and value are greatly influenced by the time it took to acquire it and its readiness for use. Information has a defined internal structure and can be rated on different aspects, such as:

- *Meaning or semantic for the recipient.* What does this particular information mean to the receiver? Why should the receiver respond to it?
- *Relative importance to the recipient.* What could be the impact to the receiver? Is this information an issue that is important to the receiver?
- *Effectiveness on the space–time dimension with respect to the receiver.* Is the information current? Is the information outdated and thereby outside the interests of the receiver?
- *Validity for the recipient.* Is the information valid for the receiver? What are the origin, reliability, and trust generated? Can it be misguided, inaccurate, or simply false?
- *Value for the recipient.* How useful is this information to the receiver?
- *Form and presentation.* Do the different ways, shapes, and forms of presenting information (e.g., numerical, alphanumerical, graphical, imagery, or verbal) influence how the information is received and treated by the recipient?

Information compilation, collection, preparation, and elaboration always seek to achieve some general and logical objectives:

- To increase awareness of the receiver about the environment, on the state of matter, or on any aspect that is studied in relation to the information provided
- To provide essential information items to individuals who must make qualified decisions on certain matters taking in consideration many parameters and a changing and uncertain environment that values could be variable
- To facilitate the preparation of evaluation and decision rules that offer control mechanisms for use by third-party application protocols requiring precise and timely information input and interpretation

Regarding this last point, it can be seen how information is used as a route to develop explicit knowledge. Information must be carefully prepared before it can be used and made available to others; however, information, by itself, does not convey knowledge. Rather, it is the individual's subjective experience that allows information to be assessed, given meaning, and organized in such a manner that turns it into knowledge.

# Using Knowledge

Knowledge is the state in which someone knows something by virtue of the meaning that is individually or commonly ascribed to the information that comprises that knowledge. It is the whole of the content that is known, and it represents the input of individual thinking, the consideration of group interpretations, and the influence of cultural wealth of society as a whole. The most common methods for acquiring knowledge are experimentation, observation, and study, all endeavors that promote the expansion of human thought and understanding. Knowledge is a relative state, as it represents the meaning of information that is subject to interpretation by individuals, groups, and societies, who determine what is considered known or not known.

The meaning ascribed to information also allows us to develop important conclusions about its users and their social values and organization. In the IT environment, analysis about the codes used and data sets utilized can offer important details about the patterns of thought used in that setting. The skills and abilities deployed in the generation and application of codes and symbols contribute to the particular meaning of information, which may constitute a true common language for those who routinely use that information. Conversely, knowledge can be quite cryptic to an outsider (or simply the uninitiated) who is not a member of the "community" involved in establishing particular meanings for the information under consideration.

As we gain valuable information about the level of knowledge, we can also evaluate the social development of peoples of the past such as those who lived in the Egyptian classical period or pre-Columbian American peoples. Looking at knowledge at a much closer level also enables us to obtain an assessment about the level of sophistication of some groups and communities that exist in our society, and who have their own distinct language. This would include, for example, unique individual users of information and knowledge such as nuclear scientists, physicists, mathematicians, biologists, and physicians.

Much of the knowledge we have today comes from science, which is the main type of knowledge source and the main generator of knowledge through the use of scientific methods and systematic efforts to obtain information as a result of experimentation and testing of theoretical statements that are evaluated and analyzed in light of the results.

However, another type of knowledge is represented by the "know-how" related to specific bodies of knowledge. This knowledge is characterized by an improvement or increase in skill and ability that results, not from learning or interpreting information, but from repetition and practice using information that is inherently known as a means to hone skills and abilities.

All in all, knowledge results from processing information, and information is derived from manipulation and calculation applied to basic data. Knowledge is important because it is acquired by using one or more cognitive processes: perception, memory, experience, reasoning, teaching and learning, and testimony of third parties that all contribute to knowledge formation.

## Using Knowledge Management

Any society acquires, preserves, and transmits a large amount of knowledge through language. In particular, writing is a system that permits the transmission of knowledge without the transmitter and receiver having to coincide in time and space. Writing facilitates the accumulation of information and the dissemination of knowledge. The same is true of other arrangements; after writing, the use of computers, information technologies, and data communications have become important means for storing and conveying knowledge.

We may also analyze knowledge with regard to the ways in which it can be acquired, handled, and distributed. Consider the following aspects of using knowledge management.

## Knowledge Procurement Procedures

- "A priori" knowledge can be innate or learned, but, in any case, it is independent of any experience and is perceived as universal and necessary truth. "Water extinguishes fire" and "Night will follow day" are common expressions of this kind of knowledge.
- "A posteriori" knowledge is derived from experimentation of the senses, which may or may not have been preceded by a theoretical prediction and is the result of an experiment that is designed and controlled or fortuitous. "The height of a tree or building can be measured by its shadow on the floor" could be an idea demonstrating this kind of knowledge.

## Knowledge Storage Procedures

- Knowledge can be stored as encoded information that captures needed details so as not to lose any information.
- Non-codified knowledge is difficult to express explicitly and unequivocally, but it can also be stored by alternate information storage means.

## Knowledge Extent and Spread Procedures

- Knowledge can be made public if it is easy to share or is the result of a process oriented its creation or dissemination that is open to the entire community of users.
- Alternately, knowledge may be personal or private when it has been prepared by an individual, and this knowledge will eventually form the basis of public knowledge, but only after it has been shared between the original preparer and other members of the relevant social or user environment.
- We can also speak of local knowledge as the knowledge developed around a particular geographical area, rather than the global knowledge that is formed and transferred through geographically separated networks or communities.

## Knowledge Nature and Genesis Procedures

- Knowledge can be oriented in reference to the causal relationships between predefined concepts.
- Knowledge can be oriented and axiomatic when it comes to explanations of final causes of phenomenon or a priori explanations of events.

## Knowledge Transmission and Codification Procedures

- Explicit knowledge can be transmitted from one individual to another through some formal means of communication.
- Tacit or implied knowledge is difficult to formalize and communicate because it is normally rooted in personal experiences or mental models and schemas with significant difficulty of replication.

Finally, we have cultural knowledge, which will be named according to the ways in which relevant groups of individuals, collectives, and organizations use associated terms, classifications, and procedures that have undergone internal agreement.

*Chapter 3*

# Perspectives on the History of Computing

Imprinted in their genetic heritage, human beings have a dual focus developed to satisfy their need for security, both as individuals and as a species. The first aspect relates to their status as social beings who enjoy the company and proximity of others, while also having among their most basic and characteristic features the tendency to be competitive in all fields and areas of life.

Individuals have therefore always sought the opportunity to be measured and compared with others in order to know, set up, and claim what is considered to be their place in society as it develops. Individuals have compared their personal strengths, abilities, wealth, and possessions, and this has created the need for basic concepts of quantity and value.

This long-felt basic human need in our ancestors is the origin of the birth of conceptual tools that make use of numbers and mathematics, which represents the first stage in the development of the information systems with which individuals might register, calculate, evaluate, and compare the distributions of goods, property, money, and community support. As societies became more complex and the wealth that a man could accumulate began to increase, so did the requirements for information management. In turn, man used his creativity to develop increasingly sophisticated tools to aid him in this work.

If we unite this basic need for information management with the volition to communicate this information beyond the natural limits of the individual action, we have before us the primal motivations that prompted the creation of information technologies and communications.

These technologies are born from the natural human desire to seek ways, procedures, equipment, and tools to aid in performing routine and repetitive work more effectively across a variety of activities. The technology of information management was created in such a manner.

Thus, since the beginning of history, man has sought ways to develop safer and more efficient routine activities for the management of personal assets and, by extension, public affairs and assets.

Over time, the emerging technology provided a variety of instruments to enable people to get the most from their social and economic affairs, with more security and guarantees, and with an effort that was affordable and compatible with their other activities. Within this framework of general development and steady technological progress lies the unique and original inventions we now know as information technology and knowledge management.

From the outset, man has created, developed, and produced machines that are becoming ever more powerful and sophisticated. They have been designed and developed to facilitate new working methods. Such developments have yielded important progress in the way information is managed, and in the creation of new and improved applications for information management. Technology components are continuously evolving to meet new and more demanding information management requirements.

It is clear, therefore, that the development of information technology and communications has been taking place over time, through a succession of steps, sometimes critical, sometimes revolutionary, and sometimes in the form of subtle improvements, but evolving and always drawing and building on the knowledge accumulated so far. This development is outlined in Figure 3.1 with the related concepts and details presented in this chapter.

With the perspective gained from the passage of time, we can observe the whole evolution process as a series of successive stages, in the form of waves or generations of development. Each stage has features that both define it and distinguish it from other stages.

Although I do not wish to provide too much historical information, I consider it important to introduce a superficial perspective or recap of the development of information technologies and knowledge management, because I am convinced that this knowledge will contribute to a better understanding of the current stages of technology evolution and more informed speculation on what could comprise the future stages of the evolution of the technology.

# Background of Computers and Information Systems

The development of our current understanding of information technology began after the World War II as a result of the need to control the Allied armies

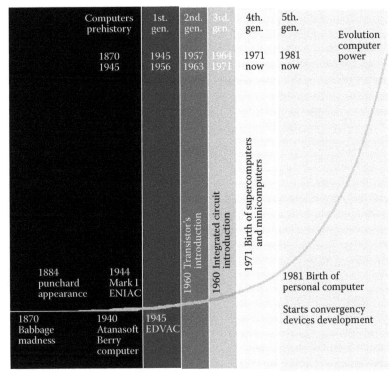

| Computers prehistory | 1st. gen. | 2nd. gen. | 3rd. gen. | 4th. gen. | 5th. gen. | Evolution computer power |
|---|---|---|---|---|---|---|
| 1870 1945 | 1945 1956 | 1957 1963 | 1964 1971 | 1971 now | 1981 now | |

Evolution of Computer Processing Power

**Figure 3.1  Evolution of computing power.**

and to manage the tremendous logistical requirements of the powerful supply network to the great military machinery deployed around the world. However, its origins date as far back as theoretical knowledge.

Among the most illustrious historical inventions and generally accepted precursors of information technology and modern communication is the "analytical engine" created by the British mathematician and engineer Charles Babbage (1792–1871). He was an eccentric man of questionable character, but he spent much of his life working to build and complete his extremely complex machinery with a purpose that was not always understood in his time. He attempted to produce an instrument that would enable the automated processing of information, a concept that was not entirely appreciated, leading to the machine being known popularly as the "madness of Babbage."

If this visionary scientist had completed his machine, it would have allowed data to be input using punched cards, a memory unit or data storage, an arithmetic unit or mill that would produce the required calculations and operations, and a unit data output process based on a printing system. Control over operations would have been based on sequential control by a program with a calculation accuracy of up to 20 digits. In other words, Charles Babbage had designed a prototype of the modern computer that contained all the elements considered essential based on the technology concepts that continued in use until the 1970s. Babbage was a century ahead of his time, but this only served to earn him the inconvenience and problems implicit in his social environ at that time.

Another generally recognized contribution to the current state of information technology and knowledge management was the work of Lady Augusta Ada Lovelace (daughter of Lord Byron, the famous romantic poet), a collaborator of Charles Babbage. It was in honor of Lady Lovelace that the ADA programming language developed by the Department of Defense of the United States of America was named. She was a woman ahead of her time but saw her gender stop her from having the recognition and prestige she deserved.

Ada Lovelace was a brilliant mathematician, who managed to correct some of the errors contained in the work of Charles Babbage. She also invented a new and original alternative approach to the design of the necessary programs using punch cards. For these contributions to the work of Babbage, many consider her to be the first computer programmer in history. However, after the death of Babbage, the development of computers was discontinued and was dormant for a long period of time.

Hermann Hollerith (1860–1929), a United States national, retrieved previous work and designed a machine that worked with punch cards, which he patented in 1884. This machine came to be known as the tabulating machine.

In 1896, Hermann Hollerith created a company called the Tabulating Machine Company to exploit the manufacture of these machines. It was sold to Charles R. Flint in 1910, and in 1911 it was merged with two other companies to form the Computing Tabulating Recording (CTR) Corporation. In 1914 it was acquired by Thomas Watson; in 1924 its name was changed and it became known thereafter as International Business Machines (IBM).

The system used by Hollerith was subsequently perfected by James Legrand Powers, also an American, and by the Norwegian engineer Frederick Bull (1882–1925). However, the functionality of these machines continued to be very basic and primary, and was based on primitive technology and an essentially mechanical nature.

In 1937, Harvard professor Howard Aiken set up the goal of building an automatic calculating machine. He developed technology that combined electrical and mechanical technologies with Hollerith punch card techniques to extend the capabilities offered so far by these machines.

Surrounded by a number of graduate students and engineers from the IBM Company, Aiken achieved his goal. The project was completed in 1944 and led to a machine known as digital computer "Mark 1," the main feature of which was that internal operations could be automatically controlled by electromagnetic relays, while the arithmetic counters were mechanical. The Mark 1 machine was the first electromechanical computer. In many ways, the Mark 1 was the realization of Babbage's dream.

The machine is to be admired for its megalithic proportions when compared with the size of today's computers and computing power. The Mark 1 had 760,000 sprockets and 800 m of cable, and occupied a space that was 15.5 m long, 2.4 m high, and almost 0.6 m deep. The machine weighed 5 tons and was covered by a glass roof that allowed its inner workings to be observed. It was controlled through a series of 1400 rotary switches, each with up to 10 positions from 0 to 9 arranged in the front panel. It applied concepts that even today are very impressive.

In a strict sense, this machine could not be considered a computer as we know computers today. It is nevertheless an illustrious precursor of today's computers, because it marks distinctly the end of the prehistory of information systems and communications, and it was the first computer built by IBM on a large scale.

The automatic calculator of the Sequential Control of the Mark 1 was the first machine capable of performing lengthy operations automatically, combining basic addition, subtraction, multiplication, and division and allowing reference to the results of previous operations. It used electromechanical relays to solve addition problems in less than a second: 6 s for multiplication and double that time for division. Although much slower than the simplest pocket calculators today, it was a breakthrough in its time.

# First Generation of Computers (1945–1956)

The first prototype to be known as an electronic computer and properly considered as such is found in the machine designed by John Vincent Atanasoft in the winter of 1937–1938. Atanasoft was a professor of physics and mathematics at Iowa State College, and faced the difficulty that none of the calculators available at the time gave him an adequate response to his requests. He decided to design and build a proper machine that enabled his needs to be met in the best way possible. To this end, and using design concepts that had been building in his mind, late one cold winter night in a roadside bar Atanasoft teamed up with graduate student Clifford Berry and began building the first computer that was clearly electronic, which came to be known as the "Atanasoft–Berry computer," or ABC. The ABC used vacuum tubes to store data and make arithmetic and logic operations, used capacitors for memory storage, and had a complex software system for its operations. Its purpose was to solve simple mathematical equations.

With the ABC was born the first electronic computer, although its utility was limited because the design was directed specifically to the very focused purpose of solving systems of simultaneous equations. However, the foundations were laid and computer development became unstoppable.

During subsequent years, Atanasoft and Berry wanted to go further and sought ways to build a general-purpose computer. During 1940 and 1941, they met with John W. Mauchly, who worked at the School of Electrical Engineering at the University of Pennsylvania, to show him their developments and work.

Mauchly, who was interested in research and motivated by the challenge, teamed up with J. Presper Eckert, a graduate student of engineering at the Moore School. Together, in the early 1940s, they organized the construction of the first general-purpose computer, which became known as the Electronic Numerical Integrator and Computer (ENIAC). ENIAC became one of most popular computers of the time, partly because of its relationship with the Colossus, the system that was used during World War I to decrypt the cryptographic code that handled the transmission of information related to the powerful German war machine.

The ENIAC computer occupied an area of nearly 167 m$^2$, and weighed 27 tons. Its operations used a total of 17,468 electronic valves or vacuum tubes, 7,200 crystal diodes, 1,500 relays, 70,000 resistors, and 10,000 capacitors. The package included 1,500 electromagnetic switches and relays; it rquired the manual operation of some 6,000 switches; and its programming, if it were to be changed, involved weeks of manual operations applied to this gigantic machine.

When the ENIAC went into operation, it raised the temperature of the room where it was housed above 50°C and consumed electricity at a rate of 160 kW. The ENIAC allowed approximately 5000 additions and 300 multiplications per second, which was impressive in terms of computational power and speed at the time. However, its operation required constant maintenance to replace fused vacuum tubes.

The ENIAC was the first electronic computer to become operational. Its development was funded by the U.S. Army and it was built at the Moore School as one of the many secret projects carried out during the war. The military was interested in the rapid preparation of tables about the trajectories of projectiles and ballistic missiles that would otherwise have been impossible or very costly to obtain.

In the construction of the ENIAC, as in the ABC machine, vacuum tubes were used, but its size was impressive. Although occupying the volume of a three-bedroom house, its capacity would be laughable today. However, the ENIAC had demonstrated abilities that were 300 times faster than any other machine of the time. The programming that controlled the ENIAC was not stored internally, but as a series of peg boards and switches located external to it. After falling into disuse in 1955, it was moved to the Smithsonian Institute to be preserved for its historical interest.

The technological progress manifested by the ENIAC was followed by a machine called the Electronic Discrete Variable Automatic Computer (EDVAC), which was the first machine equipped with memory capacity, a feature that essentially left all previous machines in the category of calculators. This machine, developed at Princeton University, was able to record, store, and restore data at any given time, using a development by the American mathematician John von Neumann (1903–1957). Its construction and operation at the University of Cambridge (Massachusetts) in 1947 were an innovation that would represent a major milestone in the evolution of computers.

Unlike its predecessors, the EDVAC was the first machine to use a binary system instead of the decimal system used by all previous machines. In addition, the EDVAC had programming that was designed to be stored in computer memory, which significantly expedited its operation. These developments amounted to the obsolescence of the other devices of the time, which still had to be exchanged or reconfigured each time they were used. The computer memory of the EDVAC consisted of mercury lines within an evacuated glass tube; an electronic impulse could come and go between the two states, thus configuring the basis to have ones and zeros as the digits to be stored.

We have so far highlighted the progress occurring in the technology race within the United States. This review should also mention the contributions of European countries. From the middle of the twentieth century, there were major European efforts that resulted in significant contributions to the development of information technologies.

In 1949, François Raymond, a French citizen, contributed some early designs for operating an automatic calculator. Konrad Zuse, a German scientist, also deserves special mention because of his development of machines such as the Z3 and the more powerful Z4.

The Z4 machine represents a milestone in the history of computers; it was the first computer in the world to be sold as a product. Until that time, computing machines were designed and built by the inventor for a specific purpose, and usually with the financing of a customer or institution. The Z4 was able to reproduce punch cards by using instructions contained within the machine itself. This made it possible to reproduce programs and programming, and it also facilitated making program modifications or the correction of programming mistakes, in contrast to earlier machines, which did not have this capability. The Z4 included about 22,000 relays, had a memory of 500 words of 32 bits, and weighed 1000 kg. It could perform calculations at a rate of about 1000 instructions per hour, and managed a comprehensive instructions set that could solve complicated scientific operations.

With all of these developments being put into operation, computer developers faced an increasingly strong demand for their products. In turn, the first marketing initiatives for this type of technology were established as a means to make products available to private-sector companies, as well as public-sector governmental organizations, including military departments.

The first punch-card-based calculators to appear were the IBM 604 and the Bull Gamma 3. The first big computers included those known as UNIVAC 1 and IBM 701. A few smaller computers, the IBM 650 and the Bull Gamma (magnetic drum), were also emerging as products at the time.

In 1951, the Universal Computer (UNIVAC) appeared as the first commercial computer; it provided 1000 words of core memory and could read magnetic tape. The UNIVAC computer would be used to process the data from the 1950 census of the United States.

IBM developed and delivered 18 units of the IBM 701 between 1953 and 1957. After this, the Remington Rand Company built their model 1103 computer, which competed with the IBM 701 in the field of science. This competition led to IBM developing the IBM 702, which had a very short duration and success in the emerging computer market. The industry of information technology was born slowly, but inexorably.

The computers existing up to this point in time used vacuum tubes. From 1960, vacuum tubes were largely replaced by transistors. The use of transistors in the construction of computers provided important advantages, including much lower energy consumption and prolonged component life. New technologies allowed the downsizing of the computers and individual components. This facilitated their manufacture, reduced costs, and enabled an emerging popularity.

The most successful computer in this first-generation era was the IBM 650, of which several hundred were produced and sold. This computer introduced a memory schema that incorporated a secondary memory and a magnetic drum as a means to advance the concept of permanent storage. This schema was the predecessor of storage disks. The IBM 650 existed alongside other machines from different manufacturers, who were true pioneers of the early computer industry, including the UNIVAC 80, the UNIVAC 90, the IBM 704, the IBM 709, the Burroughs 220, and the UNIVAC 1105.

## Second Generation of Computers (1957–1963)

So far, progress in computer development had been relatively slow, and encountered some difficulties such as overcoming the dearth of knowledge and the need to invent every tool, technique, and technology to be used in producing these new machines. However, the pace was also somewhat slow because computers of this period were very expensive, required a large amount of space, and incurred a disproportionate cost to design, build, and operate them.

With the advent of the transistor, everything changed suddenly. The transistor was invented by Bell Telephone Laboratories in 1946, and it entered into computer manufacturing in 1958. With the introduction of transistors, computers were transformed into smaller machines and began to achieve higher processing capacities and speeds that were being measured in microseconds.

The defining features of the second generation were essentially the use of transistor circuits (leading to cost savings in production and a reduction in computer size) and the emergence of new programming languages called higher-level languages. In particular, assembly languages were created to translate the instructions prepared by the programmer into machine code. In turn, this permitted programmers to generate high-level languages such as FORTRAN, COBOL, and ALGOL. The computer industry started to define how to communicate with computers, a field that was to be known as systems programming.

At this stage, secondary storage using large-capacity, high-speed printers and devices for high-speed transmission of information (magnetic tapes) were also being developed. The spread of these machines coincided with an increased capability to solve various kinds of problems. Innovation then began to focus on solving problems through the use of computers, and associated methods of information and knowledge management began to emerge.

New companies appeared on the information technology landscape as they were attracted by the business possibilities and the promise of big profits. This facilitated the appearance of many new computers at that time. Some computers, such as the Burroughs 5000 series and ATLAS at the University of Manchester, were quite advanced for their time.

The programs in this era were tailored by a team of experts consisting of analysts, designers, programmers, and computer operators, all working together as if in a very special orchestra. They applied their abilities and knowledge to solve problems by specifying the calculations required. The end user of the information had no direct contact with computers in this period. Programming, providing detailed instructions required for the computer to operate and obtain results, was limited to those brave pioneers who liked to spend a good number of hours writing the needed instructions and running the resulting program. This effort included checking and correcting errors or bugs that appeared in endless sessions of computing work.

Computers representative of this generation included the following:

- The Philco 212 (developed by a company that would disappear from the market in 1964)
- The UNIVAC M460
- The Control Data Corporation Model 1604, followed by the 3000 series
- The improved IBM 709 and the newer IBM 7090
- The National Cash Register (NCR) NCR 315
- The Radio Corporation of America (RCA) Model 501 and, later, the RCA Model 601

## Third Generation of Computers (1964–1971)

In the late 1960s, the integrated circuit was developed, and this was crucial in that it enabled the construction of new computer components that integrated multiple transistors on a single silicon substrate into which the interconnecting cables were soldered. This allowed for a reduction in the size, number of errors, and price of computers. It became a widespread technology that we still enjoy today in our homes, in our cars, and in every imaginable gadget that makes our lives better and easier.

Integrated circuit technology led to the emergence of the microprocessor in the mid-1970s, and this gave way, in turn, to even higher levels of integration, efficiency, and safety, for example with large-scale integrated (LSI) circuits and, later, with the very large-scale integrated (VLSI) circuits. These circuits provided components with several thousand interconnected and soldered transistors on a single silicon substrate. This enabled significant progress in reducing the size of new equipment and in increasing the speed of calculations by implementing different technologies for the integration of transistors and other solid-state circuits.

This era also saw the development of further high-level languages, including PL1, BASIC, RPG, and APL. Operating systems for the new machines were also developed as a means to profit from the new capabilities provided by the progressive miniaturization and increasing level of integration. Structured programming, strong compilers, and interpreters were built to translate symbolic language into machine code, and this became widely used in business management in new tools consisting of software packages, programming libraries, and databases. New techniques for increasing the capacity of machines appeared in the marketplace, to include such things as time sharing and multiprogramming, with businesses now able to take advantage of such technology features.

Peripherals become widespread in computer architecture, providing computer systems with a highly modular capacity and making use of teleprocessing, floppy drives, and optical readers to allow users to move data and programs easily from one computer to another, from one location to any other where data and information might be needed.

The defining characteristics of this generation of computers lay in the fact that machines were designed and built based on the use of integrated circuits, with the scale of integration increasing progressively, management was carried out by control languages provided by operating systems, and the scope and sophistication of these devices in delivering appropriate solutions to the new requirements demanded by users increased significantly.

In 1965, the IBM 360, highly refined and capable of solving more complicated problems, represented the beginning of what can be called the third generation of computers. The IBM Company produced the IBM 360 series with a wide range of models (20, 22, 30, 40, 50, 65, 67, 75, 85, 90, and 195) using special techniques in its processor, tape drives with nine channels, packs of magnetic disks, and other features that are now standard. The operating system of the 360 series had several configurations, including a set of techniques for memory management and a processor that quickly became standard.

In 1964, Control Data Corporation (CDC) introduced the 6000 series of computers, with the 6600 model considered for several years to be the fastest. In the 1970s, IBM produced the 370 series (including models 115, 125, 135, 145, 158, and 168). UNIVAC remained a competitor with its 1108 and 1110 models, while CDC produced its 7000 series (highlighted by the 7600 model). These computers were characterized as very powerful and fast machines.

At the end of that decade, IBM produced the models 3031, 3033, and 4341 from its 370 series of computers. Burroughs produced its 6000 series, with the 6500 and 6700 models having an advanced design, and these were replaced by the Burroughs 7000 series. Honeywell also participated by introducing several models of its DPS computer.

The concept of minicomputers was introduced, to include the following systems:

■ PDP-8 and PDP-11 from the Digital Equipment Corporation
■ VAX (Virtual Address eXtended), also from the Digital Equipment Corporation
■ The NOVA and ECLIPSE models from Data General
■ The 3000 and 9000 series from Hewlett-Packard (with models from 36 to 34)

Products from Wang, Honeywell, and Siemens (Germany) were also introduced, as was the ICL (manufactured in the UK). The Unified System of Electronic Computers series was developed in the Soviet Union and has subsequently gone through several generations of development. This series of computers were essentially clones of the IBM 360 and IBM 370 models.

# Fourth Generation of Computers (1972–Present)

Advances in miniaturization techniques and the use of large-scale integrated circuits prompted the microprocessor revolution, which resulted in the size of computers reducing to one-tenth that of the previous generation, processing speeds that increased by factors of 10, 50 and even 100 times that of previous machines, and extremely small memory sizes, all thanks to large-scale integration (LSI) technology.

In Silicon Valley, the Intel Corporation produced the first microprocessor, known as a "chip." The chip is characterized by its very small size and includes thousands of electronic components that can perform any logical task in the central processing unit of a computer. In conjunction with the introduction of the chip, the Z80 microprocessor, Motorola 6800, and others were released to the marketplace, signifying a definitive revolution within the hardware field.

Microprocessors facilitated the development and sale of computers for personal use. In the January 1975 issue of the magazine *Popular Electronics*, there was a description of a build-it-yourself computer that could be bought for US$395, unassembled. If preferred, this same computer could also be purchased assembled for US$650. It was called Altair 8800, and it was based on the 8080 microprocessor manufactured by Intel. Its designer and builder was Edward Roberts, who founded a little company in the garage of his home in Albuquerque, New Mexico. Roberts was surprised by the success he achieved; he expected to sell only a few hundred Altairs, but ultimately received thousands of requests that he could not fulfil.

Another story of business success of spectacular proportions in the history of technology in the United States was that of Apple Computer, Inc. (now Apple, Inc.). Shortly after the appearance of the Altair computer, two friends who were passionate about electronics, Stephen Wozniak and Steven Jobs, 25 and 20 years of age, respectively, founded Apple Computer. Using a meager budget funded from the sale of a car and a programmable calculator, along with a small credit loan, they initially produced and sold a computer at a unit price of about US$500 and sold 175 units. They accomplished this despite the fact that the device was very difficult to use because it had no keyboard or terminal. In 1977, these pioneers and Apple Computer released the Apple II model, which was a resounding success. In late 1983, sales of the Apple II computer achieved a turnover of one billion dollars.

In recent years, new machines have appeared continuously, and almost all large electronic equipment, office equipment, and calculator companies in the United States, Europe, and Japan have tried to gain a foothold in this burgeoning but difficult market. Sometimes, companies in Silicon Valley and in technology parks in other geographical areas have been broken by tough competition in the field of advanced technologies.

Although there has been significant development in personal computers, progress in the field of large computers and supercomputers has also continued, offering brilliant results. This includes machines such as the CRAY-1, designed by Seymour R. Cray, which had an internal memory of more than 8 megabytes and the ability to perform more than 200,000 operations per second. The CRAY also came with memory upgrades to 20 gigabytes. Other supercomputers that appeared in the marketplace included the Japanese FALCOM and the Numerical Aerodynamic Simulation Facility.

This generation also includes two notable events: the emergence of Kenbak-I and the introduction of IBM's Winchester disk technology. The Kenbak-I was manufactured in 1971 by John Blakenbaker of Kenbak Corporation in Los Angeles. It was built four years before the Altair was launched. This personal computer was built to address the needs of the education market. It had 256 bytes of RAM, and its programming was carried out by means of levers (switches). It was a dismal failure and only 40 units were sold.

Winchester disk technology was introduced by IBM in 1973 in association with its 3340 models, and they soon became an industry standard. The Winchester disk operated with a small head used for reading and writing. It had an air system flow facility that allowed the read/write mechanism to move very close to the surface of the disk.

# Fifth Generation of Computers (1981–Future)

The fifth generation of computers began in 1981 with the advent of the IBM personal computer, and it is this era in which we find ourselves today. Computing power has emerged from computing centers and into business offices and homes, allowing it to become personal and ubiquitous.

In addition, there are many research projects and experiences already completed or in progress in the field of artificial intelligence (AI), and expert systems that are searching for new ways of using and interacting with these technologies. Meanwhile, the chipsets residing in today's computers continue to demonstrate breakthroughs in communication and information processing through the use of microelectronics, which is providing integrated circuits with ever higher densities and speeds.

Microcomputers based on these circuits are extremely small and cheap, so their use is spreading to the industrial market and reaching individuals in the form of personal equipment. Such personal computers now have enormous capacity and capability, and have greatly influenced the business world, and indeed society, to produce the so-called "information revolution."

In 1981, IBM launched, with much delay and also caution, its personal computer (PC). This was commercially available in three models: the PC with floppy disk drives, the XT with a 10 MB hard disk, and the AT with a hard drive of 20 MB. In the first year, 35,000 units were sold. In 1983, the sale of 800,000 units enabled IBM's PC to achieve first ranking in the sales of business microcomputers.

In 1976, Steve Wozniak and Steve Jobs invented the first microcomputer for mass use, later forming Apple Computer, which was to become known as the second largest company in the world, preceded only by IBM. Today, it is still one of the five largest companies in the world. In 1981, Apple Computer sold 80,000 personal computers, and sales rose to 1.4 million in the following year.

Between 1984 and 1987, there were around 60 million personal computers in existence, so there is no doubt that the impact and penetration of personal computers have been tremendous. With the emergence of personal computers, software and the systems that manage it have undergone significant developments, providing progressively better interactive communication and interfaces with the user. Software applications like word processors, spreadsheets, and graphics packages began to appear in the computer marketplace. Software industries serving the needs of personal computer users also grew very quickly. Gary Kildall, creator of the Control Program for Microcomputers (CP/M), and William Gates, architect of Microsoft products, were for years devoted to developing operating systems and methods for the easy use of microcomputers.

Although microcomputers have a distinct presence, minicomputers and mainframes are still in development. The smaller machines of today far exceed the capacity of the mainframes of 10 or 15 years ago, which required expensive and specially equipped facilities. However, it would be wrong to assume that large computers have gone. On the contrary, their presence remains virtually inescapable in all areas of government, military, and heavy industry. The huge series computers such as CDC, CRAY, Hitachi, and IBM have been able to serve several hundred million operations per second, making them essential for banks, governments, and a wide variety of companies of size across industry.

In 1983, Japan launched its "Agenda of the Fifth Generation of Computers," with the explicit objective of using innovation to produce computer machines. The United States is already active in a similar program to develop parallel processing through architectures and designs using special high-speed circuits, and to use natural language and artificial intelligence systems. This makes the foreseeable future of computing very interesting, and it can be expected that science will continue to receive priority from governments and society as a whole.

On August 12, 1981, IBM launched the personal computer (PC). Since then, changes in the landscape of computers have accelerated to produce an absolute dependence on this technology in meeting the everyday needs of individuals.

The popularity of the personal computer market, growth with a diversification of needs and applications, as well as the progressive dependence on information systems by companies and governments have produced two different but related effects on computers:

- The first effect is the concentration of hardware platforms into a small number of hardware architectures, with a technological oligopoly supplying computer processing chips to all computer manufacturers around the world. Central processor manufacturers have now been reduced to a number that is small compared to the diversity of existing computer designs and technologies. Today, the best known of these current manufacturers is Intel, maker of the Pentium processor series. In many ways, Intel has been responsible for establishing many of the standards.
- The second effect is a similar concentration of software platforms, which has been facilitated by the standardization of hardware platforms.

The proliferation of Windows-based environments, which provided quick and easily learned interfaces, reduced the training needs of individuals. This made it possible for a neophyte to start working with a computer without any significant training or preparation. In addition, the virtual standardization of these tools has created a situation where the computer environment from one company to another does not change very much, thereby reducing user training and employee adaptation time.

Among the factors that have contributed to the ease of learning is the extraordinary work invested in the development of graphic environments that are more intuitive and more natural, leading to the simplification of software utilization and management for users. The introduction of the mouse led to a reduction in the use of boring and tedious command line instructions or mandates that were previously needed to specify a cumbersome syntax fraught with parameters that were difficult to memorize and use.

The reality is that the current picture of the computing environment has been reduced to a small repertoire of operating systems and tools that bring together most of a broad spectrum of the solutions currently used in business management. Operating systems show options that are reduced to, for example, Microsoft Windows, in its many versions. Unix, Linux, the Mac OS from Apple, and the limited presence of IBM's OS/400 also have shares of the operating system market.

These factors have contributed to improving productivity in the organizations that use computers, and have helped create a community of basic-skill computer users in many organizations. When the skills and capabilities of the computer users community are considered, this provides the opportunity to replace one skilled user with another skilled user for either short- or long-term benefits. That removes the aura of expertise that computer professionals held in the early days of computer system development and implementation. In turn, organizations have been able to steadily reduce costs in the form of wages and salaries, while making them more comparable among technicians and users of information systems.

In recent years, there have also been significant savings from the use of hardware and software derivatives, which have caused prices to be reduced consistently, promoting expanded global use. At the same time, computer facilities and locations, once more or less stagnant, have now been extended to virtually every desk in the workplace and into many homes for personal use.

Today, the personal computer is being converted into portable configurations to enable employees to maintain computing power on trips or when otherwise out of the office. To this end, laptops have followed the same trends as desktop computers. They have evolved to have enhanced performance and smaller size, much the same as the evolution of departmental mainframes and minicomputers into the desktop personal computers of today.

In the late 1980s and early 1990s, the Internet appeared on the scene as a network of networks. The Internet owed its design to the military's need to create a network with a topology that would allow the loss of nodes without dramatically affecting its operation. It then began to be used and developed further in university environments to facilitate the sharing of information and documentation for investigation and educational use.

Internet experimentation also facilitated many rapid changes that have made it what it is today. The organizational hierarchy helped users in finding and retrieving online content quickly, while the evolution of related systems enabled online access to multimedia content.

Another important contribution to the evolution of the Internet was the definition of hypertext markup language (HTML), which soon became a factual standard. It allowed the creation of content and facilitated Internet navigation so that each user could use the Internet in the manner most convenient to their needs. Improved Internet multimedia capabilities and increased capacity of communication lines provided the means to use not only documents, records, and books, but also photos, videos, music, and all kinds of content in multiple formats.

Users began to see the Internet as more than a repository for information, and this change of perspective revolutionized the Internet and the World Wide Web to give rise to new concepts of its usefulness. In the new concept of the Web, content is produced in a democratic way, by the whole community, which is self-regulating and self-censored to maintain the content at an adequate quality. This is exemplified by open source projects such as Open Office, a project sponsored by Sun Microsystems, or Wikipedia in which the community builds a solution under its own criteria, voluntarily organized, and without a hierarchical or organic dependency.

This new paradigm created a dependency around the Internet that was unthinkable until the lifestyles and habits of society were transformed, leading to an uncontrollable impulse for being always online and staying connected 24 h a day, 7 days a week.

Contributing to this ever-present personal computing need has been the introduction of new devices that have made this aspiration possible. The personal digital assistant (PDA), Smartphone, netbook, and other highly rated devices have provided mobile convergence between information technologies and communications, with an operating capability that sometimes makes it hard to distinguish whether the device is a computer on which you can hold a phone conversation or a telephone that lets you use applications like word processing, Web browsing, and others.

The features of these new devices include access to social networks where users can record and share common life experiences with their friends anywhere in the world. These features offer me a new concept of neighborhood and friendship in which one can establish a close relationship with a group of friends located in Finland, South Africa, Singapore, and Santiago de Chile, while not knowing the names of the parents of classmates of my son, or my neighbors. These features promote a world where distance has no meaning in itself, but where the engine of the relationship is represented by the sharing of interests, hobbies, and many other more subjective and subtle factors.

The convergence between the worlds of information systems and communications, and its dual relationship for business and leisure, is now a reality. Proof of this is characterized by the latest devices that have appeared in the marketplace, such as the iPad from Apple, which has made a significant contribution.

# Chapter 4

# The Systems Development Life Cycle—Introduction

Methodologies currently used to develop technological projects try to cover the elements of the system's development life cycle (SDLC), which is essentially the succession of phases or stages that a system passes through from its inception until it is removed from operation and replaced by another newer or more adequate system that is needed to address business needs.

Each methodology prescribes this life cycle process in a different way, dividing the process into more or fewer steps, describing the activities in greater or lesser depth, and considering the application of many or only some technologies. However, all the various processes seem to reproduce a similar life cycle progression to be used for system development and implementation. Figure 4.1 illustrates one version of an SDLC methodology that can be used.

Such methodologies are essentially a compendium of good practices that the author, developer, or even the organization tries to spread among the rest of the project management community. In turn, good practices help prevent a recurrence of any mistakes that have been identified; to apply a known, effective solution for the conditions encountered; to draw on lessons learned that reduce its impact on the project; and to remove accessorial and circumstantial elements to simplify and share the solution with those who follow the same methodology.

Methodologies and life cycle guidance can also fulfill another role within the professional technology community by providing the basis for necessary training and explicit reference to process the steps. This facilitates the effective introduction of new team members in shorter time frames. It avoids the traditional learning curve based on direct experience or through trial and error mechanisms, which are much

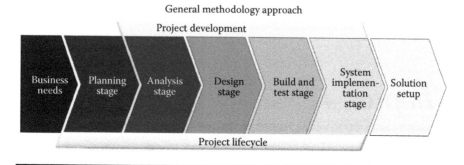

**Figure 4.1 General methodology approach.**

slower, frustrating, and unpredictable in their outcomes. System development methodologies are communication vehicles that can also serve as powerful tools for spreading and implementing organizational culture in an open and lively manner.

A methodology is not a dogma that we must inevitably follow under penalty, but it must be considered a guide for action based on the experience of others who have performed similar work before us. It provides an orientation about how to solve the common problems that are encountered, and if properly followed, it will allow us to effectively reach the established objectives. The methodological approach is not always the most efficient or shortest path to the goal, but it is the surest way to achieve the system development goals. However, with few exceptions, the only thing we can always say is that any methodology process is better than none. We should assume that the methodologies available for the technology project work we do are general approaches that should be carefully evaluated and customized for each project, as needed.

In fact, the result of the project in terms of success or failure and, of course, in terms of achieving cost and resource goals and delivery dates will be distinctly influenced by the adaptation of the methodology process that is applied. Adaptation includes considering the technologies used, reviewing the project's objectives and scope, examining the characteristics of resources, the client's personnel, and technology uses within the client's organization as elements to be taken into account before starting any project. With these things considered, the methodology can then be modified for more precision or less rigor, according to the needs of the project at hand.

This consideration of methodologies as open guides requires from all of us an attitude committed to process enrichment to be achieved through sharing of knowledge and awareness of project circumstances. This helps individuals discover when something exceptional happens and to identify solutions from lessons learned that may be of interest to other professionals. This requires project managers and team members to take the time to analyze what has happened, and to assess whether any lessons can be drawn from their experience. If so, that information must be compiled and shared with others, providing feedback to nourish the experience of using the methodology.

In our examination of the methodology used for system development, Figure 4.2 shows that methodology use is a business investment. The diagram shows how that business investment is generally distributed across the SDLC. The investment or cost for system development projects should always be considered early in the SDLC, and must be effectively managed throughout the entire SDLC. These steps will be considered further in discussions of each system development stage in the following chapters.

There are many elements and tools that can help us organize and perform the work of analyzing the current status of an organization. If we have enough insight and knowledge, this may be sufficient, or we could even rely on sensibility and intuition.

One of the tools that can deliver results more effectively and easily is the strength–weaknesses and opportunities–threat (SWOT) analysis. This tool combines the analysis of positive and negative factors in the internal and external contexts of the development effort to provide a schematic and balanced picture of the strategic situation. Depending on the nature of the business, this analysis should be implemented from four specific perspectives, rather than as a global analysis that may be lacking in necessary focus. Using the SWOT tool maintains a level of detail to provide us with relevant information of higher value when

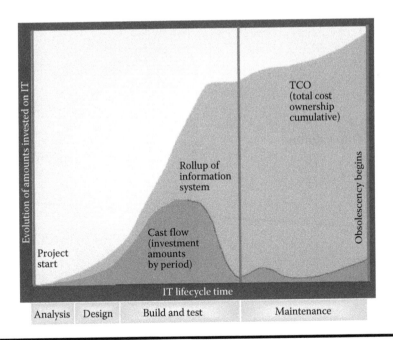

**Figure 4.2  Information technology life cycle.**

transformed or otherwise used in the planning process. The four perspectives of SWOT analysis are illustrated Figure 4.3. The elements of the SWOT schema and its use are discussed further in subsequent activities of the system development planning process.

As we begin our examination of the planning process, we must recognize how important it is to study, analyze, and understand the challenge of the development effort relative to the external strategic context of the project. Every organization operates in a context that has important preconditions for development. These could include an examination of the following:

■ The rules and regulations that exist within the organization or within the associated industry
■ The level of competition that exists in the market sector pursued by the organization

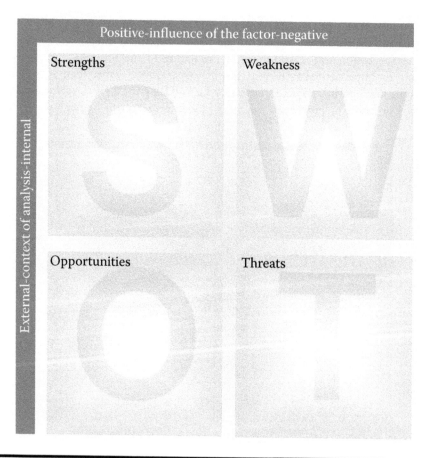

**Figure 4.3   SWOT schema.**

- The level of requirements or customer willingness to allow elasticity with regard to price changes
- The level of maturity and standardization of the market as a whole
- The barriers to marketplace entry for new competitors

The examination should also review restrictions that prevent, make it impracticable, or make it very expensive to tackle new business challenges in any market, or any of the other forces acting in any market. Michael E. Porter considers these forces and defines them very well in his book *The Five Forces*, now considered a classic of management.

All in all, the planning process necessitates careful and detailed scrutiny that allows us to know the frame of reference of where we are and the influences and forces we are exposed to before taking any action. As we gain a better understanding of what is happening around us, in the immediate business environment of the organization, we are then able to predict the reactions and results as we apply the initial planning steps to the subsequent design and development steps that give us a more coherent and effective systems development plan.

# Chapter 5

# The Systems Development Life Cycle—Planning

The first step envisaged in existing methodologies for information technology and communications is the planning step. Planning is an essential step before starting any project. It helps individuals and teams acquire the best understanding of the project in terms of the needs and expectations that justify its launch, in terms of the support and interest required from business managers, and in terms of the nature of the work to be pursued.

The purpose of this life cycle stage is to provide a framework in which to strategically place the project with regard to other candidate projects. This is done in order to select projects that will ultimately be approved and planned to support business needs and interests.

Each systems development project must have a clear plan that is defined with sufficient precision to guide the actions taken both within the project and in relation to other projects. In fact, this step helps identify project dependencies and relationships as a means to reach a desirable synergy between the different projects and actions prescribed by management.

In this step, information is somewhat scarce, and little is known about the candidate project that we are studying for approval to go forward with planning. Some of the general level requirements to be fulfilled may be known, the systems that must communicate or establish interfaces may be identified, and generic business processes may be specified. Otherwise, there is only some circumstantial and anecdotal project information, and few other things that are useful.

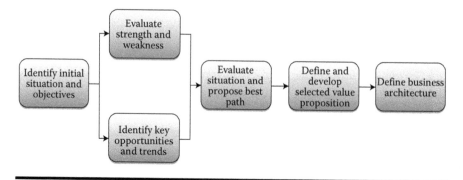

**Figure 5.1   Planning stage diagram.**

With the few information elements that we have, we need to first create a high-level model of the information system of the organization. This includes outlining the technological architecture that will support all information systems in the organization and preparing an approved project plan that addresses tasks and their durations and possible interactions. A project calendar is also created to show restrictions such as holidays, personnel vacations, and other similar dates.

Thus, each project in the planning stage is defined and delimited as accurately as possible. Where does information system development start? Where does it end? What is the project's scope and what does it include? What is outside the scope of the project? What is the purpose of the project? What is the project goal to be attained? Who receives the project deliverables, and how are those "products" generated and delivered by the project?

A systems development project plan should also always have a strategic business orientation, rather than just a technological perspective. Therefore, the project plan seeks to be consistent with the organization's strategic business plan, and this is accomplished by examining the information systems as tools to support the business operations of the organization.

The systems development planning process is illustrated in Figure 5.1, and the key planning activities are described in each of the following sections of this chapter.

# Identify Initial Situation and Objectives

A detailed description of the current situation from a strategic and business perspective is needed. It will focus on defining key aspects of the situation that exist today, and it will help prevent the detraction of essential process elements within the organization. This description and the wisdom used to produce it will be key, because it will constitute a primary reference to establish the sequence of events we want started in order to lead the organization to its target.

At this point, let us look at some general considerations regarding how a business organization could be analyzed from different perspectives:

■ Define the organization as the set of relationships, both internal and external, that have commercial and business interests in a given population, region, or country, and include indications of how the organization ensures coordinated actions to obtain synergies and produce a result greater than the simple addition of individual results. Sometimes the examination of an organization chart will provide some insight in this area of analysis.

■ Consider the possibility of developing a joint product that entwines the services offered by different companies, where the client can be offered an integrated solution for ease of operation. This essentially hides from the client the complexity of the project and the probable risks associated with the business contract.

■ Review legislation, laws, and regulation systems set for the geographical area or for the industry, which, by their nature, could cause an undesired attraction or rejection about the organization or their products or services among primary or target customers.

■ Examine rules that may specify the level of effort (rigor) or define the responsibilities of companies operating in a specified location or territory that mandate organizations provide guarantees for customers to ensure that customers have special protection relative to their interests. Likewise, understand the tolerance of local authorities about acceptable business behaviors and attitudes for organizations operating in their country or legal jurisdiction.

■ Determine and provide the skill training and professional development needed by human resources that will be assigned to analyze and manage the human aspects of the system developed to meet the needs of customers. In this sense, the professionalism of the personnel providing services to the customer will guarantee customer satisfaction. Also, knowledge of languages and the ability to establish an empathetic relationship with customers will also be beneficial to the performing organization, and could provide some business benefits in future work for the customer.

■ Identify relevant technology and information systems that will be used, and develop technical competencies and provide the technical skill training needed by technicians involved in the systems development effort.

■ Review customer relationships using established methods and tools that identify customers and match them with the services offered, always documenting the history of the customer relationship and the outcomes of previous customer work.

A detailed description of the business situation can be prepared by using information derived from an analysis of each of the perspectives listed above. A set of models representing how information flows and circulates throughout the organization can also be created so that we can visualize the effects that will be produced by the proposed projects, including the extent of their impact in measurable terms.

Upon completing the description that helps in understanding the current situation, managers can then proceed to defining the objectives for the development effort. It is necessary to identify, understand, and properly document the objectives to be pursued because they represent the purpose of the project. In general, when objectives of the development effort have been achieved, then the associated project is usually considered to be completed.

When identifying objectives in this activity, each objective should be characterized by at least two key features: objectives should be *specific* and *measurable*. An objective is deemed specific when it clearly describes the outcome to be achieved. An objective is deemed measurable when it provides a clear numerical or logical value as an attribute of the specified outcome. An objective could be considered accomplished when, for example, the operating budget is reduced by 10%, when five new engineers have been hired, when the executive board votes to continue into the next project stage (a yes/no decision is achieved), or when business revenues grow to US$4 million or more per annum. These are measurable values.

## Evaluate Strengths and Weaknesses

Just as we need to analyze the external environment to understand the environment in which the organization is evolving, we must also analyze the internal dimensions of the organization, in terms of its positive and negative factors, to ensure that the organization is in top form to operate with the efficiency that is required.

In this context, it will be important to review key aspects of the strategy: mission, vision, values, and principles, as well as policies and procedures, business processes, human resources requirements, financial status, and technical innovations and applied technology to ensure that they are all aligned with each other to be synergistic in achieving the challenges facing the entire organization.

In performing these reviews, opportunities can be identified in association with the project under consideration. They should be listed and sufficiently described on the SWOT diagram (or in a separate document) to adequately convey the actions and concepts that could be applied to help realize the opportunity.

In turn, this activity also prompts consideration of internal weaknesses within the organization that could impact or impair the successful completion of the project. These items should also be listed, to include an appropriate description of each weakness identified and a recommended course of action for reducing or removing its impact or influence.

# Identify Key Opportunities and Trends

By analyzing the internal and external situations, we can obtain high-value information that will allow us to clearly identify the main opportunities for performance improvement. We can begin this analysis by looking at the entries inserted in the boxes labeled "Opportunities" and "Weaknesses" in the SWOT diagram prepared earlier.

Regarding the "Opportunities" box, we can see a listing of conditions, events, facts and environmental circumstances that offer the possibility of business growth for the organization. This business growth could be defined in terms of financial growth, marketplace growth, customer growth (expansion), or corporate recognition within an industry. Therefore, to not take advantage of opportunities could impact business growth potential, and many would call that simply a blunder.

The "Weaknesses" box shows us the internal aspects of the organization that can be considered and perhaps even require consideration for improvement. When we identify these items in the purview of the organization's internal context, it becomes clear that we, in principle, should have or should obtain the necessary authority to take definitive action to change the organization's internal processes and operations to stop them from acting as negative influences (weaknesses) in the business progress of the organization.

This activity is intended to identify the opportunities for improvement that exist within the organization and in association with the project at hand. The consideration of these opportunities may be discussed, but usually only the most interesting and most beneficial opportunities will materialize within projects. At this moment in time, the most important thing is to generate as many ideas as possible so that in a later stage we will be able to measure and evaluate each one of them. In turn, we will then choose those that have been assessed to offer the greatest potential for business growth and for improving the organization.

This activity is also intended to identify threats that will be faced by the project if it is selected to go forward. Here we want to identify and examine things that could adversely affect the project's completion and outcome, along with things that have a negative influence on business growth or performance improvement.

The combined input of the SWOT analysis and the preparation of the situation description and objectives, both conducted above, will help managers review and select projects that have the greatest business value and potential for performance improvement. This evaluation is performed in the next activity.

# Evaluate Situation and Propose Best Path

For each identified improvement opportunity, we need to specify and conduct a study of alternative solutions. Alternative solutions should be identified based on a combination of realism and creativity, and they must provide viable options for achieving the desired benefits of the project and for fulfilling the specified opportunities for improvement.

Having a single opportunity to improve, with only one possible course of action for any return on investment or other cash value for the organization, is the simplest formula. In this instance, when the solution has been identified, work can proceed to fulfill the improvement opportunity. Once this solution is chosen as the course of action for the specified opportunity, some people tend to stop looking for alternative solutions. Instead, additional work should be accomplished to identify and evaluate alternative solutions, as a means to find and select the best solution.

The identification and evaluation of alternative solutions should be repeated for each of the improvement opportunities on every project that is contemplated within the information technology environment.

It should be understood that throughout this process, you must keep the proper orientation of considering the business objectives, as defined in the strategic business plan of the organization. This helps us fully understand the business challenges facing the organization and to use that guidance when developing the solutions and plans for each project. If the project does not contribute in some measure to the achievement of business objectives, the project will have no meaning and should not be pursued. In some cases, this is recognized after the project has already started, and, if business needs and interests are not being properly addressed, the project may be suspended or terminated at any time.

Once all alternative solutions have been developed, they should be reviewed and compared in an examination that enables the selection of the best solution. The selected solution is then used as the basis for subsequent detailed project planning. In essence, the outcome of this activity is a preliminary project plan that highlights the preferred technical solution.

## Define and Develop Selected Value Proposition

The business case is an instrument that is used in project management to show the value to be returned from the selected project. In many cases, having a business case can be the difference between the success and failure of the project. In essence, it is used to manage the project from a business perspective.

The cost–benefit analysis, in many instances, is the primary component of a business case done at this early planning stage. It is used to assess the pending projects as a means to identify those projects that offer a better cost–benefit relationship or, in other words, the best return on investment (ROI) or the best net present value (NPV). Too often, once the project has started, this fundamental document tends to fall into oblivion. However, effective project management practices should prompt its review and update throughout the project, as a matter of managing the business aspects of the project.

We say that the business case is a crucial document because it fully defines the nature and importance of the business interests in the selected project. The business case provides the necessary business information and financial foundation for selecting one particular project and not another as worthy of receiving the investment needed for development. Therefore, it is important to use effective cost–benefit analysis practices to achieve results that are formally credible and also realistic.

In terms of business case analyses, there is an approach often called the "strictly economics-oriented" analysis. When identifying the benefits of the project effort, this analysis includes only those factors that can be measured in monetary units, and this analysis is usually accomplished by an assessment specialist. This analysis approach is used as a means to ensure that project monetary benefits will be realized, whereby projects will normally start very predictably and with a gradual, incremental improvement in performance in the marketplace. However, these projects will hardly initiate any revolutionary products that can provide a substantial business advantage to the organization.

Another business case analysis is sometimes referred to as the "sellers of smoke," because of the far-reaching exaggerated benefits that are identified. People using this analysis face new ideas with the ability to see their full potential, and they try to incorporate the cost–benefit analysis without discriminating in any way. They give equal weight to the immediate benefits to be achieved from the project's development, as well as considering benefits from the project's outcomes that may or may not be achieved at some time in the future. Managers who use this method do not usually have the same level of sensitivity to see the less obvious costs of the project, so their decisions can end up being very costly to the organization relative to the uncertain outcomes that are identified as a result of this analysis.

A third type of business case analysis could be called the "danger seekers everywhere" analysis, which has a similar bias to the sellers of smoke but with an opposite focus of caution rather than optimism. In this instance, individuals have a special sensitivity to identify threats, costs, risks, and dangers of any kind in any aspect of daily activity, and they apply this sensitivity well to their examination of projects. If the business decision depended solely on this type of analysis, the organization might never begin a new project. It would never be the right time as they perceive the costs and risks as absolutely real, while the benefits are seen only as potential outcomes, subject to compliance with conditions of uncertain realization. However, this apparently negative attitude should not, for a moment, make us think to keep this type of professional away from our projects. Their unique ability to identify the hazards can be a valuable asset to the organization.

The business case must be properly analyzed in a manner that identifies all the costs and benefits. It should provide a sufficient explanation of the analysis methods used and the analysis results obtained. The analysis results should be properly structured and arranged so that managers can examine and take into account all information when making decisions about both the selection and initiation of the project, as well as subsequent decisions regarding the continuation of the project.

## Define Business Architecture

In the planning of systems for business, their relationship with the global business model and the scope and performance of the technology architecture that supports it should be known. This is accomplished in this step, which defines the business architecture.

The systems development project is planned in the context of the complex systems that currently exist, and with consideration for systems to be implemented, including system interfaces that exist externally in a delicate and sophisticated world of technology. It is therefore necessary to gain a comprehensive understanding of terms and concepts at a high level—what we call the business architecture of the development environment and its relationship with the global model. In other words, in this step we define the way the results of the project will be implemented throughout the organization, and we try to assess the key issues at the onset of planning, to include such system development issues as feasibility, integration, necessary adjustments, and additional requirements involving the development of satellite system projects.

If this is not done early in the system development life cycle, in this planning stage, we could find roadblocks to project completion, resulting in undesirable situations that may be discovered too late in the project to provide for effective recovery of the system development effort. Some issues that could arise include the following:

- Learning that the new system needs items that are not available within the organization (e.g., data, people, or other resources)
- Finding that the system generates valuable information that cannot be analyzed due to lack of an effective organizing tool
- Seeing the system produce results in a new process that the organization lacks human resources to administer
- Using the new system takes advantage of new technologies to create a "marketplace" for suppliers, but the organization has no access to the network used by suppliers to manage the products in that marketplace

In short, issues and situations related to the business architecture need to be identified and solved during this planning step to provide an early and lasting answer to any problems that may arise.

## Chapter 6

# The Systems Development Life Cycle—Analysis

The analysis phase is a very important stage in any technology project. In this stage, detailed knowledge is obtained about the problem to be solved, with activities focused on preparing a conceptual approach that will make it possible to implement the proposed solution.

This phase is crucial, because any mistakes made at this time could be loosely and unknowingly carried forward to the remainder of the project. Such conditions might cause teams to work blindly in developing products and solutions to problems that are unknown or poorly understood. This makes the development effort a game of chance, where the resolution of the problem is more the result of good luck than technical knowledge and rigor. Mistakes at this stage could generate a progressive series of unforeseen consequences that might reasonably lead a doomed project to utter failure.

Performing system analysis work is not something that is easy or trivial. In particular, it is difficult to find good analysts, because it requires a rather odd profile that combines a delicate balance of analytical and synthetic capabilities with rare interpersonal relationship skills. The analyst must obtain full knowledge about the current situation and learn associated implications from users that have a limited awareness about the planned system. In a relatively short period of time, the analyst must diagnose the problem and formulate potential solutions.

It is essential for the analyst to discern the facts, rather than anecdotal information, by means of an effective process for collecting information. In some circumstances when an analyst is gathering information, some development partners may tend to distrust the analyst's capabilities and intentions. Therefore, the analyst must earn the trust of the involved development partners, who must convey their particular visions of the problem. In this process, the analyst will often find contradictory perspectives and opinions that are sometimes charged with emotion. So, extracting the essences of each partner's thoughts, evaluating alternatives to propose a solution, and dealing with pressures from internal and external managers and stakeholders that all too often do not see the inherent value in the proposed solution all provide for a vigorous and rigorous analysis stage.

At this stage, the basic tool for completing the analysis is the personal interview, the results of which will provide input to assist in such activities as data modeling and process diagramming. To a large extent, the data collected by the analyst will also be used by other staff members in subsequent stages of the development effort.

Before starting analysis phase activities, it is good practice to review the planning output from the previous stage to ensure that an essential number of preconditions have been adequately met. This includes reviewing the following steps to ensure they have been completed and are understood.

- A project plan has been prepared to reflect and properly consider all dimensions of the project to ensure they are adequately managed and controlled, individually and as a whole.
- The project and its plan should be agreed to and supported by relevant managers in the organization. Such support indicates that the project or development effort has been formally selected and approved to proceed to the analysis stage.
- A coherent and transparent business case has been prepared for the project, approved by management for cost and funding authorization purposes, and reviewed for understanding by project leaders and relevant team members.
- The project plan contains an explanation of the paradigm used to draw up the solution framework, and these concepts and considerations are available for review by the analyst and other relevant team members.

Specific and measurable project objectives have been prepared to guide the systems development effort. In conjunction with project objectives, the elements of project scope, a very preliminary project schedule, project assumptions and constraints, and perhaps project business risks have been identified and made available for review.

The systems development analysis process is illustrated in Figure 6.1, and the key analysis activities are described in each of the following sections of this chapter.

# Identification of General Requirements

Before specifying the solution to the problem faced, the first activity of the analysis stage is the identification of requirements. The requirements represent the

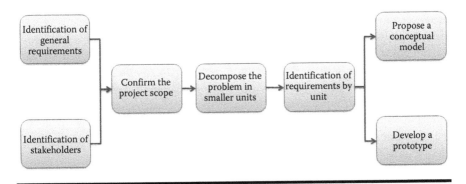

**Figure 6.1    Analysis stage diagram.**

demand and need for features and functionality of the system to be developed. However, requirements can also address issues of cost, schedule, and the quality associated with the development effort. Requirements are made regarding the products and deliverables of the project (e.g., systems, subsystems, and system components), and requirements can be stated in different ways with different expressions. All requirements should be given priority attention for awareness and understanding.

It should be clearly recognized that each project requirement that is expressed represents a limitation of some type for the design of the solution. A valid solution is one that meets all the requirements included in the specifications. Requirements can be functional when they:

■ Relate to the functions or services that the end product provides to users
■ Refer to technical aspects of the solution such as the technological environment in which the system must operate
■ Specify performance characteristics in terms of response time, number of concurrent users, or any other characteristics that deliver capacity to their users and security that guarantees integrity, availability, and protection of system vulnerabilities

This short list shows some frequently used requirements classifications, but there are many others. However, the taxonomy used to classify needs and requirements is not the most important issue. The more prominent issue is the thoroughness with which we address requirements and the rigor that we apply to evaluate and prioritize the requirements. In this sense, the ideal is that requirements are prioritized according to the needs expressed by the users themselves, but sometimes conflicting interests and perhaps irreconcilable differences arise that must be resolved through a negotiated settlement or compromise.

Please note that if a requirement is represented as a condition to be accomplished, then it creates a limitation of freedom in the design of the solution. If such a requirement is removed, its absence then allows us a broader degree of freedom when designing the solution.

The prioritization of requirements is also essential, because frequently we will find contradictory requirements or requirements that are difficult to harmonize. Sometimes we can strike a compromise with the stakeholders who included them as a means to indicate the priority of requirements. However, requirements management could be easier by having a prioritized requirements inventory, which will help us define the solution and avoid many hours of discussions and tensions from negotiations.

Once all the requirements have been specified, we must ensure that their specification is conveyed and communicated to all stakeholders in their entirety. We also must ensure that requirements are not lost through communication difficulties, either in the transmittal process or in each stakeholder's understanding of the requirements and the priorities that have been established. This distribution of requirements allows one group of users or stakeholders to see the requirements established by other stakeholders.

In any case, once the inventory of requirements is completed, it must be closed, and we can go on to define the possible solution, with the assurance that we have a clear comprehension about the conditions that it must accomplish.

## Identification of Stakeholders

The project plan and objectives, along with the specification of requirements, should be examined relative to the expectations that are held by the different stakeholders who have a vested interest in a successful project outcome. This includes looking at the role that each key stakeholder plays in the overall systems development process, but particularly in the acceptance of the project deliverables.

The following key stakeholder roles should be identified for inclusion in the systems development effort:

- An essential role played by one or more stakeholders is that of "project sponsor," which will be the person or group that drives the project, and will likely be the most interested in seeing the project achieve its objectives and produce the maximum potential benefits. The sponsor usually resides in the organization that is performing the development effort, and asserts approval authority for project costs, schedule, and resource utilization.
- The "buyer" is another stakeholder that should be clearly identified. The role of the buyer is to represent the customer organization and obtain the resources and services from the performing organization, which is usually managed by a formal contract or agreement with the performing organization. The sponsor should not be confused with the buyer in the customer's organization.

In contrast, the buyer asserts approval authority for acceptance of deliverables and payment for services rendered.

- Finally, we have a third more or less ubiquitous group of stakeholders in the project that comprises the "users." The users play a role in implementing and using the technical solution (e.g., system) that is delivered as a result of the development effort. The project will affect users in one way or another, because they will use work products resulting from the project in their daily performance of work.

In addition to the above key stakeholders, other people or groups may emerge to show interest in the development effort and in the outcome of the project. For example, we can view corporate shareholders and company owners as stakeholders, because if the project provides the expected benefits, those outcomes can increase the return on investment for these stakeholders. We can also look at service providers, contractors and consultants, and suppliers as people who have a vested interest in a successful project outcome, primarily in association with their contributions to the development effort. This stakeholder group could also be affected by changes in project scope, in the delivery of raw materials, and in the logistics plans specified for the project; they too would have stakeholder interests.

In short, anyone who might be concerned in any way, can and should be considered, in principle, as an interested party or stakeholder. Knowing in advance that these stakeholders exist and have particular interests in the project outcome will help avoid jeopardizing the project because one or more of the stakeholders decides to act independently to influence the project direction or outcome.

## Confirm the Project Scope

The process of preparing the technical approach requires great creativity and rigor, and looks to the analyst to provide a number of solutions, including those that are already known and those that have been newly designed specifically to solve the problems that face the organization. This needs to be achieved while maintaining certain precautions and safeguards about implications and risks that are important to the quality of the work that will be performed.

The development of solution alternatives is guided by the specification of the project scope. Such alternatives must show solutions that remain within the specified project scope. The scope provides the analyst with an understanding of the project boundaries, which are identified in a complete and accurate manner. The analyst also uses the scope to clearly define what is included and what is excluded in the project work effort. It is the analyst's responsibility to determine what is inside and outside the scope, and to ensure that the corresponding solution, as well as alternative solutions, are consistent with the specified project scope.

In this activity, the analyst will review the developed solution and alternative solutions to ensure that they are consistent with the established scope. The analyst may also meet with planners to clarify the scope, as needed, and perhaps to make recommendations for acceptable changes to the specified scope.

## Break Down the Problem into Smaller Units

This activity provides for a deeper examination of the problem and the solutions that are needed to resolve them. In this activity, the analyst will break down the problem previously defined at a relatively high level into smaller units of analysis that could be described as subsystems. In turn, each subsystem will be subject to its own analytical work. When starting this detailed analysis, trying to define the most suitable tools usually entails the use of specialized techniques, standardized as unified modeling language (UML) diagrams, process diagrams, or with other tools that would be most appropriate to the type of project under consideration.

This analysis of subsystems should be as detailed as possible, in an effort to remove any possibility of ambiguity and potential confusion. The analysis must ensure that specifications are understood by all stakeholders, particularly users who are outside the technology disciplines but who are still needed to develop the project. In some instances, stakeholders could lack a specific knowledge that is required to understand the true scope of the specifications, and the analyst should make a concerted effort to inform these stakeholders through the analyses that are prepared.

For this reason, it is particularly important to use plain language whenever possible at this stage, with special care to avoid, unless deemed essential and unavoidable, the use of technical terms and jargon that do not add anything to the explanation and can act as a barrier for effective communication between the development team and users.

## Identification of Requirements by Unit

The way forward will now be to proceed from general to particular, from outside to inside the system. Thus, we begin identifying unit requirements by defining the interfaces and communication channels needed for the new system to operate in the existing environment. In particular, we must define in detail what information flows in each direction on each occasion when communicating with all other systems. We also need to identify the specific interfaces needed to facilitate such intersystem communication.

These interfaces constitute some of the essential requirements about the new information system that we build, and we will avoid a lot of difficulties if we define all of them as early as possible in the development effort. Other existing systems will not change their operation with the introduction of this new system, so the new system's interfaces will have to take into account the requirements of other systems. The new system must be adapted to operate in the work environment defined by the set of current systems of the organization.

Once we have defined the interfaces with other systems, we will be able to start preparing the functional specification. This includes an analysis that ranges from the perimeter of the system toward the center of the system, and from the general to the particular requirements of each component. The specification first considers the resolution of aspects related to the outside requirements, where external dependencies can affect the operation of our information system. The specification then turns to focus on the resolution of internal aspects, where we have a greater freedom to define the system's mode of operation.

We begin this analysis effort by examining the system from the perspective of the subsystems it will likely contain. This takes into account specifying an appropriate approach to the analysis effort. The approach should be one that seeks to identify a manageable number of units of smaller dimensions, more controllable functionality, and, above all, more homogeneous problems of lesser complexity, allowing us to simplify the job.

As a manageable number of units is achieved, a review of the interrelationships between those different modules should be carried out in a manner similar to how we examined the system's external interfaces. In particular, it is necessary to ensure that the information needs that now appear relative to these modules remain consistent with the requirements of external interfaces previously defined. Thus, we continue lowering the level of detail to break down the specification to the most basic functional components representing simple business transactions such as receiving an order, issuing an invoice, accepting a return, or recording a payment from a client.

In conjunction with this detailed analysis, a good practice is to take into account the origin of each requirement and always maintain a clear traceability of every part of the analysis. We must clearly define which requirements are those that have given rise to every part of the functional specification. Conversely, it must be possible that each requirement in the specifications can be validated and properly and adequately considered. This ensures that there are no parts of the functional analysis that have been included as a whim of the analyst, without a specific request by users, or any consequential increase in the cost of the project without a defined benefit for the organization.

## Propose a Conceptual Model

A key activity in this analysis phase of the project is the preparation of a conceptual data model that clearly identifies the entities to be considered to operate the information system. An entity in a data model is simply a conceptual representation of a subject or object from the real world for which we have to manage the particular information, attributes, or traits associated with that entity. Thus entities may be customers, suppliers, employees, products, orders, invoices, invoice lines, or many other elements that may have to be managed and considered separately in an information system.

In our previous analytical process, we separated the problem into its basic components. In constructing a data model, we essentially reverse that analytical process as we integrate all the modules, functions, and interfaces with each other in a data concept model. This helps verify that the system component set that has been defined is consistent and has no fractures, holes, or defects that may call into question the feasibility of implementing the information system later in the project.

When developing a concept model, it is necessary to address an aspect of analysis that is somewhat peripheral to the core system to be implemented. This aspect of analysis represents an examination and specification of the user interfaces that are needed as a means for users to interact with the system.

There is a whole specialty focusing on this discipline, known as the human–computer interface (HCI), which aims to study how interface components must be designed to facilitate the system use. It prescribes creating functionality in a clear, accessible, and intuitive way that facilitates user learning without requiring costly user training and preparation. The user interface is something similar to the skin of the system, and, as such, it has a vital importance because it defines what the system users will see when using the system. It also defines the complexities of the internal components and other hidden features that the system users will not see.

I will try to provide more specifics about the design criteria for a user interface by presenting some information system design concepts using current technology. To that end, consider the following three aspects of user interface design:

- *The specific work environment.* This aspect of user interface design considers the environment in which system users will reside to perform assigned work. System users often work in an office, and they will need a desktop computer that has connectivity to the new system. The office environment should also include adequate lighting, temperature comfort controls, and minimal noise distractions, as well as telephone access that provides interoffice and customer contact capability. In some instances, the required telephony may have to be integrated with the new system as a means to service customers better or to provide for more efficient internal communication.

    Other work environment factors could present user interface design challenges when the system is to be deployed in an industrial environment, or on vehicles of any kind. Such environments usually require users to be more attentive to their work and environment and less on computer system use, where computer use is often a part-time activity. Therefore, the computers used may need to be portable, and possibly hardened to endure travel. System features and functions also presented to the user may need to be adapted for use in a particularly busy or high-risk work environment.

- *User interactions with the system.* This aspect of user interface design considers the interactions that must occur between the system and users. When considering such events, the analyst will identify the information that the system provides to the user, and the information that the user provides to the system. Here, the specific data elements will have to be defined according to the nature of the work performed. The analyst will also specify any alerts, notifications, or system status information that needs to be automatically generated by the system in response to user input or, in some cases, user inactivity.

■ *User interface design.* This aspect of user interface design considers the results of the previous two analyses, and then attends to the actual design of the user interface for inclusion in the conceptual model.

## Develop a Prototype

It is essential that users and managers understand the new system's features and functionality, as well as the objectives, scope, and benefits that are being defined for the project during this phase of analysis. This can be accomplished by developing a small prototype that illustrates the core system with some level of detail. It will also indicate the existence of secondary or peripheral modules of the system at a higher level of detail. This prototype can then be presented to key stakeholders for review and approval, along with any supplemental documentation that is prepared to accompany this model of the system.

The prototype provides early, tangible support for the system development effort by allowing stakeholders to see and use a sampling of the functions and features that will be built into the full system provided to users.

## Chapter 7

# The Systems Development Life Cycle—Design

The purpose of the system design phase is to define the equipment, appliance, or device to be developed and set up to resolve the problem, including the design of each and every component, and specifying how they are integrated to solve the problem at hand. In the previous phase, we sought to better understand the problem to be solved, and we produced specifications to allow us to determine the boundaries of the problem in all its dimensions and aspects. Now, in the system design phase, we will prepare the design for the proposed solution to the problem, according to the discussions, decisions, and outcomes from the previous phase.

The resulting device, appliance, or solution may be composed of several components of various types and numbers that will vary depending on the complexity and nature of the problem. Thus, for some projects, the specifications will prompt a simple design for the solution to the problem. In other more complex projects, the specifications may warrant a more extensive and exhaustive design.

For example, the prescribed solution could be as simple as installing a basic item, data, or activity tracking and control mechanism, one that requires users who access it to perform some simple actions. The design for this mechanism would be relatively simple to accomplish, and may already be available from other sources in the organization, or from other system development efforts for which the same or a similar mechanism was designed as a subcomponent.

In contrast, the solution could be a very sophisticated system with multiple system components and subcomponents, and multiple system and user interfaces. The design for this solution would probably occur over an extended period of time and require a much more rigorous design effort to ensure that the primary system and all associated components and subcomponents are accounted for and properly addressed.

For example, consider a solution that requires the development and implementation of a sophisticated customer relationship management (CRM) system. The CRM system could integrate both the care of our customers as face-to-face interactions in the office, or as incoming customer telephone calls; either type of contact could prompt a wide variety of business transactions that the CRM system would be expected to support. The CRM system must be designed to allow the registration of all queries raised by customers, and, in turn, to generate relevant reports from the knowledge obtained during these interactions. This includes reports to management as well as reports that share knowledge and information among individuals that have customer service responsibilities.

From a technical perspective, the design will need to show how the various communication channels, system components, and user interfaces are to be integrated. This could require the adoption of a range of components, including computer telephony integration (CTI) devices, together with a digital private (automated) branch exchange (PBX), which is used to route calls to particular agents or service personnel who are in the best position to assist the customer. The system could also require the integration of an interactive voice response (IVR) system as a means to reply to specific customer queries based on a structured interaction from a series of simple questions with short answers from a limited number of potential alternatives. These components illustrate some of the complexity that could be inherent in designing a sophisticated system. It shows that design considerations may have to address all types of hardware components (e.g., winches, information screens, ticket dispensers, indicators of all kinds, computers, servers, telephone exchanges), software components, as well as consulting services needed for system development and implementation, and routine and specialized training for system users.

In the field of information technology, there is no absolute solution or single panacea to solve any global problem or specific needs related to information system design. Rather, each new systems development effort, small or large, simple or complex, warrants its own time in the design phase. System design can often be a rigorous and time-consuming process, and anything done to shorten this process, either in terms of time or effort, threatens the quality of the resulting system.

The systems development design process is illustrated in Figure 7.1, and the key design activities are described in each of the following sections of this chapter.

## Define System Architecture

The first activity in the process of designing the information system is the definition of system architecture from conceptual and technological perspectives. This activity identifies the different subsystems that comprise the total information system, the

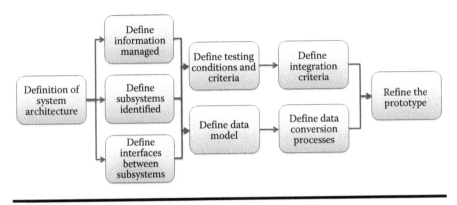

**Figure 7.1  Design stage diagram.**

technological environment in which the system will operate, and the operational scope and integration of each subsystem with the primary system and with other system components.

Each subsystem is identified and associated with the applicable requirements for its development. Sometimes, consideration is given to exceptions or contingencies that may break a defined architectural rule, but the subsystem must still be responsive to operational test requirements, while providing the features and functionality contained in the specifications.

Dividing the system into subsystems allows the design to be organized around simpler and more manageable elements. This allows developers and customers to examine and review components for acceptance before they are integrated together in an increasingly complex and sophisticated multilevel system that requires substantial understanding of the performance of system components.

Subsystem designs can be classified as *specific*, which includes components of the core system, or they can be classified as *support*, which are the peripheral components needed for a system to integrate with other applications and systems. These designations provide a means to simplify the identification of system components, and to facilitate the resolution of interactions related to the elements in the underlying technology architecture. Generally, specific subsystems correspond to the modules defined in the analysis phase. The supporting subsystems do not usually appear in that analysis, but may be the result of the insight and intuition of the person responsible for the design, someone who will identify the need for such subsystems based on personal design experience, technical knowledge, and the capacity for synthesis.

After defining the different subsystems that make up the conceptual architecture of the system, we then proceed to add detail to the design specifications. We begin with the specific subsystems, followed by the support subsystems. For each subsystem, we will create a catalog of requirements, to include all requirements identified in the analysis phase, and other additional requirements that can be identified in this stage as requirements are derived from the definition of the conceptual architecture of the system or the technology platform that will support each subsystem. During the specification of the specific subsystems' requirements, we will also identify the constraints that will be placed on the requirements for support subsystems. This is why we must begin with specific subsystems, from major to accessory, to eventually finish with support subsystems specifications.

In this process, we must identify all components that make up the system, and that should be carefully defined in order to facilitate the subsequent construction. Also, design activities should include a review of all the elements of analysis involved in each subsystem design to ensure that they are properly represented in the design and updated, as necessary, to refine their content and maintain their traceability relative to each system component. Accounting for system integration and necessary interfaces will also be important in ensuring that there will be minimal problems, if any, during the build phase.

In some instances, the design process may detect needs that warrant modification of the interface or integration requirements. Organizational norms will dictate if you can go back and make such changes to the requirements produced in earlier stages of development. However, in many organizations this would be considered unusual and exceptional. Of course, if any changes are made, a rigorous review and approval process would be needed.

## Define Information Managed

In the process of defining the system architecture, we must identify the information necessary for the operation of each subsystem, and the specification of the different modules where that information will be located. The system requires a global model of information management that gives it the necessary coherence and integrity, and which includes a physical database design.

In the design of the physical database, we should include all entities that comprise the system and the different attributes that define the associated data within those entities. According to the technological environment in which we are working, we can use different tools for this specification, such as entity–relationship models and class diagrams, among others. Creating a physical data model is an iterative and orderly process, which usually requires several cycles to achieve the desired results. This repetition of cycles helps the design specialist examine features of the system and the data required by each subsystem to fulfill the required functionality. Each cycle specifies processes that examine a deeper level of detail relative to the location of data in the physical database.

The first elements to consider will be the data sets, which are simplified representations of real-world information. Examples of such data may include the customer, the shipping address, product ID, order number, billing information, collection information, storage and transportation status, sales figures, sales region, and product descriptions. These data are recognized because they usually have a direct relationship with the same data or information used in the physical world.

There might also be occasions when a system will need multilingual support, and this may be specified as a requirement. This forces the inclusion of a language entity in the system that provides the ability to express textual elements in different languages. The system will need the appropriate functionality to ensure the timely translation of all text into the different languages used by the system or any subsystems.

Finally, data or information generated by the system or one of its subsystems comprise a data set that also needs to be managed. Examples of such data may include system-operating time, data transfer speed, system down time (outages), and system maintenance particulars. These data are used primarily by technical personnel, who are responsible for operating and maintaining the system and its components.

These various data elements can be specified according to their intended use by each subsystem component. The output of this effort is essentially a list of all data sets that will be required for system operation. These data sets can be compiled using a data dictionary, which simply identifies and provides a brief description of each data element to be used by the system.

## Define Subsystems Identified

The subsystems identified in earlier phases of the systems development life cycle are reviewed and subjected to additional design scrutiny. In this activity, the design specialist will examine the details of the technical specifications as a basis for creating subsystem designs that will achieve the specified performance requirements for the system, subsystems, and components.

In effect, this design work will be represented by the generation of system and subsystem construction specifications. These specifications should consider issues such as the construction of the system environment, a thorough description of the primary system and each subsystem being constructed, and the identification of interdependencies among the subsystems and their components. The details of these specifications will usually be determined with consideration of the technological environment and the particular technical standards of each organization.

## Define Interfaces between Subsystems

The subsystem interfaces identified in earlier phases of the systems development life cycle are reviewed and subjected to additional design scrutiny. This includes specifying hardware and software needed for intersystem communication and data exchange, and in some cases this could include communication with external systems that may or may not be owned by the performing organization.

In a manner similar to the design of subsystems above, this design effort should produce specifications for the installation and use of interfaces between subsystems. To a large extent, this design will identify the hardware needed to create each interface point. This process should also address connectivity protocols relative to each interface point, and also provide a specification of any data or signal conversions that are needed at either the exit or entry interface points. This effort may require the identification of either firmware or software that is needed to manage such conversions.

## Define Testing Conditions and Criteria

It is standard practice to test the features and functionality of every new system and subsystem before it is placed into full operation. The types of tests, frequency of testing, and test criteria to be used should therefore be identified and incorporated into the construction specifications of the information system being developed.

It is usually the case that the operation of each subsystem is tested independently; for example, do the lights come on when you turn on the system? The subsystem is then tested under loaded conditions represented by connectivity with other subsystems. Sometimes, components are built and tested before they are incorporated into subsystems, and this represents another layer of similar testing that must be specified and conducted. This is sometimes referred to as unit testing. Finally, after all components and subsystems have passed their designated individual tests, these subsystems are then connected together or connected to the primary system for another series of tests that evaluate the total system.

A variety of tests may be needed to ensure that specified requirements for system operations, as well as features and functions, are achieved. Therefore, the following types of tests should be considered: individual, integration, functional, load and stress, and user or acceptance testing. In some projects, acceptance testing is required for both component and subsystem testing as well as for total system testing.

In addition to specifying the tests to be performed, this activity is also used to specify the criteria that will be used for each type of test. The criteria are applied to measure the level of performance or capability that the system must demonstrate in order to pass each test, and to ultimately be deemed operational and accepted by the customer.

## Define Data Model

In this activity, the design work performed in earlier activities is compiled and a data model is created to illustrate and guide how data will be managed by the system being developed.

Once the data and information sets have been identified, we can then proceed to establish the relationships between them. We can do this using several methods and representations, but the fundamental purpose of this effort is to show how one instance of a data set in one subsystem relates to another data collection in another subsystem.

For example, a data element called "Client" can be used in one subsystem to relate to different data sets in other subsystems. In particular, the "Client" data element in one database can be used to identify relevant attributes about the client that are contained in another database. Establishing this data relationship will allow users to enter "Client" on one system as a means to retrieve and view client attributes such as name, account number, business address, business town or city, business postal code, established payment terms, order fulfillment preferences, invoice and billing preferences, form of payment, credit card information, and any other relevant information that should be associated with the "Client" data element.

The resulting data model should be reviewed to ensure that it properly represents and responds to the data and information needs of the subsystems identified, and that it also provides consistency across the primary system. The result of this review may require certain data entity designs to be adjusted; for example, it may be necessary to separate a data entity that is seen initially as a single entity into more than one entity as a means to improve the data management capability.

## Define Integration Criteria

In this activity, the design specialist will examine the overall system specification and the subsystem interfaces to ascertain the aspects of system performance that are performed more or less concurrently by two or more subsystems. The purpose of this effort is to identify the data requirements and protocols needed for such concurrent operation.

In turn, data, information, and even applications are examined, and relevant inputs and outputs are specified. Criteria are then defined to show the format, content, and protocol requirements for data that are to be transferred and used in functions across systems, usually in an automated manner. If a particular subsystem performed a function, used a database, and did all of this totally within that subsystem, then there is no need for integration with other subsystems, and no need for associated criteria. The criteria developed in this activity are used to specify what is needed for the proper exchange and handling of data and information between connected subsystems.

It is usually appropriate to incorporate integration criteria with the data model for easy reference.

# Define Data Conversion Processes

When a new information system is developed, it is rarely installed as an isolated system in an untouched systems environment where elements of information management did not previously exist. Rather, new information systems usually represent a next step or next generation in the evolution of previous or existing systems within an organization. Those previous systems may have become obsolete, or they may have incomplete data-handling capability, but they still contain valuable information for the business and for the organization. That data and information needs to be incorporated and possibly converted from the starting point of the original system and loaded into the new system, to begin operations under the new management paradigm.

Therefore, the design phase must take into account the need to apply this data conversion process by designing the method migration process needed for the timely implementation of the new information system. The design of the migration and initial data load must clearly establish the equivalencies and relationships among the data available thus far in the organization, and must also include the components of the new physical data model.

These relationships can be direct and immediate. (The client code or postal code can have the same structure in both environments, for example, and not require any processing.) The relationship might also require small changes or more sophisticated elaborations that can affect the entire generation of data with arbitrary values if the data were not available in the previous system.

Depending on the type of transformations to be performed on the data for migration from the previous system to the new information system, there may be a requirement for a definition of modules and data conversion components of varying complexity and sophistication. These must be designed and constructed just as any other part of the information system, but their usefulness is transient and limited in time. The actions needed for data conversion are specified as an outcome of this activity.

# Refine the Prototype

A prototype helps the users and decision makers of the organization validate the system design specifications. In this design activity, a prototype is created (or the previous one is refined) to present a more complete and detailed representation of the system under development. It will likely include additional features that were not included in the earlier prototype model.

This refined prototype will focus on specific subsystems, essentially leaving aside support subsystems. If necessary or appropriate, with considerations such as size or system complexity, this effort may result in several prototypes being developed to illustrate the partial functionality related to specific groups of users or particular departments within the organization.

Therefore, it is not necessary that a prototype be created to reproduce the entire system. Instead, it is sometimes appropriate to simply offer an overview of the system in order to demonstrate the operating capability of the system. It will be very important for the prototype to show how the new system will resolve the issues and rectify the problems for which it was developed.

# Chapter 8

# The Systems Development Life Cycle—Build and Test

The building phase of the system is the core work of the information system implementation effort. It will normally consume more resources and time than all other life cycle phases. However, despite the significant effort, one must avoid the temptation of thinking that it is the most important phase. When the importance of other development phases is ignored, the result can be a system riddled with errors and inconsistencies, which might require patches and improvised on-the-spot changes to correct analysis and design defects. The analysis and design phases are equally if not more important, and due consideration and effort must be exerted in those stages of system development.

In the build and test phase, all activities are aimed at developing the hardware and software (including programming code) needed to implement the established specifications and to resolve the problem for which the project was initiated. It is the phase in which we can see the results of the efforts invested thus far, as we see the analysis and design turned into an information system that meets the various features and functionalities specified.

The systems development build and test process is illustrated in Figure 8.1, and the key build and test activities are described in each of the following sections of this chapter.

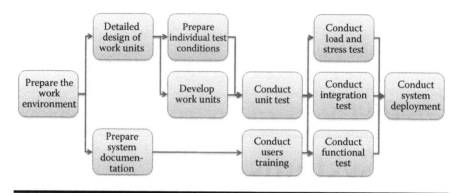

**Figure 8.1    Build and test stage diagram.**

# Prepare the Work Environment

The first step in building a new system always involves preparing the work environment. The work environment may be more or less complex than the technology being introduced, but the following activities warrant consideration when preparing the work environment.

- Tools are needed to manage the source files and control versions, as amended. The source file editor may be a general-purpose application or more specialized depending on the source language. These tools may be simpler if the team is small and concentrated in one physical space, where they can informally share information and coordinate their activities. In turn, tools may be more complex when circumstances change and the team is scattered at different physical locations. Appropriate tools must be used and care must be taken when the development team size is increased. This can make it difficult to control changes if more than one programmer is simultaneously modifying the same source, and this situation must be managed to avoid conflict and change overlaps in subsequent updates.
- A database manager needs to be assigned to facilitate the identification and management of the database that will support the information system. Currently, we normally use a relational database to accomplish the storage and retrieval of data. This allows us to define certain logic to ensure compliance with some general restrictions of the application, thus easing checks to the application programs. A database manager with skill and expertise is needed to accomplish this effort.
- In general, we need to create an environment or framework that allows us to compile the different elements of software, translate them into executable code, and then conduct performance tests under a structure that frees us from cumbersome tasks and allows us to concentrate on debugging code and mistakes.

# Detailed Design of Work Units

Although we are working in the build and test phase, this activity provides a final review of the system design for the purposes of adding design details that ensure each unit design is usable in the build process. It is very important that this effort is based on validated specifications, because any errors that occur in this stage will likely multiply the costs associated with error corrections. Possible impact areas could range from a section of code in a particular source to multiple parties from different sources.

We must therefore insist that all efforts to refine the specifications made in the analysis and design phases are completed in this activity before starting construction. This will be critical to the progress of the project and the management of its present and future costs. It will also help avoid mistakes and shortcomings, which, if identified later, become more costly to isolate and correct, and will cause more risk to the information system development effort.

# Prepare Individual Test Conditions

As detailed specifications of the different components of the information system are developed, we can prepare the test conditions that will be used for testing each system component, as well as for each module or subsystem. Such tests need to be performed as proof that the solution is suitable for fulfilling project requirements. The identification of these test conditions, properly organized at different levels, types, and test cycles, will become our test plan.

The test plan will identify each test to be performed, and in this activity we will concentrate on establishing the conditions for performing the following prominent tests:

- *Unit/individual tests.* These are tests that will focus on verifying that each component, considered individually, complies with the specifications prepared for operation. The responsibility for carrying out such tests is the programmer or programmer analyst who is developing each component, and the purpose is to ensure that the component is working properly. Unit test results should provide reasonable assurance that the component is working according to specification. However, this test does not offer any conclusions about how this component will interact with the other components of the global system.
- *Integration tests.* These tests will be performed by personnel with advanced experience relative to those involved in unit testing. Their responsibility will include testing the subsystem or module to which those unit components belong. They will review validated unit test results, and then perform the designated integration testing to ensure that the different components can

handle the required maximum load and level of stress and that they are properly integrated and interact correctly to result in a functional and operational subsystem that meets the test indicated in the relevant design specifications. This process is repeated successively at progressively higher levels of integration, ending in a complete system test.

The test plan should also include provisions regarding the actions to be taken when a unit or system test fails. The plan should specify the variety of incidents that could cause modules and components to be returned to technical teams for correction and rectification. It should identify the process for doing this, and for arranging the repeated iterations of tests needed until we have an information system that is clean of errors.

It is very important that the various test conditions are defined from the perspective of customer acceptance. To that end, test conditions should correspond to the criteria for product acceptance, and as such should be discussed and approved by users who have defined the behavior of the system they are seeking to obtain. This allows information system testing to engage all relevant stakeholders in the process, which facilitates public awareness and the accountability of everyone involved in the testing activities.

This test plan is used in the subsequent activities that specify the performance of particular component, subsystem, and system tests.

## Develop Work Units

Once we have defined the work environment and completed the detailed design of the work units, we can integrate the various components in a framework for the production of software, and then begin our work on code generation of the information system components. This work represents the fundamental purpose of this project phase and will absorb most of the effort and dedication of the team members. It will also take the longest period of time to complete, and consume most of the project budget.

The output of this activity will be the developed work units (subsystems and components), and the overall system that is made ready for the variety of tests that lie ahead in the system development process.

## Conduct Unit Test

The test plan developed in a previous activity (see Section "Prepare Individual Test Conditions") will be used to guide the conduct of all required unit tests. This test of system components is the first test in a series that will subsequently be applied to components, subsystems, and the overall system.

This type of testing is performed on the source code of work units to determine if the application is working properly, without bugs, and that the application performance produces the desired results. In a sense, the unit test represents the first step in a bottom-up testing process that ultimately considers and tests the total system. The unit test provides assurance that the component is functioning properly. In turn, successful test results can be used in higher-level system tests to eliminate the previously tested components as the cause of any problems that are encountered.

Unit tests are applied to each work unit that is developed. There could be a few or many such work units. Therefore, it will be important to distinguish the work units being tested, and to separate and maintain the test results that are achieved for each work unit. In some instances, unit test results will contribute to the preparation of component documentation.

## Conduct Integration Test

The test plan developed in a previous activity will be used to guide the conduct of all integration tests. For integration testing, system components (work units) are combined to form the larger system. This can be done by adding components and then testing the successive "growing" system, or the components can be combined together at once to create the total system for testing. The approach to use should be specified in the testing plan, and will be based on the number and complexity of components to be integrated.

The components and subsystems are combined to define the full system, and this integration of components must be tested to validate their ability to work together. This includes tests that examine component interfaces and communication. It also considers the automated transfer or generation of data between relevant components. Integration testing is performed in conjunction with the load and stress test and with the functional test. Sometimes, these specific tests are included in the plan for integration testing. For our purposes, these two related tests are briefly described in the subsections below.

## Conduct Load and Stress Test

The test plan developed in a previous activity (see Section "Prepare Individual Test Conditions") will be used to guide the conduct of all required load and stress tests. Once we have verified that an information system meets the specifications and is validated by the satisfactory completion of successive test cycles, we must ensure that the system will be capable of withstanding the most demanding operating conditions. To do this requires the preparation and conduct of a set of load-testing and stress-testing steps.

Unlike the previous tests conducted in the development environment, these load and stress tests should be performed in the production environment or in an environment as similar as possible to the planned system-operating environment. This testing subjects the technical architecture to increasing operating loads as a means to determine the threshold of its operating capability. This testing verifies the technical architecture issues on the burden of increasing operating loads as a means to determine the threshold of its operating capacity. The test continues until the threshold is reached, and falls within the expected demand for the information system.

This process may require the use of simulation tools to assist in and effectively control the test in order to obtain results that can be reported as valid test outcomes. These tests will carry the system, or at least the critical elements of it, to the boundary of the most demanding conditions and the worst case that the system is expected to bear. This helps identify if any operations are blocked or if any exceptions occur that render the system unresponsive to users in such circumstances.

## Conduct Functional Test

The test plan developed in a previous activity will be used to guide the conduct of all required functional tests. Although stakeholders, particularly customers, may be involved in many of the tests performed, the customer's end users are likely participants in functional tests.

Although the interfaces, connectivity, and communications between components and subsystems have been evaluated in previous tests, particularly the system integration test, the functional test examines the actual inputs and outputs that will be needed by system users. It may also be used to examine the graphical interface presented to users. All in all, the functional test ensures that the features and functions of the system will fulfill user needs, and verifies that they have been developed and perform according to design specifications.

## Prepare System Documentation

Following the completion of all tests, it is time to prepare the product for delivery to users, and an important part of the product comprises the manuals and documentation generated during the development effort to make the system understandable and usable by different user groups. This includes information that will be provided to project engineers responsible for the administration and operation of the information system, technical people responsible for the evolution and corrective maintenance of the information system, and system users responsible for completing necessary system training to enable their subsequent use of the new information system.

For this purpose, we must collect, classify, and review all relevant system documentation, including consideration of the following document types:

- Installation, loading, and system management documentation is provided for the technical staff that must deploy the information system and maintain its operating capability for system users. This documentation will provide guidance in resolving incidents that may arise in the technical environment from the falling off of software services to the restoration of certain system components. This type of documentation should also provide instructions and guidance for conducting system backups, restoring a failed system, and routinely updating external components, such as versions of base software products and databases that interface with other systems.

- System development and maintenance documentation is addressed to the technical staff, and should facilitate the subsequent development or bug fixes that have gone unnoticed in the various tests and specifications. This documentation contains information about all the system levels that must be considered, and it should assist the technical staff in understanding system operations, in predicting the impact of any problems that arise, and in defining the most appropriate solution to problems that do arise.

- Information system training documentation oriented to the explanation of the information system, its capabilities and features, and its operation is provided to system users. This documentation is used by system users both in training sessions and as a reference that presents adequate guidance for informational and educational purposes. It will need to include examples and cases to facilitate the understanding of users receiving the documentation, and may take different forms: user manual, reference manual, user documentation online with contextual help, or facilities and support material for training.

## Conduct User Training

A plan that presents the strategy for training various types of system users is prepared for the purpose of conveying information about system characteristics, features, and functionality to the potential user population.

If the system is designed for "self-service" use, where users generally reside outside the organization and access the system via Internet portals, for example, then there is no point or particular need to train such users. However, some learning aids should be incorporated into the online experience, and those aids should be strengthened through the use of contextual online documentation that helps the user find the information needed to use the system.

If users of the system are a relatively small group, more or less localized geographically, and with a level of knowledge that is homogeneous, then we can apply a general training strategy for all users. This training strategy may account for users that have different roles and positions in the organization, according to the different individual needs for user access to the system.

However, if the number of system users is high, or if user geographic locations are broadly dispersed, then it may be necessary to adopt a segmentation strategy for user training as a means to provide the different users with adequate information system training that falls within reasonable and assumable costs for that training.

It is also possible to define a special user group that represents proponents of the information system. These users will receive intensive training in order for them to acquire a deep working knowledge about the information system, knowledge that they can later spread to other users. They become system "apostles," who evangelize and promote new information system use, offering help and support to their colleagues when needed.

In addition to the training strategy, the training plan should also identify training dates and locations for training individual users and specially identified user groups. If appropriate, instructions for notifying users and their managers of their participation in system training can be included. A training program registration process can also be specified according to the normal training process used within the organization.

It is then time to conduct user training according to the strategy and schedule presented in the system user training plan.

## Conduct System Deployment

Once the information system achieves or surpasses all the technical tests, we can conclude the development process of the information system and have a reasonable certainty about its readiness to be delivered to users for final validation.

When the system is ready to be delivered, we must prepare the data migration and initial system load to allow its setup and later entry into operation, and to facilitate its implementation. This is discussed in greater detail in the next chapter.

# Chapter 9

# The Systems Development Life Cycle—System Implementation

The purpose of this phase in any project is to accomplish the effective implementation of the project's products or deliverables. Whatever their nature, their implementation represents some level of transformation in the ways that business operations are performed in the organization.

This deployment of a new system, subsystem, or component represents the introduction of a change into the organization that has the potential to produce both stress and a rise in individual resistance to that change. This reaction is almost inevitable in the system implementation phase. Therefore, implementation necessarily involves managing the acceptance of change in addition to acceptance of the new system. This phase may include a period of instability and some risks associated with change could occur until the new system is fully implemented.

The implementation process therefore needs to be effective in resolving severe difficulties associated with the acceptance of change. The most prominent difficulty lies in the subjectivity of users, which leads them to perceive both real and imagined consequences from the change that occurs. To that end, these perceptions, along with diverse attitudes, expectations, and personal impacts, need to be recognized and managed in a forthright manner. The success or failure of the implementation effort (and the project) will often rely on management's responsiveness to these issues. Management actions should help to achieve the desired open collaboration that is needed in this phase; indeed, management inaction

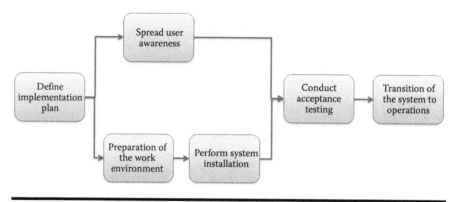

**Figure 9.1   System implementation diagram.**

could raise suspicion or mistrust among users who are already wary of the new system. The implementation phase is distinctly a time for visible management presence and support.

The systems development implementation process is illustrated in Figure 9.1, and the key implementation activities are described in each of the following sections of this chapter.

## Define Implementation Plan

The first step to successful implementation is to devote adequate time to thoroughly study and carefully prepare the implementation plan. An implementation process that provides for thorough preparation and detailed planning will reduce the potential for problems. Also, with effective planning, any problems that do occur should have minimal impact, with less distortion of planned activities. This planning activity is performed to specify the actions and activities needed to accomplish system implementation. It also provides for risk assessment and contingency planning that will provide remedies to some problems that might occur.

We can begin this activity by reviewing and considering all of the project's general requirements to ascertain whether they have all been achieved, or if any requirements are still unfinished or incomplete. Moreover, in this phase, it is time to make final decisions on issues that remain unresolved, such as server locations, the best strategy for implementing the new system, and the reconciliation of details or designs that might have changed in the course of the development effort and now require reconsideration. The final decisions on these items should be presented in the implementation plan.

The implementation plan should also include a fundamental schedule of implementation actions, or reference to the same in the overall project schedule. This plan should specify activities and tasks that accomplish the following:

- Preparation of the user's IT work environment
- Installation and setup of newly developed systems in the user's work environment
- Arrangements for acceptance testing
- Procedures for making the system operational

However, planning for implementation will not be adequate if it simply comprises the preparation of a schedule of milestones, activities, and tasks; instead, it must also consider objectives, outputs, and constraints, and the requirements derived from these elements. Therefore, the implementation plan should ensure that project outputs (i.e., deliverables) can be deployed effectively, according to the requirements and specifications. The nuances and findings relative to these issues should be included for reference in the implementation plan.

Moreover, any uncertainty associated with system implementation should be identified and examined by performing a risk assessment on the elements of the implementation plan. This may be accomplished in conjunction with the risk assessment performed for the overall project, or it may be accomplished as a separate effort. When risks are identified, they should be analyzed for the probability of occurrence and potential impact on the planned implementation effort. The resulting risks should then be evaluated for their total potential impact on system implementation, which helps prioritize them in order of importance.

For each risk that is identified, analyzed, and prioritized, we then proceed to develop a contingency response—what we will do should the identified risk actually occur. Such risk response strategies can be developed to eliminate or reduce the probability of risk occurrence or the intensity of risk impact. The following are common risk response strategies that can be examined and considered for each identified risk:

- *Risk avoidance*: actions that can be taken to remove the probability of risk occurrence, usually accomplished by specifying an alternative course of action
- *Risk transfer*: actions that are taken to move the risk responsibility outside of the performing organization, which is represented when contractors and consultants are used to perform highly specialized project or development work
- *Risk mitigation*: actions that are taken to closely manage the risk event, which is accomplished in a way that minimizes the risk's probability of occurrence or its impact
- *Risk acceptance*: decisions that are made to accept the outcome of a risk event should it occur; usually reserved for the process owner or management levels, according to the impact of the risk

The collection of these responses can be compiled into a contingency plan that is relevant for the system implementation effort; this plan can be appended to the project risk management plan.

All of these risk management actions provide the necessary checks to evaluate uncertainties, and offer new insights that can be included in the plan for system implementation. This plan will then constitute the road map for system implementation, and can be integrated into the primary or overall plan for the project.

## Spread User Awareness

One key aspect of successful implementation in any project, regardless of whether the purpose is construction and implementation of a new information system or simply an alteration of any work routine, lies in the acceptance of the new system performance by users. They must leave the comfort of their previous routine to accept and adopt the new processes associated with the new system. For this reason, various types and gradations of awareness are needed for these users, and possibly include information dissemination, education and training, and specialized programs that promote the acceptance of the changes that affect the users.

To achieve this awareness, we should identify appropriate awareness programs within the implementation plan. Training programs represent an appropriate means to help users deal with the strategic importance of the new system and the circumstances of the solution. Most users will know about the project and its system-oriented products through participation in system user training. With actual implementation, we want users to know and reasonably understand how the new system can help them in their daily work, what advantages they can expect from using the system, and how the new system will benefit the organization. Therefore, a training program should be specified in this plan and presented to users with a focus on why the system is desirable, why the change is needed at this time, and what user contributions are expected and needed for the successful implementation of the system.

This plan should also provide the means to convey relevant information to system users and project stakeholders. In particular, reporting on key uncertainties and their implications or potential impacts on users and stakeholders should be transparent, and inform them about what contingencies or specific plans have been implemented to counteract each of the possible problems identified. This transparency will make it easier for users to appreciate the work done and to assess the benefits of the functional change that is being introduced in the organization. This contributes to early acceptance, and encourages the more enthusiastic individuals to play an active role in the implementation, acting as promoters of change, defenders of that change among their peers, and even "apostles" and drivers of the new system introduction for the rest of the organization.

## Prepare the Work Environment

This activity is performed to ensure that the work environment is ready to receive the systems to be installed or deployed. It begins with a review of the provisions and procedures prescribed for introducing system components into the production environment. This includes reviewing the prescribed sequence and order of component installation (deployment) to ensure that the various components are installed properly and work without difficulties or incidences.

Preparation sometimes involves introducing new hardware that may be essential to system operations. This could include ensuring that required electrical inputs are available, that necessary air quality and conditioning equipment is installed, and that receipt and installation of all specified equipment is accomplished. Connectivity and communication capability for the new hardware also needs to be established, and such activities should be accomplished when preparing the work environment.

Usually, system deployment will not consume too much time once all the elements of the technological architecture are prepared and verified, so time is taken to make sure this is done in this preparation activity. This will be helpful should it become necessary to repeat the deployment process more than once, which could occur in order to resolve problems that are found when the software is updated to include changes that incorporate new requirements, or when errors and problems identified in the user-testing process need to be rectified.

A final preparation activity is accomplished to confirm the system installation with the relevant department and its users. This takes the form of communicating the intention to proceed with system installation, as was planned and previously announced. To that end, user participation in the installation process is reviewed and initiated.

## Perform System Installation

System installation begins with the introduction of the new system, subsystem, or component into the information system environment in a manner that allows user access to its features and functions. Therefore, system installation includes the processes that physically install applications and any peripheral software on relevant hardware in the information system environment. This is accomplished according to the established configuration specifications and system requirements.

This installation is often designed as an automated process using appropriate tools that generate the installation files as a package. Then we only have to invoke this process in order to deploy our software with apparent simplicity.

Every time a new version of any software is deployed, it should be accompanied by several types of documentation containing relevant information about the installation.

- Deployment files must always be accompanied by their installation instructions. These instructions must provide sufficient information to enable proper installation planning, including prerequisites or peripherals related to the products that must be installed, and they must be configured so that the deployment will be successful and free of any incident or inconvenience.
- We must also include all configuration requirements documentation, which provides steps that have to be taken into account to ensure that precautions and warnings are followed, and to ensure that proper settings and configuration parameters are identified and used. This will result in a system that loads, starts, and runs properly.
- We should also include documentation concerning the contents of the deployed system, which can take one of two forms depending on the nature of the installation and how installation events unfold. In the first, the installation represents a major or new version, which will introduce radical changes to the previous features and functionality. The documentation associated with this type of installation needs to fully describe the new system. In the second, the installation represents a minor version change. For deployments that introduce only isolated or limited changes or improvements, we can simply provide documentation that briefly describes the improvements in features and functionality, identifying what is new in the system and what requires some kind of attention from users or technical staff.

The final step in the installation process provides for loading data on the system in the production environment. Although system component installation may be repeated because of issues or problems that arise, data loading in the information system operating environment will normally be done only once, or perhaps twice under extenuating circumstances.

Data that are loaded into the information system include the setup of system files needed for acceptance testing by users. This is done in order to facilitate the acceptance-testing process. It includes introducing a variety of test data that allow testing of all possible conditions resulting from system operations, and precludes the need for actual business operations data. However, real-time business will have to be introduced at some point in time during system installation.

## Conduct Acceptance Testing

System acceptance is managed by the technical staff, but it is performed by users within the organization. This testing is conducted for the following purposes:

- To confirm that the new or revised system meets the quality specifications and criteria defined at the beginning of the project

- To verify that the new or revised system contains the features and functionality that are specified in the product requirements, as presented in the test conditions that were agreed at the start of the project
- To enable users to evaluate and determine if the new or revised system resolves the problems, issues, or conditions for which it was developed, and to provide feedback to the technical staff in that regard

The documentation cited earlier will present knowledge and information about the new system, and facilitate system evaluation and review by users and technical staff. Evaluation results will ultimately determine whether or not the deployment effort was justified, and if user needs and any requested changes have been incorporated and work properly.

A common mistake occurs when the test conditions to be met by the new system are not defined until reaching this stage of the development effort. This places an unnecessary burden on the technical staff and users alike, who must try to agree on test conditions just before or as testing is being conducted. A still worse scenario arises when test conditions are not specified, and acceptance testing reverts to something like converting test results into a show about information system capabilities without any real testing being performed. This could result in using the attitude and willingness of users to give their approval for the product in place of formal testing. In such cases, acceptance is achieved based on the user's mood, affinity toward team members (and technical staff), or personal insight or experience with acceptance testing.

Of course, proper acceptance testing should apply a rigorous testing plan that sets out the tests to be performed, the input data to be used, the measurement and compilation of values achieved from each test in contrast to expected results, and is therefore applied with total objectivity, to provide a comprehensive check to determine if the system works according to plan or not.

## Transition the System to Operations

The final implementation activity is represented by the production pass or placement of the system into operational mode. This involves entry of the information system into service for the accomplishment of business needs, and the beginning of its routine use for work by the system users.

This activity, according to the nature and scope of the project, may mean the end of the project and the dispersal of the project team, but it could also be just another milestone in the design process. Sometimes, the design strategy calls for iterative system development in which there is a defined series of successive phases; then this implementation represents just one of several progressive and wider range system implementations. From a core of essential and basic system functionalities, successive implementations are used to extend the system capabilities available to users. This gradually enriches the users' information technology environment while work is being consolidated into essential and central parts of the system. Subsequent implementations are also influenced by exposure to opinion and constructive criticism of users, based on the daily use of the operational system in their daily work.

# Chapter 10

# Managing Problems Related to Information Systems

A critical look at the everyday reality in any modern organization offers us a good basis for our analysis about how information systems are currently used in organizations, with insight into the processes of design, development (build and test), and implementation (exploitation). We can then build a picture of a landscape full of problems, tensions, and difficulties that will lead us to believe that this profession cannot be described as mature according to its results.

This is especially true when the field of information technology is compared with other disciplines. For example, if we consider engineering (mechanical, electronic, industrial, aerospace, and telecommunications), it is clear that if we direct a specific question at two engineering experts on a particular subject we would assume that we would receive two identical or at least similar responses, with minimal variability.

Professionals in the field of information technology and knowledge are developing their work within the framework of a young profession with serious difficulties to overcome in the definition and delimitation of their scope of responsibility as well as a substantial amount of controversy inherent in its ongoing development. It is a discipline that has progressed dramatically in the last 20 years, but still encounters serious problems, some of which are unacceptable. To that end, in this chapter, we will examine the types and natures of information system problems.

The implementation of a new information system in any organization invariably introduces organizational change in the way people conduct business operations, and that change may have a range of impacts depending on the strategic or operational nature of the project and the general or specific scope of the project, and this in turn may cause significant reactions in individuals in terms of cultural and human factors.

We can consider the effects of transience, which is inevitably associated with the introduction and implementation of the change process, with its beginning and end clearly defined. Then we also need to bring into play and consider the multiple skills and abilities that are normally located in different areas of the organization or even beyond, and the need to organize all components in a specific way to achieve the planned objectives. These matters contribute to some level of uncertainty as each new project is launched, as we build the structure and form the project team, bringing together capabilities that were scattered before and are now assembled to work together for the purpose of producing the required change.

When projects of this type in modern organizations are analyzed, a terrible conclusion can be drawn: according to some international agencies such as the Project Management Institute or the APM Group, both dedicated to promoting the project management discipline, no more than 10% of projects end in success, with 90% of projects that were started not achieving their planned objectives. These statistics are devastating, especially if you consider that the skills and knowledge normally deployed in managing an information technology implementation project are not essentially so different from the skills and knowledge used in other types of projects such as constructing a building, setting up a new production line, or creating a new product.

So, what happens with these information technology projects that causes their results to be so disappointing? Where is the problem? Is the problem related to an intangible condition or is it more related to the production methods? Let us take an analytical look at what happens to projects before venturing to diagnose the overall problem, which has many angles.

## Discovery of Difficulties Associated with Defining the Scope

One of the factors that may cause more conflict in projects that develop information systems, and which occurs with unacceptable frequency, lies in difficulties arising from the contrasting understanding that customers and development team members have about the scope of the system development effort. What is the perimeter of the system and what implications does that boundary have? In other words, what is included in the information system, and consequently in the project, and what is excluded from it? In this way, the scope and the perimeter define what is within and out of the boundaries of the project.

This problem inevitably arises in any project, whether developed internally or performed with the participation of an external company. It becomes much more evident in the latter scenario, because noticeable conflicts of interest arise between the client and the external provider of system development relative to their respective perspectives. This conflict can take many forms, such as the late addition of new requirements, when the project is already in advanced stages of development, or when unanticipated requests for changes are made and claimed as essential. This can break the patience of development team members because it can be very irritating, and also because some of the requested changes are not adequately defined. In some instances, requested changes will vary between alternatives, if the petitioner has a doubtful character.

Just a few months ago, I had the opportunity to lead a project for a group of institutions of higher education. The purpose of this project was to build a new information system to replace the independent systems that each university had been operating thus far. These information systems allowed them to manage the process by which students who wanted access to higher studies must pass some tests to probe their knowledge and competencies, the results of which would determine the careers they could subsequently follow.

These tests, also known as "access proof," are held annually across Spain under the authority of the regional government. Tests in 2010 involved the participation of nearly 15,000 candidates, and about 115,000 tests were needed to validate the educational level achieved by these young people. The test results determine if these aspiring individuals will be able to receive a higher education in public universities after their years in high school, and will also enable them to obtain guidance about their abilities and their options based on the preferences they have expressed.

This project involved the first collaboration of these five institutions of higher education, which, despite sharing geographical space in a noncompetitive environment, had never worked together on any matter other than when forced to do so by the public administration office responsible for higher education in each community. However, on this occasion, they were compelled to do so for two primary reasons. First, a new law at the state level was published, indicating that the tests had changed. This declaration automatically rendered obsolete the information systems that these institutions had used in previous years. This was done without giving the institutions the opportunity to manage or negotiate their current applications. Second, an extraordinary budget constraint was added to the traditional restrictions that we might call structural, and that resulted in a heavier-than-normal burden on the institutions because the global economic crisis had further deteriorated the revenues of the government.

The project was conceived and planned over a period of 6 months, which seemed a meager term. However, given the circumstances, it was determined to be possible because it was assumed that certain conditions would facilitate the work, including the following:

- The project would develop a new information system based on the specifications and software currently used by one of the institutions that had more experience and whose leadership was recognized by the other institutions. The other basis for the specification of requirements would be the text of the new regulation that had recently been published.
- The technology platform to be used for this project would be defined by the team, which would be given full freedom to define it, with the only condition that it should be a Web environment developed in three layers and with use of the Java language.
- The universities would define an authorized person who would be responsible for making project decisions. This person would represent the development team in collaborating and negotiating with colleagues from all of the involved universities with regard to aspects of the project that would affect them. This would free the development team from the burden of having a multiple dialog, and facilitate a central point of contact for discussing and reaching required agreements. This adds value, because the clients were distributed across the entire region, with more than 200 mi. between their respective locations.

The project was given the necessary priority and attention from all participating institutions, because the dates of the entrance exams were already published in the new law, and the institutions had to implement their systems solution within 6 months. The new law ruled every detail of the new process to be implemented, and the ability of the participating institutions to reach the goals established by the new law required a full commitment from all parties.

However, despite all the efforts invested by all participants, the day when the new information system was presented to the heads of all the institutions as well as the competent public administration, less than 2 weeks before the day on which the tests that would definitively validate the success of the project, a surprise situation was encountered. At the end of the meeting, as people were leaving, one of the attendees suddenly announced that the system was not working properly, and he referenced an enrollment report that was used and still needed in his institution to identify areas in which students were enrolled. This was an issue related to scope.

The coordinator of the institutions, the technical team members, and the various institutional representatives, including the representative from the same institution that identified the problem, were all unaware of the problem. Fortunately, given the small scope of change required, it was determined that this feature could be introduced on time; indeed, it was made available, on time, to all users, and more than 15,000 young people passed their tests without incident.

Nevertheless, this circumstance produced some negative effects among the technical team members, both specialists from the consulting firm and technicians from the participating educational institutions. Some concern also arose between users of the system and those responsible for its operation. The project team saw how its work was questioned as a result of apparent communication failures, and were concerned about why the representative who announced the problem would not have known to identify the requirement at the time when the scope of this information system was being created and approved.

If the communication process had worked properly, it would have allowed this person to expose his requirement for consideration at the outset of the project. That would have been the appropriate time to discuss the reasonability of the requirement, leading to it either being included in the system specifications if accepted, or if not accepted, being given an explanation of the conditions resulting in that decision. All in all, inattention to the established scope created a dilemma during the final stages of the development process.

The users also expressed a growing unease and discomfort because they perceived the new information system as one that did not resolve the needs of the participating educational institutions. They began to view the development team as one locked in a glass tower, insulated from the world, and working outside the reality of the business needs of the universities. The problem caused a perception among some users that the system was developed without considering the needs and requirements of users.

Of course, this absolutely did not happen, because many of the users of the five institutions had actively participated in providing requirements and in performing intermediate product reviews with varying degrees of involvement. However, despite the feelings of excitement and satisfaction at having succeeded in creating the new information system in a record time and with the active collaboration of the five entities, some mistrust, some frustration, and the occasional withdrawal by members of the core technical team did occur. All of this happened because of an unjustified and surprise "attack" from one of the users, who never explained his requirement or need until the final review meeting.

Differences of opinion over the scope of a system arise in many projects, and this occurs according to the management style and leadership provided by the project's sponsor and other responsible managers, and depending on how well they assert the scope. The second half of a project, in general, or the end of the project, in most cases, is when the project team begins to deliver the specified system products that require validation and approval from users, as shown in the example discussed above.

So when users begin to review the information system that is announced as a final product, they will likely look for the features and functions that were present in the previous version of the information system, along with the new features and functions that they requested to improve their work performance. They could also look at the new system and find that the requested features and functions are not there, and that the system does not have the desired and appropriate characteristics to meet their goal of improving user productivity.

These problems can be divided into two different types that are equally unpleasant and have similar consequences for users, but that can be distinguished by their different contractual consequences: (i) functionality is insufficient or inadequately built into the information system, and (ii) issues related to integration with other systems in the information technology environment have surfaced.

In the first scenario, the problems may be considered according to their potential effect on routine operations within the organization. They are *critical problems* when a system failure or malfunction causes an impact that prevents the normal functioning of operations and business of the organization. They are *important problems* when a system failure can be remedied with some manual or alternative operations that provide a temporary solution that allows the organization to continue normal business operations. These problems usually impact business operations in terms of comfort at work or cause only minor problems in the organization, and can be solved without difficulty indefinitely, if necessary.

In the second case, any integration gaps and deficiencies that are identified may require an extraordinary effort on the part of system users to overcome them, and although this can be done, the burden on users can be assumed only for a limited period of time. Integration issues also represent an additional risk for proper system operations because of the possibility that discrepancies between the different subsystems will undermine the trustworthiness and confidence of the informational output coming from a distressed information system.

This disappointment on the part of users and any subsequent claim against the information system, its development, and the project that produced it may arise at different times and may be due to a variety of practices or absence of practices. A nonexhaustive discussion of problems encountered in the information system environment is presented in the remaining sections of this chapter.

# Discovery of Difficulties Affected by Timing

Projects that implement new technology-based information systems must follow a very strict process to ensure the quality of products delivered, and that process is defined by the methodology that is used to manage the project. However, despite the fact that a reasonable application of methods allows the detection of many difficulties in the early stages of the project, during the system analysis and design phases, the fact is that too many problems are detected much later, when the cost to rectify difficulties is much higher and sometimes even prohibitive. There are many problems that go unnoticed throughout the project and appear only at the end, when the system is finished and ready to be put into operation. Sometimes problems do not surface until the system has already been launched and the users find them as they begin working with the system.

When a functional problem reaches this point, problem resolution often requires an effort that is much larger than would have been needed originally. This is because the development team must perform a complete process that identifies new requirements from the affected users, review the overall specifications of the system to include the new requirements, and ensure that the inclusion of new requirements has no collateral effects on the rest of the system's functionality. Also, any new features and functions must be retrofitted into the analysis and design documentation and included on the software components that comprise the new information system.

Once the development of the new functionality is finished, the functionality along with its integration in the system should be tested. These tests must take into consideration the whole system and must not just be focused on the part of the system providing the new functionality. However, testing must consider a much broader scope in order to ensure that required and needed changes are adequately incorporated, and also that these changes have not had a negative impact on the rest of the information system. This can be achieved through so-called regression testing. This additional testing effort often represents a considerable cost, particularly if the test has to be repeated several times. Each additional test can raise project costs to multiples of the original estimated project cost.

The impact on the costs of the project, together with the anxiety of the users who want to see their problems or issues resolved as soon as possible, will produce an additional source of tension among participants in the project. Issues will be raised and they will become the cause of many discussions and meetings about these project deviations. The supplier will try to group identified issues and problems into packages of amendments, known as versions or revisions, in an attempt to reduce the cost impact by controlling the number of times that system retests are needed. In contrast, the client requires an immediate resolution of the issues and problems in order to maximize the usefulness of the new information system as soon as possible, and to avoid the disruption that these deficiencies present to routine work and business operations.

## Discovery of Difficulties Identified by Users

It can also happen that deficiencies are detected earlier in the process of implementation, and are discovered and disclosed before the system is launched, during the training process for users of the new system. When this happens, it creates a problematic situation where the user tends to offer resistance to the implementation of the system. It is often the user's sense that when functional requirements are not achieved, extraordinary measures must be taken to rectify the situation, such as the following:

■ The assumption of an additional, extended project work effort

- The simultaneous use of two alternative information systems, the new and the old working together in combination to accomplish work the new system should be able to accomplish alone
- The need for additional manual operations, which are used to fulfill the functionality that was missing or that works unsatisfactorily
- The need for repetition of data loading and subsequent and ongoing validation of system operations

Because training is often oriented to using the software to perform routine business operations, the learning process led by the instructor is followed in a very strict manner where fixed content about features and functionality is explained, process itineraries to be followed are discussed, and data to be introduced and managed are reviewed. This usually precludes users in training from veering off to find previously unknown discrepancies in system functionality.

This training orientation and its focus on the curriculum and learning content makes it somewhat difficult for the user to identify any problems arising from gaps in the features and functionality of the information system, but it does allow the identification of problems arising from faulty solutions for those features and functions, as may be uncovered in the training program. Otherwise, discrepancies in features and functionality that have been omitted from the training route can remain hidden until users uncover the issues and problems during operational use of the new information system.

If the identification of missing features and functionality occurs in the process of training users, this can make system implementation difficult. However, if those difficulties are identified during the presentation of the system to executives, it could be deemed something near to a cataclysm. When this happens, it usually indicates that somehow the requirements were changed by executives, but those changes were not adequately communicated in a timely manner for the project team to incorporate them into the information system development effort; this can present a serious conflict.

The main problem is that the late detection of problems, or more precisely the attempt to rectify problems, can create a multitude of undesirable effects that could cause the system to acquire undesirable properties. When we try to fix deficiencies in system functions and features, we can sometimes introduce additional problems of a different nature and more difficult to resolve. Should our system difficulties expand, this serves to foster subjective or emotional responses that represent a loss of confidence, which causes the climate around the project to deteriorate as it promotes resistance to the final implementation of the new system.

Rectifying system features and functionality problems will likely include an increase in the cost of system development. It will also present a need to extend the deadlines for system delivery and entry into production mode. It also gives cause to subsequent discussions, confrontations, and general unpleasantness that could contribute to delaying and perhaps even preventing the organization from obtaining all of the benefits initially expected from the project effort.

It is common for an information system development project to have most defects detected in the testing process. After all, that is the purpose of testing, to subject new system features and functions to scrutiny in order to identify any defects, errors, and dysfunctions that may have been introduced during the production process.

## Discovery of Difficulties Involving Collaboration with Suppliers and Contractors

The most relevant case that comes to my mind is a project conducted for a public administration office, which hired a consulting firm with a world-class reputation and recognition to accomplish the design and development of an information system. The firm was brought in to develop a system that enabled the administration office to manage services and benefits, in an integrated way, where this administration served the interests of certain disadvantaged groups in society. In particular, the administration office wanted to reduce the risk of excluding any individuals or families that were qualified to receive their services. The national government had recently enacted a new law to protect these people and the challenge for the administration office was to create an orderly and systematic process to achieve the mandates of that law. A capability was needed to administer services and benefits according to the different levels of program participants, and that process would be dependent on budgetary considerations and the availability of material resources. In turn, the distribution of funding to the local office would be based upon locale or region, population, and the national budgetary balance for this program. The change that was needed as a result of this new law was to create a systemic approach to add new services to those currently existing, thereby creating mechanisms for universal and equal access to these services and benefits regardless of the country, city, or town where the person requiring help lived.

The multinational consulting firm did an analysis of the situation and prepared a complete high-level design of the new system. However, as the development effort entered into the build phase, negotiations with the consulting firm unexpectedly broke down. For that reason, new players were introduced into the development effort. Domestic companies entered the picture and started negotiations with the administration management using the design prepared by the consulting firm. This was done in order to determine what must accomplished in order to reach the construction and implementation of the information system in a shorter period of time and with a lower budget than that previously estimated.

At the end of a short negotiation process, the project was entrusted to a national company with international presence. That company began work on building an information system with a defined scope that was limited to a system that had to integrate functionality and data currently supported by different applications, with the aim of creating a unique platform on which to build the remaining and expanded system functionality, data model, and associated integration interfaces at a later date. To meet these objectives, the project was replanned to be completed within 8 months and with a budget close to $400,000. This cost estimate represented a significant adjustment to the original budgetary plans, but took into account that the revised project must revisit the analysis and design phases.

Because the priority was to integrate all the information scattered in different applications, much importance was given to the preparation of an overall design that was able to achieve the final scope of the system, with all its features and functionality.

The new system had to obtain all information necessary for its initial loading of data from the subsystems that carried out the management of the various services currently provided. This had to be done with a level of absolute certainty to avoid any disruption or discontinuity in service for citizens. It also had to ensure there would be no loss of control by the regional administration, which was responsible to the national government for correctly applying the new law as well as for transferring funds to the service providers of the citizens.

The development team was now focused on preparing the overall design and they did truly a commendable job, in general. However, they did not involve the customer's technical personnel, who independently began to develop additional modules and functions driven by pressure and requirements from users and citizens. The extraordinary actions of the technicians and users, along with the failure of the communication mechanisms provided by the development team, prevented system start-up. Every time the team presented and explained the information system to responsible individuals on the client side, they were told that the system did not meet current user needs. This demonstrated conflict with the established scope, which had been agreed to earlier, and this was exacerbated by the client's technical team's effort to develop new applications and functions that "they could not do without" now. The goal of the project was continuously moving further and further away from the original specifications every time an effort was made to implement the new information system.

This difficulty led to an agreed delay in the implementation and to the subsequent extension of the project to include the new features and functions required by the corporate users. However, as it happened in the fable of Achilles and the tortoise, the technicians of the public administration organization, ignoring the request of the corporate users in order to respond to the demands of its own users, continued developing additional modules and modifying and extending the features and functions of the previous ones. This was done without warning or any collaboration with the company with regard to the changes being made.

When new software was introduced a few months after the first attempt, it had become obsolete yet again. It had been passed by the interim solution, which had evolved faster than the solution provided by the services company. This highlights how effective system solutions definitely need strong and frequent collaboration among participants of the technical teams involved in the effort.

# Discovery of Difficulties Associated with System Testing

It is common to identify deficiencies related to the scope of information system functionality during the performance of the various tests that must be passed by any information system before it can enter into operation. Testing is a critical stage in the information system's life cycle. It checks the suitability of the developed system to perform according to established requirements and specifications. For this reason, different types of tests are used to check various aspects of the information system and its production process.

The various checks that are performed could include individual testing, integration testing, functional testing, user testing, stress testing, load testing, and acceptance testing, among others. Each of these tests should be carefully planned and reviewed with the client and project managers. Test criteria are established and agreed, and the associated test results will determine whether the system should be allowed to proceed to operation mode and the production process, or whether a backward step is needed when failed tests are encountered.

Thus, if testing plans for each of the prescribed tests are as complete and detailed as they should be, including regular updates by users, they will provide a systematic guide that can be used to detect any system functionality problems or feature discrepancies at a much earlier time. This early identification and detection will preclude significant additional project costs, and will enhance product quality and promote greater customer satisfaction. This requires the timely preparation of test plans at a reasonable time before testing actually begins. This allows not only sufficient time for the proper development of the tests, but also sufficient time for negotiating test and acceptance criteria with the customer and with other relevant stakeholders.

One of the most interesting considerations in this area is depicted in Figure 10.1, an illustration that represents my own elaboration of the Method-V Model. This model was developed to regulate the software development process by the German Federal Administration, and it is named for its primary utility as a verification and validation test model. The model depicts each level of testing as having a corresponding level of specification, and therefore it tries to validate specifications at different levels by planning and conducting tests that correspond to those specifications.

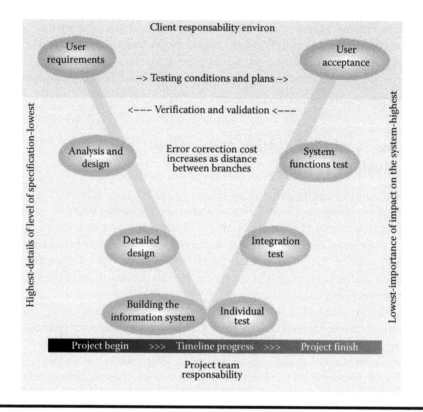

**Figure 10.1  Verification and validation model.**

The systematic approach to testing, such as that presented in the verification and validation model, can provide significant advantages in the system development effort. Consider how the following advantages could be achieved on your projects:

■ *Reduced project risk.* A systemic-testing approach would bring a greater transparency in process control and production management, allowing the technical staff to clarify the expectations of all stakeholders from the beginning of the project and in a transparent way. This helps when defining the roles and responsibilities of all people involved in the project, and it provides a comprehensive, understandable, and free-from-ambiguity vision of the products that will be obtained from the project. In turn, this approach also allows for early detection of deviations and risks, which helps avoid increasing costs associated with correcting deviations and gaps in functionality in the subsequent implementation of the system.

■ *Improved product quality.* An effective testing approach helps guarantee the adequacy of the system under evaluation in meeting the needs and expectations of users and responsible managers. It ensures those needs are achieved through an evaluation of system performance relative to quality specifications. To that end, even intermediate products can receive an early check to observe and measure the quality of system features and functions. That will facilitate the final product review and, again, reduce the costs for corrective actions when they can be implemented sooner rather than later.

- *Reduction of total costs.* A structured approach to testing can lower costs over the full life cycle of the system development effort. Formal and informal testing can be performed to achieve early detection of problems during the analysis, design, development, and production of software. Technical work teams can have specialized expertise in areas of information system implementation, but they may also be ignorant of the client's business needs and interests. They can, however, use structured tests and reviews to identify and resolve the system problems as early as possible, before costs become unmanageable. We can see that in the information technology environment, the later in the project that an error or defect is identified, the greater the multiple of cost that will be incurred to rectify the problem. Structured testing can be used to prompt the early detection of problems.

- *Improved communication.* Structured testing helps improve communication among all relevant project stakeholders. It facilitates clarification of stakeholder expectations about the developing system based on a uniform and detailed description of every one of its relevant components and project deliverables. Structured testing, and particularly the associated testing documentation and test results reports, facilitate a common understanding about any defects or errors that may occur. The dissemination of this information among stakeholders eases frictions and reduces conflicts.

# Discovery of Difficulties Associated with System Transition to Operations

Another point in the system development effort when system performance difficulties are too often discovered is during the final interactions between users and analysts during the system implementation phase. As the technical members of the staff are trying to close the details of actions related to implementation, they will sometimes go to users to confirm their understanding of the features and functions of the total system. Unfortunately, it is not unusual at this time for users to find gaps or perceived hidden functionality. This presents a last minute requirement for the technical staff to address these issues, sometimes with simple explanations and sometimes with modifications that bring coherence to the total system.

This late detection of feature and functionality defects (or perceived defects) may be anecdotal, as happened in the case described earlier about the system developed for the five institutions of higher education. In that instance, resolution of the problem identified at a late stage required a mere modification of a report. Late detection can also sometimes prompt substantial adjustments in the features and functionality of the system. Such changes may impact the very foundation of the system, making it wobble like a building in an earthquake, and forcing a complete rethink of the system modules and elements from their basic design and foundations.

## Discovery of Difficulties from Other Sources

After making a cursory examination of the most common problems affecting the scope of the project, one sometimes wonders why we cannot effectively contain recurring problems if they are detected so frequently? Problem repetition should make it recognizable, detectable, and potentially manageable. The answer is that although some problems are very common, their causes are varied, diverse, and subtle, making it difficult to detect the signs or symptoms of the problem as a basis for diagnosing the effects that it will have on the project.

As we identify the most common causes of scope problems, we can find a fuzzy definition of the project presented in informal documents and lacking a consensus of support among the project stakeholders. A lax project definition can have different explanations, but usually arises from not making a complete and exhaustive specification of the problem, which is needed to establish project goals and objectives, and for the preparation of a comprehensive project scope statement that garners the commitment of all project stakeholders.

For example, it is often perceived that the new information system is simply the evolution of a previous system. However, the older system, which is already obsolete, is usually considered the best source of requirements for the improvements and changes that users have requested. This prompts the technical staff to reference the documentation and performance of the previous information system as a foundation for the new system development effort. Therefore, previous system documentation is modified in lieu of creating a new set of requirements and specifications for the new system.

This approach, essentially a system reengineering effort, may have worked in simpler times, but in today's advanced information system environment it can provide a multitude of problems and difficulties. When you extract the requirements from a previous system, you can obtain a fairly good idea of the features and functionality that are working for the application. However, this representation is a flat image, and we can miss critical information such as the different information requirements of the new system, or the reason or purpose for each function or system component specified for the new system.

In many cases, this behavior results in the survival of features that were incorporated anecdotally, the only purposes of which were to solve a specific need isolated in time and circumstances. They therefore continue into the new system as a result of a lack of critical questioning about their true usefulness and value to the organization.

This problem has always existed, from the inception of the information technology discipline until today. It will probably exist as long as Moore's Law continues to influence executive IT managers. From their perspectives as heads of information systems departments, they are focused on keeping the project on schedule, they are under pressure from users and budget constraints, and it is more economical to increase production capacity by installing more powerful machines without devoting the necessary time to identifying and verifying the obsolescence of the software components installed on them.

Gordon E. Moore was the director of laboratories at Fairchild Semiconductor in 1965 when he first stated his theory. In the summer of 1968, Moore, with Robert Noyce from Intel, reiterated Moore's original statement: to paraphrase, "the number of transistors that can be used per unit area in an integrated circuit is doubling every 18 months, and, consequently, the price of hardware is reducing by the same proportion." This statement has turned out to be fairly accurate. Moore's theory has been applied over time, and in the past 40 years it has been cheaper to simply expand information systems rather than to review and debug the software and data, or identify and remove programs, applications, files, and databases that have become obsolete and will never be used again. In a sense, the effects of Year 2000 computer issues and potential problems served to promote a considerable cleaning of this type of "zombie software," which brings nothing to business but survives on systems, occupying payloads and resources that could be used for other purposes.

## A Personal Perspective on Difficulties in the IT Environment

In 1996, I worked for a company that received a request for assistance from a financial institution. The institution wanted to revise and convert all of its software to ensure that they would have no problems with the potential dreaded effects that were speculated to occur at the onset of the Year 2000 event. The financial institution was working with a technology platform based on IBM mainframe computers, which supported the operations of the branches' personal computers network, emulating the operation of the 3270 terminal, while offering users a friendly working environment and increased productivity for routine tasks. The application software was written in the COBOL language, with some features still running in ASSEMBLER language, and data were stored in a DB2 relational database. All of this represented what you would expect to see in the IT environment of a mid-sized financial institution.

The company for which I worked at that time had established a competency center, a software factory that specialized in work related to the problems arising from the advent of Year 2000. This factory had the best tools and a perfectly standardized work process that ensured greater efficiency and predictability of process performance. It used a structured approach defined from the knowledge and experience of technicians assigned to a series of highly specialized cells.

A colleague serving as a manager in the factory accompanied me to a meeting with the director of the bank's information systems department to assess some qualitative aspects of the upcoming work effort. This included costs associated with the possibility of process automation for the impact analysis and the subsequent conversion of software. The process was so defined that when the client asked us about the cost of the conversion process, my colleague replied that it depended on the number of lines of code they had to work with, and the importance of completing a cleaning operation before any efforts to reduce this volume were made. The director also inquired about ways to reduce the volume of 7 million lines of code, with awareness that significant amounts of "dead code" were included in that estimate.

My colleague shared our experience in another financial institution with similar issues. In particular, he suggested that when end-of-month reports were prepared they should be made available to users according to demand instead of by means of mass distribution. Users would go to a central location to pick up only the reports that they wanted or needed. The institution could then identify the reports that were actually useful and necessary, as well as copies that were no longer needed. This would also save much money on paper as the organization discovered that there were reports that nobody used. This experience had yielded spectacular results in other client organizations, where it was found that as many as 70% of the distributed reports were not read and therefore not needed.

The director was hesitant, because he believed users would be clamoring to his office when they found reports missing from routine distribution. However, he agreed that it was worth trying as a starting point for the identification of obsolete software and the reduction of the conversion budget for the Year 2000 event. His surprise was considerable when the following month he found, indeed, that almost 75% of the reports were left uncollected and unclaimed. This subsequently prompted a significant reduction in the number of lines of code and the cost of the Year 2000 project.

In contrast, when the information system responds to a new need in the organization, it can also cause difficulties if the scope does not clearly delineate the purpose of the system. A request for proposal (RFP) is often used to provide a rigorous definition of the system.

However, it is also possible to find some RFPs that try to define the full functionality of a new system in terms that are reduced to simple expressions like "the system should be integrated with other applications in the organization…" or even "the system will generate reports required from the information available in the databases of the company…." These expressions reflect a lack of detail that can be explained only by irresponsibility and a lack of commitment by project executives, project managers, and project team members who drafted or reviewed the RFP. The simplicity of these types of expressions is a prelude to problems and conflicts of all kinds that will end in inevitable tensions and considerable frustration for all project participants.

The first consequence will be that the project manager who has to estimate the project will face a dilemma that will force him to choose between being too conservative or too aggressive in preparing project plans, but especially in estimating the project's cost and schedule. In a market that is rather cold, with few business opportunities, suppliers receiving such an RFP will tend to be more aggressive, because clients tend to select more aggressive responses that represent less cost.

Another consequence is caused by the limited information that is provided in such an RFP. When the supplier's project manager finds such simple expressions in the RFP, he might think that there will be only two or three simple system integration efforts involved in the project. In fact, there could be eight or nine integrations involving the execution of complex transactions. The response can be conservative or aggressive, but either approach places significant risk on the performing organization when preparing a cost and schedule estimate in response to the RFP. Once again, it is likely that the most aggressive approach will have a lower cost that is below the offers of other potential suppliers, and contracts are usually awarded to the bidder with the lowest cost.

For these reasons, we should strive to define the scope of the project in a precise manner. We should likewise strive to help our clients describe their needs and requirements accurately.

# Chapter 11

# Managing Problems Related to Project Management

Information development and implementation projects are always dealing with important issues associated with the condition of their deliverables. These projects involve intangible product development and, as such, they are subject to scrutiny represented by hard-charging subjectivity and interpretation that can be different for each project stakeholder. These differences occur in spite of efforts to provide details and a comprehensive definition as a common frame of reference.

However, without taking away the importance of these difficulties, they tend to be accompanied by other problems that provide uncertainty and potential conflict from a project management perspective. Therefore, effective project management practices must be applied to control the established strategies and to ensure appropriate project oversight and management.

## Stakeholder Perspectives on Project Management Problems

Speak with any member of a project team involved in information system development and implementation and you will probably find that the ability to meet deadlines is a recurring project management issue. It seems to be an issue that has a high frequency of occurrence. This problem can have different causes, depending on the role of the observer with whom you speak.

Technicians, programmers, and analysts will tell us that the customer is not aware of the effort required by the project and therefore maintains an uncompromising stance on timing, which can cause an extra burden of stress for the team if effective project management practices are not followed. In other cases, the technical staff might say that the project manager or person who sold the project based on preliminary planning did not take into account the real complexity of the project. That will result in a delivery schedule that is essentially impossible to meet without extraordinary effort. This extra effort will usually require long working hours, every day and on weekends, and can lead to some self-defeating effects on the project.

The customer's representative will probably have opinions that are very different from those of the technical staff, and will include claims that the technical team did not have the necessary training when they were assigned to the project. The customer has been known to assert that they believe the current effort represents the technical team's initial effort in training on the tools and techniques to be applied. The customer may also express concern that certain aspects of the project should not be charged to the project because they can be considered training for the project team and not productive work on the project.

The customer's representative may also show concern when, from time to time, changes are made in the composition of the project team. Although it may occur less frequently, it is possible that the customer will complain about technicians having low productivity or making slow progress. This usually prompts ongoing reviews of work carried out by the technical experts on the project team.

If the question about project difficulties is posed to the project manager or project leader, yet another set of issues arises? First, project managers often become concerned when customers appear to be changing requirements on a frequent basis. Changes will make the project progress more slowly than desired, and change introduces an extraordinary burden that involves a constant review of work already done, to reflect the changes made by the customer. Therefore, project managers need to ensure that effective procedures are in place to manage project change as a means to avoid this dilemma or otherwise reduce its impact on the project.

Some project managers may view initial planning as unrealistic, and may cite that as the cause of certain impacts on the progress of the project. This makes it necessary for the project manager to be involved in the planning effort as early as possible. Also, when project managers express concern about initial planning, they should recognize that such plans are not immutable and indisputable, and they can take actions early in the project to question and even facilitate project plan modifications. It is better to do this early rather than waiting for defects and problems to emerge later in the project when the costs needed to rectify defects and problems increase.

Project managers will sometimes identify difficulties when forming the project team. The issues here usually revolve around the effort required to create a cohesive project team, which often requires an extra effort to properly address team member experience and training.

## Project Management Planning Problems

At the onset of the project, high-level plans are constructed, and particulars such as cost, schedule, and resource utilization are approved by management with expectations that these planning elements will be maintained throughout the project. These early plans are prepared at a high level far removed from the concrete reality of the project. Sometimes it appears that the fundamental project definition (i.e., objectives, scope, assumptions and constraints, risks and initial cost, schedule and resource utilization estimates) is a standard template that is applied to a variety of similar projects. This adds no value to planning the current project and does not distinguish the current project from others. Therefore, it must be recognized that initial planning, including estimates, will need to be adjusted as more details become known about the project deliverable and the project work effort. Expecting project estimates to remain unchanged throughout the duration of the project is probably unreasonable, and perhaps impossible to achieve.

The preparation of early, initial project plans will achieve broader acceptance when the individuals who perform this work have two particular attributes. First, project planners and estimators need to have extensive field experience complemented by a broad and deep knowledge of all aspects of the project (i.e., market, industry, company, business area, functionality, features, objectives, and corporate culture). They also need to have an understanding of the problem and the alternative solutions that are available, the technologies to be used, and the equipment and partners that should work together to complete the project. Second, these individuals must demonstrate leadership based on being a recognized authority in their technical field, and they should garner recognition from team members as a means to earn the respect of everyone involved. This will increase the value of their work and their opinions, and reduce the questions and uncertainty of planning at later stages in the project. Organizations could have some difficulty in finding individuals with these attributes or qualifications, but the benefits are well worth the effort. In some instances, organizations can even be proactive, helping to develop these attributes in-house, as individuals are trained and mentored as a part of the natural course of their career progression.

## Project Work Plan and WBS Construction Challenges

There is broad acceptance within the project management discipline that the project work plan and the project work breakdown structure (WBS) are among the most valuable tools available to the project manager. For many practitioners, the work plan and the WBS are one and the same. In effect, a WBS is constructed to specify and delineate the work activities, tasks, and subtasks that are needed to achieve the project objectives. A work plan is then created simply by adding estimates of cost, schedule, and resource utilization to the lowest level work elements of the WBS.

The process for accomplishing this effort can be specified as a series of steps in the project management methodology that is used, or as a separate procedure. In either case, this planning should be done with care and with sufficient attention to detail in order to properly account for all project work that needs to be accomplished.

The following steps highlight and discuss this planning process:

- *Review project objectives and requirements.* Creating a work breakdown structure starts with an examination of the project objectives and requirements. This step provides planners with an essential understanding of what the project is supposed to accomplish. In turn, planning can be done to ensure that the project objective and requirements are achieved. In contrast, work that is not related to achieving specified objectives should not be included in the project WBS and work plan.
- *Determine the planning approach.* Top-down planning is a very common and preferred approach for most project management practitioners. It represents a process of work decomposition that is made gradually in layers. This is almost like peeling an onion, and involves an examination of the upper layer and avoids thinking of the next layer until the current layer has been completely defined.

  For example, if we tried to define the work required to build a house, we would start by defining the different areas or phases of work, to include house design, site preparation, foundation building, and house construction. Once the phases are identified, we are ready to move across those phases to break down each one further to provide greater detail and definition of the work to be accomplished. This represents the identification of project work elements as phases are decomposed into activities, activities are decomposed into tasks, tasks are decomposed into subtasks, and so forth. This work decomposition continues until we determine we have reached a level at which we can effectively manage and control project work performance and the development of the required products.

  Using this approach ensures that we do not forget or miss any aspect of project work that is essential to achieving the project objectives. This approach provides for a consistent examination of project work at increasing levels of detail. It will help us control project work performance after the plan has been approved, when we are in project execution.

- *Organize the WBS work elements.* Once we have broken down the project work elements (i.e., phases, activities, tasks, and subtasks) to the appropriate level of detail, we should then use preferred methods to organize them. In general, phases will normally represent successive periods of time, providing for some organization at the highest levels of project work. It is often good to select an initial activity or task in the first project phase for the start of the project. We can then consider and create groupings of activities and tasks (under each phase), and organize them in a meaningful way, perhaps according to a timeline. This exercise will allow us to create a preliminary WBS that shows generally how our project work will be organized. This will be used to create a more precise WBS as we proceed to define tasks and incorporate cost, schedule, and resource information. The WBS becomes usable when we finally create all of the task dependencies that are needed to indicate work flow, as described later in this effort.
- *Prepare WBS task definitions.* When a definition is prepared for each task, it provides the purpose and an understanding or description of what is to be accomplished by each task. In some project management environments, task definitions are prepared using a format called the WBS Dictionary. As a result of this effort, the project manager, project team members, and, for that matter, any project stakeholder can review the task definition and understand its purpose, what is to be achieved by the work effort, when it will be done, what resources will be assigned to do it, and sometimes even the process that will be used. This ensures there is no conflict or misunderstanding about task performance.
- *Incorporate time estimates (schedule) and set task dependencies.* It is very important that the time estimate is expressed in measurable units of work effort that are manageable and unambiguous. Therefore, for a typical project the time estimation should be reflected in man-hours, meaning the hours per person needed to complete the task. As needed by the size of the project or by standard organizational practices, the time may be expressed in terms of days, weeks, or months of work, as appropriate. Nevertheless, the estimate always refers to the individual effort of each team member dedicated to the project relative to the task or activity considered.

  Sometimes task duration estimates are represented as elapsed time. This can be done for initial estimates, before the workload is sufficiently defined to enable resources to be assigned. But it is undesirable as a routine or final approach. This method of time estimating must be used with caution, because it is the number of resources assigned to each task that has a prominent influence on the task's duration.

  Finally, the full project duration (project schedule) cannot be established until all task dependencies have been set. Every task has at least one other task that precedes it, even if that is the "start-of-project" task. However, it is more likely that tasks will have dependencies on intermediate tasks rather than going back to the "start-of-project" task. Therefore, tasks dependencies need to be identified in order to see the true project work flow and the resulting project schedule. As task dependencies are created, perhaps where one task must finish before the next task can start (a finish–start dependency), you can see the constraints that may require an adjustment in the task duration or in the work effort of the subsequent task. There are also other variations of the finish–start dependency that can help to move into the work plan all the project complexity and relations.

■ *Incorporate resource estimates.* In this planning step, the resources needed to perform each task are identified and appended to the WBS at the lowest task levels. Depending on the project's progress, these estimates can include the names of specific project team members, or generic titles such as System Analyst II can be used until specific individuals can be identified. The identification and alignment of resources with tasks could result in changes to the project schedule, and this process is sometimes used to make desired changes in the project schedule.

Resource estimating allows us to manage the assignments of individuals assigned to the project team on a dedicated basis. Therefore, if work conditions permit it and we have adequate staff free of assignment, we can implement resource changes to add resources and shorten the task effort, and ultimately, the completion date of the project. Likewise, if resources are not all available when needed, we can make changes to extend the task duration or the project if it is necessary to share the assignment of certain resources on more than one project.

■ *Incorporate cost estimates.* Once the work effort is defined, the task duration estimates established, the resources identified, and the task dependencies specified in detail, we then have sufficient information to prepare the cost estimates that will become the overall project budget. Project costs are estimated for the lowest-level work elements in the WBS. Here the work effort and resources required to perform project work are examined, and the cost needed to perform the task is specified. Usually, project resources represent the primary costs for most project tasks, and this could include the cost of external consultants and suppliers. In some organizations, costs for materials, supplies, and equipment are also included as a means to see the total costs for the project in one place.

Once the costs for each task are determined, the total project budget can be calculated. This calculation is a simple addition of all tasks, made vertically from bottom-level tasks (represented by the work elements having resources assigned) to top-level tasks (represented by the project phases). To that end, costs are aggregated or rolled up to produce the total project budget. For example, all tasks under an activity are rolled up to show the total cost of that activity. In turn, all activities within a phase are rolled up to show the total cost of that phase. Phases are rolled up to show the total cost of the project.

This effort produces the work plan and WBS needed to manage the project. Together they identify the work that is to be performed to achieve the project objects and product outcomes. Project management happens when the project manager ensures that work is accomplished according to the established plans. These tools will help the project manager to monitor work progress, to identify deviations from the work plan, and to take actions to control the work effort and restore it to the correct track, as needed.

There is an alternative to the structured planning approach described above, which is to conduct the planning effort in reverse to the "natural way." In this approach, the project manager begins planning based on the prescribed end date of the project (the date on which the client or user needs to have the new system available for use), or on one or more of the project's milestone dates for interim planning. The time interval between the current date and the selected date is identified, and this interval then determines the duration of the project (or the portion of the project selected for planning). To that end, planners must adapt the work plan to fit within that time period, while maintaining the proportions and relations usually found in such projects.

This approach can offer some significant challenges. For example, the work plan still needs to include a more or less general set of normal activities that specifies all needed work to accomplish the project objectives, and those work efforts still need to have their dependencies defined. Therefore, task dependencies are extended or contracted to fit the default time period in a manner that produces a credible project schedule and achieves the prescribed project end date.

This approach usually provides an artificial solution, because it has nothing to do with the reality of the project work effort. Project timing, duration, and calendar are results of force-fitting the project's work efforts, and that causes a condition in which project work can be arbitrarily and perhaps randomly defined. In some instances, needed work may be omitted from the work plan because of time constraints. This prompts concern about when such work is actually done, and how the end product is affected if that work is not done.

Such plans can be shown to management and to the client in a fairly effective manner using a graphical diagram, usually a Gantt chart, to present project activities, their dependencies, and timeline bars that define the duration of each activity. This is usually done to present the project's work effort at a high level. However, it does not show how detailed information, estimates of work, and workload distribution between different team members are not well addressed at lower levels of the project work plan. Plans developed from prescribed mandates can still have a nice graphical presentation, but they do not have the rigor of examination and calculations that should have preceded the graphical depiction to justify the project's work effort, dates of performance, and assurance that objectives will be achieved.

This approach to project planning may be appropriate in some cases, such as when projects have been previously subjected to the rigor of detailed planning.

Here the project manager may decide that previous planning had sufficient rigor and maturity, and that another iteration of the plan can avoid the tedious bottom-up approach. This decision is usually made when the project manager believes that the key work elements that define the complexity of the project have been adequately addressed, and that only the portion of the work plan that needs revision or update will be considered in an additional planning effort.

In many cases, the requirement to use this approach does not originate with the project manager. Rather, it comes as a concession to pressure received from users or customer representatives who require an immediate response from the project manager. It can also be used because of external conditions unrelated to the project that have some type of impact on the project. This could include such matters as marketing requirements, competitive influence, government regulations and mandates, and sometimes even the weather. However, as far as possible, the project manager should make every effort to resist planning shortcuts, because these will only cause difficulties in the course of the project, usually beginning immediately following the start of the project.

Some may ask what role technical methodologies play in the planning process. If you have not yet discovered this, we can say it clearly: technical methodologies are not strictly necessary for any project—what is critical is to ensure that the project is addressed in a methodical way, using effective practices in project management.

## Project Management Methodology Challenges

Methodologies can play an important role because they facilitate the accomplishment of a standard and repeatable process such as the one for WBS construction described above. In general, technical methodologies are used to design and develop a quality product that meets technical specifications and requirements. In contrast, a project management methodology is used to plan and track project performance; its purpose is to manage and achieve project success, which usually means achieving the business interests of the organization for each project. In some organizations, a standard project management methodology is used across all departments. It serves as the "umbrella process" for the technical processes used by each department. This concept is illustrated in Figure 11.1, which shows the general relationship of methodologies that could be used within an IT department.

Here is a sample of some of the benefits to be gained from using an effective project management methodology, from the perspective of technical users.

- ◾ It provides guidance for building the WBS to show project tasks and activities in an orderly and logical way. This ensures that no significant aspect of the project is overlooked, and delineates work associated with intermediate and final products as well as the project activities necessary to produce them.

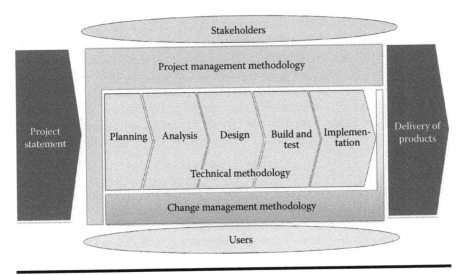

**Figure 11.1   Diagram of methodologies.**

The WBS should represent the reasoning and good sense of the project manager when the WBS and work plan are being prepared.

■ It provides the process to be followed and descriptions of the main techniques
to be applied in the conduct of major project activities, and it specifies the
requirements to be met for starting or ending every task or activity.

■ It provides templates and forms for many of the documents to be produced
across the project life cycle phases, and it presents detailed explanations on
how to use them to make the most of the document preparation effort.

■ It creates a common language, and a common frame of reference that can be
shared and used by all project participants and stakeholders within the organization. This results in more effective communication and avoids any ambiguity of key concepts that could affect the project's progress.

■ It presents standard practices in project management, to include the knowledge accrued by experts in project management on best practices. These practices, and associated knowledge, are made available to all who use the
methodology. This facilitates the introduction of new team members, giving
them immediate insight into the procedures to be used. It also facilitates the
incorporation of more junior team members, who have limited experience
and require closer management and detailed guidance as they learn their job
responsibilities.

Benefits considered, the introduction and use of a methodology cannot be
done in a simplistic manner. Methodology deployment is much more than sharing
a collection of activities and practices as they appear in diagrams. It represents an

organizational commitment to accomplish projects using a structured and standard process. Therefore, methodology deployment means questioning the validity and applicability of every aspect of the processes, procedures, and tools to be included. Avoiding this rigorous examination and determination of need would be a severe mistake, with profound negative effects. Poor methodology implementation could end in a well-intended effort growing to unexpected and unmanageable proportions, and that would likely nullify all the user advantages mentioned as well as the organizational benefits.

## A Personal Perspective on the Consequences of Poor Project Management

Consequences can arise when project management is deficient, as when the tasks and activities of the project work plan are not properly managed or precisely followed. Omitting planned work exposes the project to unnecessary risks that deflect the project manager and project team members from the attention needed to manage objectives, tasks and activities, dependencies, products to be delivered, and the associated work efforts. In turn, management simply establishes new timelines and milestones to counter the effects of poor project management. If those project management deficiencies continue, this creates a dynamic that could be called a "vicious circle," which then creates an atmosphere of distrust and hostility on the project that just adds more difficulty to the project management effort.

Some time ago I was in a position to take charge of a project launched and managed by a friend who was recently fired from the company. In turn, he had received it from another colleague who had also left the company some months earlier. The project's client was a publicly owned entity that managed a business complex devoted to leisure and tourism. This was a key investment for the city in which it was located, and included several facilities in a collection of buildings and open spaces that offered visitors the chance to enjoy many different experiences related to popular science, with programs oriented to families and young people.

The client had a very high profile, relevancy, and social visibility highlighted by several factors, of which the most important could be the relationship with the local municipal government. Besides being the owner of the business complex, the client also used its installation as flag facilities and as a symbol of progress. This led to the client's facilities becoming an icon of the city in which they were located.

The project had been sold about 4 years prior to this time, with a plan that product development and implementation would not exceed 9 months. The project's contract was originally valued at nearly $500,000, but the actual costs to date exceeded $1,000,000 without any sign of being near to project completion. Now, after more than five times the expected project duration had elapsed, the challenge was to finish the project before another year passed, and without costing more than an additional $100,000.

When the client decided to start new system development in 2005, the organization was using a solution that satisfied the existing needs. That solution was based on standard software that provided a viable response to business management and access control to the most emblematic of the facilities. However, the design and content of the aging solution was considered less attractive to visitors when compared to the new facilities that were about to be opened.

The cost of maintaining the standard software being used seemed prohibitive, and this served as the trigger that promoted the new project. The maintenance cost was high due to the volume of transactions that were being processed. As plans for new facilities were implemented, it was expected that there would be a significant increase in the number of visitors, and the maintenance costs of the current solution for ticketing and sales would also therefore increase.

With the intent of reducing operating costs, but especially to avoid the increased costs that would have occurred with the launch of new facilities, the client decided to introduce a new system solution, and the project was established. The aim for the new project was then to reduce operational costs, and a date was set for completing the project and implementing the new solution. That completion date was aligned with the open day for the inauguration of the first of the new facilities.

With this specific objective, a project schedule was created to include a full collection of intermediate milestones to ensure effective management of the development effort, and to ensure that the new information system would be in operation by the opening date for the new facilities. It was expected that the project outcome would eliminate the costs of licensing associated with the previous solution, and allow recovery of the investment in record time.

However, when the project started and the project team started to collate user requirements, the team encountered a user group that was given absolute freedom to specify requirements for all the features and functions they wanted. They were encouraged to create the most flexible system possible, to include both current needs and any future needs that they could anticipate. Users were asked to define an information system that would respond to all current operational needs and any potential needs that might be required at some time in the future. Of course, like many other utopian dreams, this excess essentially devoured the objective and intent of the project, which was ruined when the client lost focus on the opportunity at hand.

The new information system included the usual features of selling tickets for single or multiple products to individuals, groups, and families both by cash, or through hotels and agencies with cash, card, or voucher. It provided functionality to periodically settle these accounts, and it produced an extensive collection of reports that allowed every operational aspect to be managed and controlled. The system also had connectivity with other systems in the organization through a series of interfaces provided for this purpose.

The new system included requirements to enable combined product selling, which offered customers the opportunity to enjoy more than one facility with the purchase of a one-day ticket, as well as season tickets that allowed the customer access to the facilities for a year. As one of the facilities required the sale of numbered seats, the client requested that the system have an entry module with a graphical interface that would show the distribution of seats in the room and enable selection of available seats.

All this meant that the requirements specification phase was much longer than originally planned, that is, until it was determined that the addition of new requirements would not allow the system to be completed in time for the inauguration of the first of the new facilities. That led to creating an exception action plan that was used to implement an interim system that would support the operations of the first new facility in its early stages. This was done because the facility opening had already been announced, and a first-order media campaign had been used to invite prominent guests, who had already confirmed their attendance. These circumstances did not give the client any leeway for changing the dates established for the opening.

Therefore, project management was essentially carried out independent of the established scope, identified equipment, and specified requirements. That led to a succession of awkward situations that produced a climate of tension, confrontation, mistrust, misunderstanding, and cross-accusations by the end of the effort. All of this could have been avoided if the client had kept in mind the original design and development objective, which was unfortunately distorted from the first day of the project.

Project scope, milestones, and timing are very important planning elements that may prove crucial to achieving the value expected by the client. These elements are dimensions that help define the project along with budget, equipment, requirements, and other conditions. They are not something separate in themselves, and should be considered as a geometric body with many faces, where every change in one will result in changes in the others. Therefore, we must understand that when we fix one dimension of the project, we are also setting all the other aspects that correspond in some way to that dimension. For that reason, we can qualify that a mistake was made in managing this project because after the deadline for submission of the main product was set, users were allowed to make changes that expanded the scope and the acceptance requirements without consideration of the impact on the project.

A modified system solution was delivered more than 4 years after the date on which it was expected to be launched. Nevertheless, as the project neared completion, users continued to demand changes that modified the design of the reports, and they did this without blushing just 2 weeks before the end of the effort. The project leader attempted to manage the delivery date, but did not visit the users to determine if the late requested changes were critical to project success. When issues were raised, the project leader always got the same answer, "You must comply with the dates and if you need more staff, look for them and assign them; hire them or do what you must do, but you must meet the dates without using any other variables."

Naturally, in the end, the project ended with the breakup of the relationship between the client and the provider, and a spectacular failure was quietly resolved between the parties.

## Project Management and Quality Issues

The quality of products delivered is usually one of the first areas to be affected by informal, poor, or generally sloppy project management. Any such weak approach to project management makes it virtually impossible to deliver a quality product that has been tested and proved reliable. In these instances, the quality of the final deliverables of the project ends up depending more on how lucky or inspired the project team members were, rather than having a quality outcome that is based on the results of systematic and rational analysis and design work.

Quality problems can take many forms, but the most important may be those described as follows:

- *Inability to establish traceability of system requirements.* Traceability should provide a reliable two-way journey between requirements and outcomes by showing how a technical or functional requirement has been reflected in the discussion paper in the analysis phase, how it was translated into design specifications, how it has been developed into programming code, and how it has been examined in test conditions to monitor compliance at the different test levels. In particular, each software element should provide the means to know what requirements prompted its development, why it has the design that it has, and what problem it was intended to solve.

- *Incomplete or defective functional specifications.* The project must have complete specifications at all levels, and it cannot leave anything to the interpretation of reader. It sometimes happens that products will suffer multiple and severe defects because of weak specification preparation or when specifications are not modified when a system design update is needed. When no one remembers to modify the specifications, then that could cause major conflicts in the development effort.

   A good practice to follow is to not start the next task until the product is approved in the current task. This practice is important because it recognizes that the output of one task is often the input for subsequent tasks and activities. This approach is used to avoid troublesome situations, such as the dilemma that arises when someone changes a functional specification after the system design has already been started or completed. In some cases, this has been done even when the module is already in programming or in testing. When this happens, the project manager must decide whether or not to apply the change. If it is applied, it may cause the repetition of some work that has already been accomplished, and that has a corresponding impact in the form of increased cost. If the change is waived to avoid these extra costs, it gives up the advantages and benefits that the proposed change would have provided to the business.

■ *Inappropriate use of preliminary analyses.* The fact is that in many projects the technical team will prepare a draft analysis, with a minimum level of detail, which is submitted for the approval of users. However, users are sometimes opposed to such a preliminary document, because they do not understand its purpose and they do not know what to do with it. This usually results in one of two situations: (i) the users will approve the preliminary document without really understanding its content, or (ii) the users may express concern about the document and sometimes criticize its contents, but they generally remain silent and take no action to disapprove it. In turn, the project team interprets user silence as tacit approval, so the team proceeds with their work using that document.

This practice creates problems and conflicts in almost all projects, because the content of the discussion paper is so generic and vague that it is easily interpreted by both technical team members and users in a way that supports their respective claims. Ideally, you will find sufficient time at the end of the analysis to identify alternative system solutions for user consideration and approval.

■ *Analyses performed and prepared with little discipline.* If the system analysis is carried out without applying proper discipline, the system design will suffer, presenting a less-than-complete picture of the new system. Therefore, the discussion paper prepared in the analysis phase and used by the technical team in the design phase could have errors and omissions, such as those mentioned in the previous section. Then, these somewhat faulty component designs are distributed for development by programmers. Of course, without sufficient detail in the design, programmer skill and competency are challenged, and the rigor actually needed in the analysis stage now has to be applied by programmers in the development stage.

Gone are the days when we prepared a general design of the modules, also known as global technical design, which served as the detailed specifications needed for the construction of the system. This general design of modules was submitted for client review and approval before each module was built.

■ *Detached development work.* It is common to find some project teams in which technicians are performing development work independently of other team members. For example, consider the circumstances where one technician creates the files maintenance programs, another creates the system reports, and so on. In this way, they will be able to develop system component content and structure to achieve business requirements, but this will be accomplished without establishing any particular contextual relationship among the components. Therefore, components that should be interactive will be developed separately by different members of the technical staff.

The problem with this approach, besides avoiding the functioning of a more collaborative project team, is that the perspective of each independently developed system component will be quite short-sighted and short-term. This condition results when the team member who is programming reports does not have visibility or awareness about how those reports will be used or how they will be inserted in a module of functionality to provide an integrated solution to the problem. This condition is exacerbated when the team members begin to feel disheartened and alienated, because they realize that their independent focus on aspects of mechanical work will likely result in a low-quality product, and, perhaps, a system that will not work properly when delivered.

■ *A lax development effort.* As suggested above, the result of work delivered by some programmers is often fraught with technical errors and deficiencies that are easily detected and corrected if given proper attention by the individual developer and by the project manager or technical team leader. However, because of lax development efforts, often accompanied by lax oversight, these problems are not discovered or addressed in the development effort, but instead are detected later in the project when functional tests and user tests are performed. This occurs when the concept of individual tests and reviews of work performed are devalued on teams with lax management. In such an environment the technical team member often, somewhat absurdly, assumes that an emphasis is placed on producing massive amounts of programming code and not on creating operational programs that give systems their functionality. The end result is the presentation of code and programs that sometimes do not compile, terminate prematurely with fatal errors, or do not integrate properly with other programs.

■ *Work affected by faulty communication.* The programmer is often cited as the source of all problems, and that may not be so. The programmer tries to work in an environment of high uncertainty and sometimes without adequate support and collaboration that would help overcome many of the difficulties that occur. Rather, problems that surface are often rooted in faulty communication between the different levels and groups involved in the system development effort. The lack of communication in a systems development effort can affect virtually all aspects of the project. It can lead to difficulty in the relationship between the customer and project manager, between the project manager and members of the project team, and among combinations of project team members including analysts, programmers, and users.

In this context, we tend to think that direct interaction based on oral communication is richer than written communication, and that might prompt us to dispense with published documents, replacing them with interviews, discussions, and meetings. However, there is a tendency in too many projects to abuse oral communication to the point of making it ineffective. In particular, it can cause an inflation of meetings that have repetitive agendas, reconsideration of decisions already made, and purposes that are unclear as to who should be in attendance. Of course, meetings incur a cost related to the time and effort of participants, and those costs are not always recognized and understood. In some cases, email has become the mechanism for routine project contact and communication, but that too can sometimes become unwieldy and make things worse. Communication by email can be ineffective when there are delays in message distribution, when there are delays in reading and responding to messages, and when there is a random array of unrelated topics and discussions transmitted.

## A Personal Perspective on Project Communication Problems

Sometimes, communication problems can go beyond the issues described above. These problems are related to the nature of internal communication, which in many cases provides situations that could qualify as comical or simply absurd.

About a year ago, I was involved in a project for a customer in the north, a local government authority that used the services of the company I was affiliated with to assist them in the selection of software related to citizen service management. The customer requested my involvement after receiving recommendations from an independent consultant that I previously collaborated with on a similar project for another local government agency in my region.

The customer had a strategic plan to address public service where it set out the broad lines of action, identified the basic services that should be provided to the citizens, and categorized services according to their characteristics and constraints of implementation. The plan presented a series of high-level strategic considerations for starting the process of solution design and for the subsequent selection of software from among available alternatives.

The technicians who started the project had created a system design that did not reflect in any way its relationship with the strategic document or its contents. It appeared that they did not question or consider that document in any reasoned or reasonable way, and instead simply ignored its existence. However, in preparing the design for the creation of a citizen service center, they used materials from other local government authorities that had already completed similar projects. Their design included content that was the same as that of another project on which I had personally acted. Without blushing, they even used the same specification documents, but they did not provide a basis of argument on why this was considered an appropriate solution for the customer in this city. They did not identify what alternatives might exist, and they did not give reasons for selecting their solution over other possible alternatives.

Logically, the customer rejected this arbitrary specification and demanded a more professional approach to the work effort. The customer wanted to conduct a project in which the design was created specifically for them, and not one representing ordinary plagiarism of an external design document that was previously used by another local government agency, and certainly not one that was poorly adapted. At this point, the customer had paid $150,000 for the project effort, and what they received was a report that showed a design for a citizen relationship management system intended for another city and a report showing that the solution must use the software of a known database leader without further consideration. The customer might have agreed with the conclusions for this selection, but the customer wanted to examine the research process, the evaluation criteria used for selection, and the reasoning about the weight assigned to every question and answer to be sure that the selected solution was truly the best.

At this juncture, the project appeared to end, but with an unsatisfied customer. However, the customer seemed interested in continuing the effort in a proper manner. That gave the possibility of opting for a different software solution than that chosen by the original technical team. Furthermore, if their software selection decision was changed, it would be very difficult and very expensive.

My surprise came when, in the process of reviewing all of the relevant project documentation, the project manager insisted that the project technicians had already given them all that they had paid for. I asked to see the offer of collaboration and the call for tender, documents that are used to define and govern the contractual relationship and that specify the scope of the project. I was told that the project manager did not have any of these documents. That meant, in the absence of these specifications, that the project manager simply proceeded to perform work typical of this type of project. Under these conditions, however, the project manager did so without considering the needs, expectations, or specific commitments of the customer.

This situation was difficult to resolve, because the project manager essentially ignored the customer, and instead focused on basic sales and delivery of a common software application product. In contrast, the customer felt disappointed when, after the work was done, it was discovered that the time was spent on illusions that produced something that was "almost standard," and something that did not meet the needs expressed and required at the beginning of the project.

As my company entered the picture, I asked the customer what they wanted to do, because I did not see precisely how to help in such a closed situation. The customer's answer was simple. It was explained to me that they believed the strategic plan was adequate after having worked on it for over a year. They did not particularly question or disagree with the original system design and the software selected as the solution, but they indicated a need for a report to act as a bridge to allow them to have a basis for the selection of that software. It seemed to me that this approach was logical and reasonable, and we proceeded to begin the work to achieve that end.

The above example clearly illustrates that problems can occur when the project ceases to be the resolution of a customer's problem and becomes simply the implementation of a tool. It is essential to remember that information systems represent business solutions, and projects, project managers, and project team members must be attuned to the customer's business needs and interests when developing and implementing such systems.

# Chapter 12

# Managing Problems Related to the Project Budget

The budget spent on information technology and communications in any public or private organization is awesome, and that can be confirmed by any executive director who is asked about the subject. Each organization prepares its budget in a different way to others depending on culture and philosophy. Some organizations have a centralized authority for budgets related to new technologies, and they have budgetary responsibility for proposing, developing, and maintaining information systems in relation to (i) equipment (e.g., computers, workstations, servers, electronic communication lines, and network hardware) and (ii) logical items (e.g., software, databases, operating systems, and all the tools necessary for system operation).

Other organizations have created responsibilities for budget management in alignment with separate business departments or technical functions of the company. In other cases, control over spending on information technology and communications is differentiated between managing the costs corresponding to the creation of new information systems, which is considered an investment, and managing the costs associated with maintaining existing systems, which is considered an operational expense. This essentially creates two budget centers within the organization.

The truth is that there is no uniform standard for budget management within an organization, and there is no particular budget management approach that has been proved to provide better results than the rest for the management of information systems. Therefore, a company or organization makes an independent selection of the budget management approach that will best serve its business needs and interests. In some cases, the approach to budget management is simply a matter of personal preference, where the influence of individuals at senior staff and management levels in the organization will determine the approach and alignment of the budget management process.

## The IT Share of the Corporate Budget

In general, if we add up all the costs associated with the management of information systems in any organization, we will find that those costs range between 3% and 5% of the corporate revenue. This, of course, depends on the size of the organization, the level of automation of its operations, the business or marketing sector in which it operates, and the current status of the business. This range can be influenced and varies when there are periods of major strategic changes taking place, which are also known as step changes in some organizations. In such periods, cost figures may increase and cross the upper limit of the range, then decrease again and, occasionally, fall below the lower limit of the range.

Spending on information technology is also influenced by the level and reputation of the company and its role in the market. A company with a national or international presence will likely have a higher spending level, which is derived from its commitment to technology as a competitive weapon and as a means to create differentiation from its competitors. In contrast, a more localized company will probably have a lower cost derivative resulting from a lower level of technology development and a lower interest in fending off competitors.

The range of budgets spent on information technology is also influenced by such factors as the culture of the company, the behavior and decisions of corporate owners and stockholders, the level of professionalism of the management team, the geographic location, and the current effects of the economic cycle on business.

In Spain, as in many countries in southern Europe, the budget levels for information technology tend to be somewhat lower than those mentioned above. This is particularly true for small- and medium-sized businesses with a sole proprietor who acts as both owner and director of the company. These are usually businesses in a local or provincial market, and the overall IT budget will be smaller, with reduced figures across the range of IT expenditures.

## Elements of Information Technology Costs

Project budgets are managed according to an approach established within the organization, and information technology budgets created for each project will contribute to the overall budget of the organization. We must ensure that all costs associated with information system development and maintenance are understood and accounted for in the project budget. The following are some cost elements that should be considered:

- *Cost of computer equipment.* This includes the servers, workstations, desktops, laptops, monitors, printers, scanners, and plotters that make up the installed equipment base. These items have associated costs, which are adjusted and annualized according to their expected useful life. If the equipment is rented rather than owned, then we have to account for the rental or leasing costs.
- *Cost of facilities.* This cost item is specifically related to rooms and buildings used to house information systems, but it also includes costs for associated data networking, network electronics, cabling, antennas, and Wi-Fi or Bluetooth, as well as routers, switches, and all electronic network components deployed for operation of the facility.
- *Cost of services.* A variety of services can be acquired to establish and maintain proper functioning of our information systems. Arising from this will be the cost associated with telecommunication lines used for communication between geographically separate components of our information system located in remote offices. These services have become increasingly critical for ensuring connectivity between all regional or field offices and the headquarters of each company, as well as between different companies. This connectivity is also needed to provide access to the Internet, to email, and to provide remote access to the increasing number of employees who are working out of the office under a "teleworking" schema.

  Also considered in this area is the cost of maintenance services needed for the various components of the system, including hardware maintenance for components such as computers, printers, scanners, storage devices, and network electronics, as well as basic software maintenance for operating systems, databases, compilers and development tools, and applications.

  A few other cost items can also be addressed in this services area, including the cost of relevant insurance policies underwritten by insurance companies to cover risks related to information systems. We must not forget to include the costs of outsourcing for the development of new functions, the creation of new information systems, or the maintenance of current applications. Of course, this may be represented as costs for the services of external consultants and technical experts who have become involved in the development or maintenance aspects of information system management.
- *Cost of supplies.* These are the costs required for the operation of information systems in an organization, and here we must consider the energy used by all electronic equipment that comprises the system, even the power needed for air conditioning and for lighting the offices where the servers are located. This budget area includes the costs of supplies used to ensure proper system

operation, such as paper for printers, binding materials for reports, and one-time consumption products for the system, including compact discs, DVDs, and other storage media. Finally, we should consider costs for furniture and any other type of equipment required in association with information systems operations (e.g., air conditioning units, fire alarms).

■ *Cost of personnel.* These are costs incurred by using resources in the functioning of information systems. There are costs for resources directly involved in system conception, design, construction, installation, maintenance, and operation (e.g., project managers, analysts, programmers, testers, trainers, technical engineers, operators, and general technical staff). There are costs for resources that serve in support roles (e.g., secretaries, data recorders, personal assistants, system users, and field technicians that solve problems for the users). Finally, there are also costs associated with the participation of the management staff, who may be involved on a part-time or continuous basis (e.g., director of information systems, development manager, implementation manager, or other roles that may have been created in different organizations to perform functions related to information systems).

■ *Indirect costs.* These costs are incurred by the organization and are generally distributed across all projects and across all operating units. They must be calculated to reflect the correct information systems costs that are apportioned to each project.

The cost of the managerial structure is an important funding element that will represent a proportionate share of the indirect costs. A portion of the salaries and operating costs of executives' and senior managers' participation in information system management is accounted for in each project's indirect costs. Also, the general uses of work space, including the amortization of any land, buildings, and construction, are also indirect cost elements. Most organizations also include the general consumption of voice-based communications (telephone systems) as well as energy consumed in lighting and air conditioning in the calculation of indirect costs. This type of allocation is needed when we are unable to determine the exact consumption for each project or business unit.

When we have identified and calculated all costs for information systems and compare them to the total volume of business of the organization, we can then determine the proportional value of our revenue that is dedicated to supporting our information systems. This calculation is generally illustrated by the following formula:

$$Rate\_investment\_TIC = \frac{\sum (direct\_costs + indirect\_costs)}{Sales\_or\_total\_income} \times 100$$

If the number calculated using the formula (given as a percentage) returns a value greater than 4%, then it is quite possible that information system operations are a key competitive lever for success, a contributor to business transformation, and a means to create new business capabilities that allow the organization to look ahead with optimism and confidence in the future. If, in contrast, calculations provide a result that is <3%, it is very possible that the technology is designed from a purely instrumental perspective, and is used simply to contain or reduce operational costs. The latter approach is more reactive than proactive, and although that indicates a hope to survive in the future, it fails to exercise any leadership in the organization's market and business environment.

## Project Management Budget Issues

There are many ways of establishing and managing budgets, and each method has its own advantages and disadvantages depending on the situation, so one cannot really say that one method is better than another with absolute certainty. Notwithstanding that we cannot establish an infallible recipe for budget management, it is clearly worth our effort to identify some of the budget difficulties encountered on projects, and to examine how these are perceived and managed by executives.

In general, most corporate budgets have a time horizon of validity corresponding to the fiscal year, which in most cases coincides with the calendar year. In some cases, the fiscal year may be based on a different period of time related to the business cycle or the season. Therefore, it is not uncommon for organizations to have a tax year beginning or ending in August. In this instance, the organization adopts a budget related to the natural cycle of its product. For example, fashion companies may use a cycle based on the trade shows that they conduct or attend, while some wineries consider a period from October to October as a means to include their recent vintages as important milestones in their fiscal year. After establishing the time period for its fiscal year, a company will then prepare recurring annual budgets for each successive fiscal period. These budgets usually represent a variation or adjustment of the actual or estimated budgets from the previous year.

Sometimes exceptions to this practice are required, and companies may apply a zero-based budgeting approach, which leaves out what happened in the previous year and requires the calculation of a totally new budget, from start to finish, for the next budget period. This technique is normally applied only to very specific parts of the budget for which special circumstances require a comprehensive review.

This approach to budget management is more or less effective because it is repeatable. However, this repeatable process also raises the concern that recurring habits, if less than effective, could present issues and problems for the effective management of projects.

The following is a partial list of budget issues and problems that could be encountered.

- Budgets are normally prepared on an annual basis, and the rigidity of the process requires projects to be considered and discussed well in advance of their planned start dates in order to include them in the annual budgets for the upcoming year. Investment projects can be introduced, and then filtered out in the normal course of project evaluation and selection. Some projects that are removed could be replaced with other projects that were not even considered at the time of budget preparation. Also, other remaining projects could undergo significant changes after the budget has been prepared and approved. This results in circumstances that can be radically different from when the projects were initially included in the budget. Such unattended changes will inevitably lead to projects with budget management problems.

- In some cases, projects are identified at the last minute, just before the economic planning process is closed. There will therefore be a lack of the necessary evaluation and reflection needed when considering projects for inclusion in the budget. This may lead to the appearance of what seems like declarations of intent rather than actual projects, because simply listing projects on a budget sheet does not provide a serious definition of the problem to be solved, an analysis of alternatives, and a logical justification for the selected option. In turn, such project uncertainties could affect product quality and cause deviations that create project cost overruns.

- The specificity of budgets that allocate resources for specific purposes on projects does not allow for future conditions that may lead to the type and number of required resources changing. Therefore, as projects become active, resource allocation and management are too often affected by the bureaucracy required to obtain the appropriate approvals. This can constitute a disincentive for project managers trying to manage in an flexible way, because it hinders the adaptation of resources, previously unplanned, to the current needs of the project. In some cases, larger and more complex projects are established as a means to "harbor" a collection of various resources that can be allocated and assigned to project work on an as-needed basis.

- Issues and problems can also arise when there is an accumulation of several heterogeneous problems in a single project. This leads to perceiving the project as a disjointed set of work elements with a questionable connection between the true purpose of the project and the variety of work elements. This type of project seems to emerge when a variety of unrelated requirements are brought together in the budget cycle in order to create a budget item, because they otherwise do not make sense as a cohesive project. At other times, the opposite can also occur, and a project that makes sense only as a unit is partitioned and managed as two or more for budgetary reasons. This is done despite the interrelationships and interdependencies between the two efforts.

- The perception that the project budget represents a cost ceiling that cannot be exceeded presents another problem for information system development efforts. This consideration is widespread in all business sectors, but particularly in the sector of public administration. When applied in a strict manner, it prohibits the inclusion of any change that affects the project budget. This limits the developer in being able to introduce new or revised functions or features that are deemed essential. Ideally, the organization will have procedures in place for effective project change management, to include the capability to update project budgets when needed.

- When a project starts to receive unusually high numbers of change requests, doubts about key system features and functions begin to surface. This tends to produce a sense of uncertainty among project managers, who begin to feel that their efforts to control the project according to established plans, along with specified project deliverables, tasks and deadlines, are being redirected. A viable response to this situation is to open a period to discuss the reasons for so many change requests. This period of examination will undoubtedly prolong the duration of the project. Therefore, with consideration of budget limits and constraints, project team activities should be reduced or stopped until the period of discussion is completed.

- Any period of work stoppage may involve the decoupling of some team members, who will be temporarily moved to other projects. In extreme cases, some personnel may be forced to leave the company. Either way, the simple decoupling of project staff members represents a significant loss of knowledge and experience, which will likely have some negative impact on future project performance and the quality of the resulting solutions.

- The extraordinary rigidity of budgets developed for specific annual periods can cause projects to be affected by the volatility of the environment, which evolves and changes on a recurring basis. This means that some projects could end up being used to solve a problem that either no longer exists or has been radically modified. This occurs when business or market needs and interests change between budget cycles.

Finally, it should be noted that as a result of these factors, and the inability of organizations to effectively overcome the issues and problems they create, projects are subsequently subjected to potential delays and sometimes potential failure.

# Chapter 13

# Managing Problems Related to Value Delivery

The problems we have considered to this point actually arise with relative frequency in the majority of technology and information systems implementation projects, and it is generally accepted that these problems do have an adverse impact on projects. We will now examine project value, a concept that offers broader differences of opinion, because it is open to interpretation based on how we perceive value and based on the different ways we have to generate or obtain value.

The value generated for a client conducting a technology or information systems project will always be difficult to grasp, complex to calculate, and difficult to prove. Therefore, project value is often the first area examined when initial difficulties begin to appear. Most other aspects of a project can be verified during the course of the project. Such things as physical devices, terminals, workstations, software, databases, applications, programs, and manuals often constitute project deliverables for which material performance can be reviewed and observed by the project team as a means to certify the fulfillment of requirements. However, the generated value or competitive advantage produced by the project deliverables can only be checked after the project has ended, and probably after the project team has been dispersed.

It is a fact that when a project is duly executed to produce the desired business outcome, it begins generating value in association with its conception and implementation. The customer, among others, will see value in anticipating the system capability promised. Then, as the project is completed, system implementation will again create value in terms of the operational effectiveness it achieves. Project value should then continue to emerge for long periods of time, typically years depending of the kind of project, and that value will be associated with the achievement of strategic business objectives and interests, the resulting positioning of the organization in the marketplace relative to the competition, and recognition of success by customers and others in the industry in which the organization participates.

Not all projects will provide direct strategic value to the organization in terms of giving a substantial advantage in the market. This is because the orientation of many projects is purely instrumental and operational, focused on supporting the business operations in an efficient and consistent way. They provide indirect strategic value, but not the same type of value that could be obtained from a project that delivers a "breakthrough" technology solution. This lack of strategic focus in the project's inception, planning, and execution does not have to be a problem as long as all involved partners agree on the operational purpose of the project.

However, too often, there is a weak alignment of project outcome expectations among the various stakeholders, and we find that individual needs, interests, and preferences will create different perspectives about the expected value of a project. We may begin the project with general assumptions and constraints that lead us to presume there are homogeneous, shared interests between the parties and across stakeholder groups, but then we come to the realization that conditions are not always as they seem, and we may not always detect these differences until it is too late to do something about it.

## Understanding Value-Related Interests of Client-Side Stakeholders

There are many causes at the root of problems affecting stakeholders' perceptions of project value. The discussion points below consider some of the more prominent and more frequent causes of negative perceptions regarding projects on the part of client-side stakeholders.

The internal relationships in any medium-sized organization tend to be complex, as well as sufficiently subtle and delicate as to be not easily understood unless you have a thorough knowledge about the evolution of relationships and the relative positions of key participants influencing those relationships. This knowledge is usually held by very few people, especially when the technical staff has limited representation at senior management levels in the organization. In this context, understanding the role of each stakeholder on the project can be very difficult, which can be a handicap to proper progress if we fail to identify the most relevant project stakeholders and their relative interests in the project.

There are three key players or stakeholders in most organizations who are concerned with client-side value interests: the buyer, the project leader, and the project users group. Each of these roles is identified and discussed below.

## The Buyer

This stakeholder provides project financing and has responsibility for providing the project budget. The buyer has the authority to impose criteria and make decisions related to economic and resource allocations for the project, and that makes the buyer the real owner of the system.

The buyer's direct participation in the project will usually be relatively distant, limited, and infrequent, and this can cause inexperienced project managers and project team members to mistakenly believe that the buyer's relationship with the project is less or more distant than it actually is. Nevertheless, the buyer is the real customer for the project, and is empowered to approve, stop, suspend, or even cancel the project. Initial project planning and any deviations or changes in the key project dimensions (e.g., budget, scope, time, and resources) must be approved by the buyer, who may also require justification regarding the project's profitability objectives as a basis for approval.

Other stakeholders are often seen working in conjunction with the buyer in peripheral support roles. However, unless the buyer's authority is delegated, those stakeholders do not usually have the same measure of authority as the buyer. These stakeholders are sometimes called project sponsors or "project godparents." They bring different levels of personal commitment to the project, and any decisions or guidance they provide will be consistent with the buyer's interests.

## The Project Leader

The project leader, or project manager, is the person who drives the project from concept to completion, and this stakeholder will devote considerable time and effort to accomplishing project objectives based either on personal initiatives or on behalf of the interests of others. The project leader will have close relationships and remain near to the buyer and the project users group, the other two prominent client-side stakeholders associated with the project effort.

To that end, the project leader will usually act as an interlocutor who is authorized to act on all matters related to the project. This includes implementing decisions and managing limitations established by the buyer, and working in collaboration with users to facilitate their input to the system design and development effort. Limits of authority are usually established for the project leader, and may include conditions when decisions must be elevated to appropriate management levels for the purposes of consultation and to obtain permission for matters that exceed the project leader's established authority limits.

The project leader's dedication and involvement in the project can sometimes create an illusion for an inexperienced observer that the project leader is the owner of the project, and that the project leader's project management authority is unlimited and absolute. However, this is a false perception that should be rectified as quickly as possible in order to avoid situations of tension and minimize potential problems for all participating stakeholders. In contrast, we should make an effort to understand the limits of the project leader's authority, and to help achieve project goals within current project constraints, so that the project leader does not have to meet further with the buyer and other senior management officials to request additional funds or additional resources.

### The Project Users Group

Finally, there are the more or less numerous users of the system that will ultimately use the system that is developed and implemented. On the project, the users will be represented by a project users group, a small delegation of users who have been chosen for their quality performance, experience, knowledge, leadership, or authority within the users' environment.

We must consider the users group because they will be responsible for using the information system to validate the design and development work of the technical work team. This group will have no real authority to independently change the orientation, size, or significant parameters that define the project, but they can use feedback and established change management procedures to influence the system development effort.

The number of stakeholders may vary according to the nature of each project, along with our level of access to them. In any case, we should always make an effort to identify all of the stakeholders that have an interest in the project, and to understand the roles they are playing on the project. Please keep in mind that it is possible for one person to play different stakeholder roles in a project; combinations include buyer–project leader, sponsor–user, and project leader–user. In some cases, we may find that some stakeholders, such as those listed as sponsors, may not be visibly present or to the casual observer do not appear to have active involvement. It should be recognized that not all stakeholder activities are obvious.

The worst thing we can do is develop a superficial and simplistic reading of the project as if it is just about two stakeholders: the developer and the client. Rather, we need to distinguish the different stakeholders on the project as a means to avoid confusion over motivations, authorities, responsibilities, and capabilities, which could hinder the achievement of project goals. The proper recognition of stakeholders and their project interests will provide a complete understanding of the intended project purpose and, with all probability, an understanding of the value they expect to achieve from the project effort.

## Understanding Value-Related Interests of Supplier-Side Stakeholders

In the previous section, we reviewed the different client-side stakeholders and their attitudes toward the project. Now we will consider the attitudes and roles that can be found on the supplier side for their value influences and contributions to the project.

Some years ago, I had the opportunity to collaborate with a group of colleagues who were working on some projects for a prominent financial institution that was very well known in the community. I was surprised to see the extent to which work performance expectations and attitudes were maintained by the project manager and project team members. The project team comprised some specialists with recognized expertise in the business intelligence environment who were developing a system of business indicators for the financial institution.

The project team came to the client from its offices in the nation's capital, and I talked with them when I also visited this client's facilities. My purpose was to understand the current status of the effort and to identify and discuss opportunities for further collaboration activities with the institution based on the project team's privileged knowledge of the client. All of this was intended to consider ways in which additional value could be offered to the client. However, after speaking with the project manager and some team members, I was informed that the project team wanted to finish the project as soon as possible, with minimum duration and scope, so that they could return to their home offices earlier. They managed to negotiate with the client to achieve a reduction in project scope. In turn, they were recognized by their executive managers for improving their margins on the project.

However, the adjustments made to this project had other consequences. It was discovered, while working at the headquarters of this financial institution, that there were two other work teams from the same company situated within walking distance. Furthermore, those teams were not aware that other staff members of the same company were working in the client's headquarters, and they did not know the nature of work in which they were engaged. Essentially, those two teams were rather ignorant of aspects of the client's business not directly related to their projects, and they did not know about any opportunities or needs of the client that could expand the current work and collaboration effort.

This condition represents a shortsighted, somewhat selfish, and perhaps limited vision oriented toward immediate financial results. This prevented the extended collaboration that could have been used to examine added value for the client. First, information about the client's business interests and opportunities that might enable the project team to expand its work was not examined, and proposals that would have offered added value to the client were not pursued. Second, where the project team had ignored the opportunity to discuss expanded interests with the client, the client had to accept the revised project outcome (albeit, as agreed to), but without fully considering a more comprehensive solution or even alternative solutions.

The previous example illustrates how the supplier-side perspective of project value can be different from the client-side perspective of project value. Here are a few additional points that represent the supplier's point of view with regard to project value.

- The supplier is sometimes seen to be dissociated from the variety of interests expressed by multiple stakeholders. The supplier is not necessarily dismissing stakeholder needs or avoiding stakeholders, but rather is focused on fulfilling the contractual requirements for the project. This perspective results because the project team is often guided by a different set of business interests, and supplier-side value is achieved when those business interests are adequately addressed.

- The supplier may show interest in achieving goals besides client-specified project goals. This is not particularly inappropriate, and it may even be laudable within the supplier's organization, as long as the supplier's effort and special interests do not interfere with the achievement of the client's project goals or result in project deliverables that are deemed unacceptable.

- The supplier will sometimes try to manipulate project resource allocations by cutting the duration of resource assignments on the project. For example, the supplier will try to provide resources on a part-time rather than full-time basis as a means to improve the financial performance of the supplier. Here, the supplier monitors revenue per worker hour, and measures margins achieved over revenue. This is simply an examination of the relationship between costs and revenues on the project, and the management of resources to produce the desired financial results.

- Sometimes project difficulties can arise when the supplier does not adequately distinguish between sales activities and development services. In this circumstance, the client feels bombarded with the ongoing effort of the project manager and project team to add new products and services to the existing contract, or to prematurely discuss the client's need for the next-generation system before the current system is fully developed and implemented. The supplier's perspective is one in which each client development effort is seen as a sales and marketing opportunity, and project teams are often called upon by management to exploit that opportunity. Problems can arise when suppliers do this in a less subtle and more blatant manner than the client can endure, as the client will sometimes see this as a diversion, with reduced focus on the current development work effort for which the supplier is being paid. It should be noted that this supplier-side issue is different from the bigger picture of client relationship management described in the next subsection.

## Supplier-Side Perspective of a Client Relationship Model

Most suppliers will state that establishing and maintaining long-term client relationships is a prominent business objective. To do this, suppliers need to understand the client's business and the client's perspective for achieving business results. In particular, suppliers need to perform projects that attend to client-side value as well as supplier-side value.

The root cause for too many project difficulties is the increasingly widespread trend among technology companies to strictly separate the function of production and the function of sales of service. This ignores the logic applied for many years by the most prestigious consulting firms—the premise of, "who sells, delivers the service." This premise recognizes the fact that in a service environment such as that of a system delivery project, there is an opportunity to provide added value through relationship continuity with the client. That continuity allows us to achieve and have in place a common understanding of client needs, and that provides real value for both parties. For example, it reduces the time constraints and difficulties of transmitting and using information needed to define subsequent project work and to conduct subsequent project negotiations.

Client relationships using this model do not develop overnight, but, instead, such business relationships are formed over time. An effective client relationship management strategy is needed to integrate client-side perspectives with supplier-side interests. In particular, suppliers will need to facilitate communication and continuity in the client relationship across periods of commercial promotion, sales, production, and delivery of services. Communication ensures that real-time information is provided to work teams as a means to improve project performance and improve quality. Continuity ensures that many of the same supplier participants are involved across the various client relationship management activities that take place. This provides the supplier with current knowledge about the client's business and a consistent understanding of important issues and expectations of the client. This knowledge and understanding can then be applied, with an ease that would not otherwise exist, to proposals presented to the client and to work efforts conducted in the client's business environment.

However, this model also raises some concern associated with situations in which the supply-side professionals who participate in the process of promoting and selling services are the same individuals that participate in the direction and management of the subsequent project effort. The concern is that these individuals will dedicate a good deal of their time and attention to selling and delivering services, and it requires individuals with relevant experience and training to qualify for this role. This approach to client relationship management has the potential to limit the growth of the company, because suppliers will incur expenses and use resources to form and train professionals in an accelerated way.

To break these limitations to corporate growth, technology companies decided some years ago to separate the two functions of sales and service delivery in order to extend their capacity to attract business and clients. It was believed that breaking this restriction would help them to grow faster than their competitors in a market where customers were competing for the attention of suppliers. This occurred in the years between 1994 and 1999, when companies were prompted to embark on large projects that focused on resolving the potential effect of the Year 2000 event on legacy systems. Many enterprise resources planning (ERP) software implementation decisions that were made at this time also have their origin in this dilemma.

This separation between the two functions caused suppliers to extend their commercial promotions with less experienced personnel who did not have sufficient seniority to accurately define the project scope and the system environment. These individuals could reasonably conduct most routine follow-up contacts to provide service presentations and product demonstrations, but these were essentially pre-packaged events that did not require the participation of the most qualified professionals. As needed, qualified professionals attended client–supplier "sales" meetings at critical times when their expertise was needed. Otherwise, these professionals were free to engage in the management and delivery of customer system solutions. Therefore, the ability of suppliers to manage business and projects was improved.

Now, many suppliers operate the two sides of the company as separate and independent business units without making a conscious effort to harmonize their performance in any collaborative way. These units are now being propelled to greater levels of performance as isolated units, leaving each unit to evolve in an independent manner.

## Supplier-Side Presales Interests and Potential Difficulties

The way in which business is managed prior to supplier selection produces some potential for problems that could impact the generation of value.

The presales period includes an interaction between the client and the supplier in which the client seeks to transfer relent information to the potential supplier. The supplier is expected to use this information to gain an understanding of the client's business needs and interests, and to define a collaborative approach to providing a solution to the client's problem. In turn, the client will compile and review responses from all potential suppliers to evaluate their proposed solutions and to select the supplier that will be used.

The supplier's response to the client could have variable size and structure depending on the culture and standards of work of each company. Some supplier responses will emphasize its use of methodology; others will cite and promote professional experience. In most cases, the client will request that certain essential information be included in each supplier's response as a means for the client to assess common factors. Clients will often ask suppliers to provide information that includes the following:

- The supplier's understanding of the problem
- The solution and approach proposed by the supplier to resolve the problem
- A brief discussion of possible alternative solutions, if any, and the grounds or reasons underpinning the choice of the proposed solution
- The benefits expected from product implementation, including indications of increases in revenue and profit, and reductions in expenditures

■ The project scope and a description of the resulting product with identification of functions and features
■ A project work plan showing the proposed work effort
■ A preliminary project schedule showing the anticipated duration of the project
■ A staff allocation and management plan to identify individuals that will be assigned to the project and to show how they will be managed
■ A project pricing proposal that represents the costs to be incurred by the client

Supplier proposals frequently offer these information details together with project planning in the form of Gantt charts or other similar graphical representations, as requested by the client. All of this content may not be essential if it does not contribute to the value of the proposal. Also, added graphical content sometimes just unnecessarily fills a portion of the document, like having too many pages dedicated to explaining internal methodology details. However it is important to include the requested information needed by the client to assess and compare supplier proposals.

Some difficulties can surface for the supplier when inadequate proposals are prepared for client consideration. For example, proposals too often have only a couple of paragraphs describing the understanding of the client's problem. Some also avoid any discussion about the benefits and value that will be generated by the resulting product. Similarly, proposals are often lacking a detailed product description for the main project deliverable, and conditions and thresholds of deliverable acceptance are not identified. It also appears that many proposals have a more than reasonable amount of work plan details to specify the work to be performed. These items have the potential to generate difficulties and conflict in early client collaboration efforts.

So, we see that in proposals of collaboration it is frequently forgotten that the goal is to show how the product deliverable will be provided, which happens when the proposal presents a diffuse response with little concrete information. In a way, this suggests that we are paying more attention to the road that will be followed and less attention to the destination we want to reach.

This lack of focus and precision in supplier proposals causes the project team to start with general and vague information that is sometimes confusing and generally of low quality. This forces the team to discover for themselves the goals of the project, product deliverables, scope and composition, and tolerance thresholds in all other details that should have been provided in the proposal for early collaboration with the client.

It is not surprising, therefore, that many projects have been completed with significant client dissatisfaction. Although the products were seemingly generated in a solid and well-built manner, this was defined in response to the criteria of end-users, which were often different and divergent from those of management.

# Chapter 14

## Managing Problems Related to Internal Supplier Issues

When we focus our attention on companies providing professional services within the framework of information technology, we find that these organizations often undergo a series of failures that hinder their performance and contributions to value generation in projects conducted for their clients. These shortcomings might be characterized as difficulties experienced by suppliers in association with developing capability to provide simultaneous services to multiple clients, to manage internal corporate growth and staff management to enable participation in a variety of client engagements, and to provide consistent and successful outcomes for each client.

In this chapter, we will examine some of the prominent issues that affect supplier performance, and perhaps gain some insight toward improving capability to manage these issues in an effective manner.

### Issues Arising from the Supplier's Human Resources Policy

Among the problems experienced by suppliers, there are a wide array of problems that are directly related to human resources. In particular, people may be employed to develop and deliver services aligned with a company's business, but are too often assigned to projects in roles unrelated to their training or technical expertise. This can result in a reduced team performance when some team members are not suitably qualified, and it is sometimes the case that these individuals do not want to be involved in a project where they cannot apply their knowledge and skills. This hampers the opportunity to form a synergistic project team that has all of the needed skills to support the client's effort. In effect, qualified project team members are replaced by a simple aggregation of resources that enable the supplier to obtain larger payments with less qualified project team members.

Among the factors contributing to this situation is the short-term orientation of human resource policies. This appears to be caused by a lack of vision and commitment to the workforce by leadership within the supplier's organization. Instead of betting on real people as the organization's repository of intellectual capital and showing value for their professional growth and development, managers seem to ignore this in favor of the alternative of managing the shortage of talent and team member commitment on a short-term, case-by-case basis.

Thus, supplier firms create human resources (HR) departments that are overcrowded and impersonal in their management efforts. Such an HR department will be constantly seeking to hire a labor force to participate on the latest project to be contracted, which has been sold as neither having the proper team and resources nor the basic skills needed to manage the challenge with a reasonable assurance of success.

Newly hired project team members are integrated with current employees, bringing together individuals with different degrees of skill and motivation. In some cases, suppliers may recycle professionals with expertise different from those required by the project. In contrast, new employees are challenged to take on key roles on the project, even those who have recently joined the staff after a rapid and abrupt hiring process in order to fulfill project commitments.

The lack of time, the pressing deadlines of the project, the lack of criteria and requirements for HR department use, and the predominant orientation to quantitative metrics prevent a rigorous process that could be used to acquire the best professionals. Instead, staff members are too often selected because they can be incorporated into the project on the required date, even though they are far from being the most appropriate candidates.

Many HR departments appear to be continually busy. This is not necessarily due to corporate growth, but rather to staff turnover. In some cases, this turnover is caused by the work environment an organization creates, one that lacks the appeal or motivation needed for staff retention. When the work environment takes on characteristics of being chaotic, disjointed, lacking in common sense, or simply undergoing constant change, it can cause a steady stream of retirements and departures from the company that requires a major effort by the HR department to replace them and to manage the moderate growth that occurs.

Many suppliers will use their institutional press statements to announce shining declarations about their human resources being a foundation of their intellectual capital. They tout people as key corporate assets, and the true source of their competitive advantage and their best guarantee of future growth and progress. However, their actions often contradict these statements, and this is particularly evident when the HR department is viewed internally as a liability rather than as a corporate asset.

The real liability occurs when HR departments are directed to use questionable hiring practices, and stretch the possibilities that legislation allows. In some circumstances, regardless of their professional category, the organization may apply practices that are very close to an improper transfer of resources. They may also hire temporary employees at higher than prescribed limits as a means to immediately optimize their financial results without any consideration for the actual resource assignments that are made. Although the work of the HR department is sometimes criticized and reviled, it can be very difficult at times to achieve acceptable quality with consistency.

The use of position descriptions can sometimes create differences of opinion. On one side, there are those who believe that it is enough to provide a general and simplistic definition of a profile based on a professional level (e.g., programmer, analyst, or systems engineer), plus a specification of the work environment in which work is to be accomplished (e.g., Java, COBOL, or Microsoft.NET). This relies on the accuracy and truthfulness of what each candidate specifies on the job application, and on the capability of HR management specialists to match professional qualifications to needed technology expertise. On the other side, there are those who want the position description used by the HR department to be more complete. This would include, in addition to the professional category, a full description of the tasks to be performed, usually in terms of preferred methodology use, along with identification of a more or less complete set of tools intended for use on the project.

Either way, these specifications do not always facilitate the work of the HR department when specialized skills and experience are needed. It is difficult to find a candidate who has all of the required competencies and capabilities with an exact match to the methods and tools to be used. So, as there is usually no ideal candidate, the HR specialist must choose the most suitable candidate, and this is too often done with complete ignorance of the technologies involved and the problems of the projects to be addressed. To that end, it is possible to select and hire a candidate whose record indicates the largest number of methods and tools aligned with the project. This is regardless of whether they relate to the most important aspects or accessories of the project, if they are project-centric or marginal, or if they lack the necessary criterion to distinguish the candidate's level of competency in the use of tools and procedures.

If HR specialists choose to rely on members of the professional staff to filter the candidates listed, this does not improve the situation, despite the goodwill of all HR specialists and information technology professionals participating in the effort. In this case, managers from the professional staff who participate usually do not have sufficient detailed knowledge of the products and tools to be used to enable a reliable assessment of a candidate's knowledge and experience, and this does not improve the selection situation.

In any case, the process of candidate selection is usually applied on a basis that is oriented toward achieving a short-term response. Therefore, it is not the candidate's potential for professional growth that is important. Rather, it is the candidate's value in relation to the immediate exploitation of their current knowledge and professional experience that matters.

## Human Resources Management: An Examination of Hiring Practices

Not long ago, in a well-known services organization recognized as a first-class company, the process began to look for professionals to create a team for a new project. The process called for a comprehensive specification of candidate qualifications. This specification included a professional profile, a list of qualification features, and the set of tools that candidates should know to successfully complete the project. These requirements included the need for knowledge of Java Server Faces, Hibernate, and Jasper, a report generator for the Java environment, a relatively popular combination that facilitates system definition, construction, and testing.

After more than 2 months of waiting, the despair of those responsible for the project was lifted when the request received approvals from the unit director of the unit, the marketing director, and the general manager. At the same time, the HR department considered the required resources, and replied that it was impossible to find a professional with this profile in the company. It had taken 2 months and four executive signatures at different levels in the organization to get a negative response that was essentially known a priori from the start.

As established corporate policy forbids hiring technical staff in this manner, they passed the opportunity on to subcontracting firms to fulfill the resource request. After two additional weeks, some subcontractor responses arrived in the subcontracting department, and they were held until the project manager arranged to interview the candidates. While the project manager responsible for the project met personally with the candidates to assess their skills, knowledge, and experience, the project manager knew little or nothing about the tool and product to be used, and, therefore, was unable to effectively evaluate the candidates' experience.

The project manager was determined to break the ongoing project delays that were beginning to try the client's patience by choosing the three most suitable candidates based on a limited examination of their solvency, knowledge, and experience. At that time, the analysis effort was well under way, and client pressure to have a coherent design and validate a prototype was constant. The entire subcontracting process was done as quickly as possible because the project was expected to finish in only 6 months, and nearly 3 months had been lost just in the staffing selection process.

One month later, problems with the development work surfaced and two of the three subcontracted individuals were released for an apparent lack of skill and experience that was not evident during the interviews. One of the individuals also displayed a negative attitude toward the project and difficulty integrating with the rest of the development team. The release of the first technician was assumed to be simply based on a lack of the skills and experience needed for the project, and no further inquiries were made. However, when 3 days later a second technician was released, the project manager wanted to make an objective evaluation of the circumstances.

The evaluation process began when the task leader was asked to provide a report created by this second technician using Jasper. The task leader was also asked to have a team member with known related experience produce a similar report. A technician that was available was selected by the task leader, but that individual who had broad development experience did not actually have Jasper experience. So the task leader agreed to provide the corresponding manuals to that technician in order to allow some fundamental work to be accomplished for evaluation purposes. This experienced technician, working from relative ignorance of the product, used Jasper to produce the necessary report in just 3 days. In contrast, the second technician, who had indicated having specific Jasper experience, had been working for 3 weeks and was still stuck in resolving the problem. The contrast between the two was distinct; the situation was unacceptable.

The technician was called to a meeting to review performance and notes of the meeting held during the selection process. The technician was reminded that when asked about knowledge of Jasper, he had replied that he knew everything, which was taken to mean he had a complete knowledge of the product. To this he was undeterred and replied, "Of course, I answered all because I knew there was more to know, but of course I knew everything I knew."

Leaving aside the gall of the technician, it is obvious that an interviewer with tool and product experience would have enabled a more realistic examination of the candidate's knowledge and experience. Even better, it would have been good to use an objective test prepared by a qualified specialist for an assessment of candidate skill, knowledge, and experience. However, the rigidity and lack of nimble internal procedures caused a significant delay in the project, precluding the development of instruments and interview questions that could be used to validate candidates' background, their interview results, and the contents of their curriculum vitae. This would help identify and eliminate those candidates with fewer scruples who try to gain an advantage by creating their curriculum vitae to show the capability and experience looked for by the company.

The result, after releasing the two technicians, was a frustrating improvisation, which significantly impacted the progress of the project, the quality of the product generated, the production and delivery deadlines to the client, and essentially led to a loss of control over the entire process. This situation incurred a significant cost, although it did not prevent the client from having the product on the date needed, albeit with a scope lower than initially expected.

## Issues Arising from the Supplier's Internal Organization

Improvisation such as that described in the previous section is often widespread across different aspects of project management. However, problems can arise when improvisation is too rampant and runs uncontained or unresolved.

There are some organizations that presume a positive value in association with improvisation. They will commend those practitioners that effectively use it, and label them as resolute when they are able to find needed, albeit informal, shortcuts in the system development process. In contrast, this can sometimes appear as showing indifference to others in the organization that follow established procedures; they might even be considered as lacking in imagination and resources to find an improvisational solution within the forest of organizational barriers.

There are real "traps" in organizations where the procedures seem designed to detect and punish those who follow the established processes and reward those who find a way to skip them or follow them in appearance only. Moreover, most of these procedures are conceived and designed from a short-term perspective, oriented to oversight and control by management rather than to support the development needs of clients. This can cause professionals to reach a point of despair, when they see their client work and projects undermined and put at risk by all-powerful procedures dictated by a bureaucratic system of management, which has a primary focus on the current reporting period (i.e., month, quarter or, at most, the year). The governing processes that should be supporting long-term business activities are imposing priorities and requirements over short-term client engagements.

Management controls have the common condition of living on the margins of customer projects. In order to oversee impacts on margins, management starts from the premise that its mission is to require functional and project managers to provide reasoning and justification for every action that is needed, including hiring staff, creating a partner alliance, purchasing a product or tool, issuing an offer of collaboration, signing a new contract with a client, or issuing a new client invoice.

Likewise, any action that requires the support of a centralized function often meets some form of resistance that requires an extraordinary effort to overcome. One would think that these centralized functions would be supportive, enabling specialists to put their knowledge together in order to achieve greater collaboration and therefore operational efficiency. Instead, these centralized functions sometimes have staff that presents self-indulgent and egocentric perspectives of their departments. They have a self-perception of their function and role in the organization as guarantors of the corporate future. As they develop a clear and self-serving exaggeration of their own importance, they sometimes become the main obstacle to normal development of business activities, and this happens within limits that are sometimes simply ridiculous.

A few months ago, I encountered a situation that dealt with such capricious and unreasonable attitudes, and which illustrates what I have described above. In an international services company with extraordinarily powerful central departments, there was a situation that seemed to be the result of personal whim rather than a result of using more or less standardized procedures or rules.

A public administration agency was working in collaboration with the services company, which had sold the agency a product license for corporate document management. The license cost had to be distributed among different departments associated with the public administration agency, and this was done in a variable proportion that had to be calculated every year according to each department's use of the product in the previous year. All operations and negotiations were centralized in a particular unit, which acted as a representative for all departments. This representation included reviewing and agreeing to the contributions of each department every year, and negotiating the license renewal cost with the services company for the next period.

To determine the contribution of each department, the services company facilitated the compilation of product usage statistics for the previous year, which served as the basis for establishing the proportion of costs that each department should bear the following year. In parallel, besides the license renewal, another line of collaboration provided for an accounting of evolutionary maintenance of services applications developed using the document management product. In particular, the various departments had agreed to collaborate and coordinate in the development of a comprehensive application that considered requirements from stakeholders in different departments. This coordinated effort would help lower maintenance costs and provide the richest possible functionality within the application.

This year, like all previous years, the account manager provided information on the distribution of effort and use of the system during the previous year to facilitate the calculation of costs that would be applicable. This was done in response to changing prices for maintaining licenses and for preparing a preliminary estimate for developing the evolutionary maintenance of service applications. With this information, the coordinator started negotiations with the heads of each department in order to achieve the appropriate participation of everyone in the financing of two activities—the license maintenance and the services for evolutionary maintenance of applications.

The agency coordinator decided to manage the effort as two operations, one for the license maintenance and the other as services for evolutionary maintenance of applications. This would consider the involvement of all departments, which included 13 parties and two concepts, which presumed 26 invoices as a means to achieve economies of scale. However, the services company, in contradiction with the agency's perception, did not distinguish between the two components, but saw it simply as the maintenance of the common solution.

When a final internal agreement was reached, the terms were collected in a proposal that specified global cooperation across the departments. As was done in previous years, this included the details of department involvement and their financial contributions, along with the data needed for billing, including recipients, amounts, and respective statements and information that should appear on invoices.

The proposal was approved and the services were started. When the time came to make payment on the first bill, the administrator was unable to compile supporting documentation customized for each department because the services company issued an invoice that did not separate the two efforts, and did not separate department costs, as was intended internally. After some discussions, protests, and arguments, the services company explained how it had never been asked for something like this before, and stated that it had always been considered sufficient to request the central collection of funds based on the proposal signed by the agency coordinator. At the end of the day, the bills were relatively small amounts, just over a 1000 or 1500 dollars each, and the departments made regular payments without any incidents.

However, a dilemma remained within the agency to satisfy procedural problems associated with billing each department for their portions of the cost. This involved the preparation of up to 26 small and different proposals that had to explain every part of the department's commitment, both for the annual license maintenance and for the services oriented to evolutionary maintenance. In consultations with the billing department, this approach would satisfy procedural requirements, and the documents to be managed and approved by the departments were prepared, but with discomfort and some anger on their part.

This situation was exacerbated when the invoice approval authority required additional documentation, and withheld payment until that was achieved. This prompted a lot of protests and dislike from departments who saw the extraordinary bureaucratic procedure as a roadblock. They balked at having to prepare 26 bills and 26 approval documents of expenditure, signed and properly matched to each bill.

## Issues Arising from the Poor Implementation of Methodologies

Suppliers are accustomed to encountering another set of problems related to how methodologies are used to manage the projects. Methodologies are generally assumed to be an inflexibility factor, and a means to provide necessary professional rigor in the project management environment.

In most cases, a baseline methodology is used to present an idealized concept that integrates the presentation of professional credentials and experience, and an explanation of the strategic definition of the company relative to its mission, vision, and corporate values. Ultimately, this baseline methodology becomes an element of marketing and communications for the company, but this is far removed from being an operational approach that is detailed, specific, and tailored to the circumstances and conditions of each individual project addressed by the supplier and client. At best, the baseline methodology may provide some fundamental details about the main products that are to be produced as a result of performing the various methodology phases, activities, and tasks. In some cases, the service provider may develop a work plan with Gantt charts to outline the phases, activities, tasks, and products to be generated, as defined in the referenced methodology.

However, although the methodological approach is offered as a means of collaboration in presentations prior to the sale, the project team will too often abandon the path prescribed by the methodology as soon as project work begins. The project manager and project team members will often revert to improvisation and practices that have nothing to do with the methodology, but are deeply rooted as habits in the team members. They might recognize the inherent rigor of the methodology, and can adjust to that, but they do not have any certainty that the methodology process will be a guarantee of project success.

The result is a superficial and esthetic application of the methodology, perhaps using only the nomenclature, forms, and documents provided by the methodology. Otherwise, project team members prefer to leave the outcome of the project in the hands of professionals who will use personal methods and expertise to achieve project results. In many cases, the project outcome will comprise a collection of heterogeneous products resulting from a lack of precision guidance that would have been provided if the methodology had been used properly. Sometimes, this prevents or reduces the realization of the benefits that motivated the client to undertake the project in the first place.

Arguments offered by team members to justify why they have minimized the use of the methodology will often comprise a series of excuses, rather than reasons related to the rigidity of the methodology, the costs of its implementation, or problems of applicability to the project. Rather, their reasons generally represent views that the methodology hinders their job performance because it is not specifically aligned with the details of their particular project.

At the other extreme, we can find those who strive to implement the methodology with all of its rigor and guidelines, and therefore apply the resultant rigidity and complexity in implementing the activities and tasks that create the products. This approach is applied infrequently among suppliers, but interest in using an effective methodology will often be found among clients who have limited project and system development experience.

In a few cases, we will find that companies and professionals alike understand the value of methodologies, and they will promote their use in the project management environment. These proponents of methodology use recognize that methodologies are nothing more than general process and practice guides, and they do not have to provide a direct and detailed link to the specifics of each of the projects in which they are used.

However, methodology use should provide for customization that considers the goals and objectives to be managed in the specific project. This includes identifying the constraints of the client and the environment in which the methodology will be implemented to manage the project. It also means adapting methodology processes to be consistent with the size and scope of each project—prescribed tasks can be enlarged or reduced, or even eliminated, to meet the needs of each specific project. This need for adaptation should not be misunderstood as a weakness or limitation of the methodology. On the contrary, it is its greatest strength, because such adaptation makes the methodology usable in multiple business environments and across a variety of projects having different problems to solve.

This does not mean that any methodology will serve, with appropriate adaptation, for any purpose or project. Rather, each methodology has its purpose and provides a framework in which it is effectively used. This framework is defined and facilitates methodology use within a certain range of problems. The methodology can be used in that range, with appropriate adaptation and customization, and it is not intended for other purposes that fall outside that range of problems. Allow me to be emphatic—there is no general-purpose methodology that can invariably serve to resolve any problem or project. This idea is an illusion and false.

Every methodology has its scope, which should be known and well-defined when selecting it for project use. Otherwise, we will be trying to solve problems with an unknown and perhaps inappropriate methodology. If we apply a particular methodology to situations where it does not effectively contribute to the solution, this will probably result in a predictable failure, suboptimal project performance, and tension and frustration among the parties.

## Problems Arising from Improper or Ineffective Planning

Poor planning will hinder the project team's subsequent ability to comply with requirements based on basic and essential problems that surface when project estimates are deficient. Therefore, project estimating is the key to effective project planning. Estimate preparation considers critical project planning elements that include the work breakdown structure, along with detailed estimates of tasks (effort), time (schedule), and cost (budget). Planning also addresses team structure and every objective dimension of the project effort required: the number of users and the number of departments affected, the number of systems that will use established interfaces, the number of functions to be implemented, the number of reports to be generated, the quantity of transactions to resolve, and the queries or information demands to be facilitated.

When the methodology used for project work is mishandled, we are likely to encounter consequences that are practically inevitable, and that will have adverse effects on the outcome of the project. Some prominent problems are mentioned below according to their frequency and importance.

## *Project Estimating*

When the appropriate level of care and attention is not given in the planning phase, the result will be an inaccurate representation of the scale and difficulty of the project in the work plan. In turn, this will cause project estimates to be erroneous. For example, an erroneous estimation of effort could cause the project to be overestimated, showing an oversized scope, size, or level of difficulty. That leads to estimates that are higher than actually required by the project. If this happens without correction, the supplier could lose the opportunity to work on the project. This may be so even if the designed solution is good, because the client will probably want to avoid additional costs, and presumably will choose another supplier that has not made the same estimating mistakes.

The person in charge of business development should have sensitivity, adequate knowledge about customer expectations, and intelligence enough to bring the customer the results of these estimates with a level of disclosure and sufficient transparency to allow them to enter into basic negotiations. This will identify the points where estimates are divergent from what is expected, and enable it to be seen with some confidence that a mistake has been made in the estimation process, which can be corrected to better represent the project.

If, instead, the business development manager chooses to adopt an attitude that is less open to dialog, this could put pressure on technicians to reduce the estimate to the figures believed to be driving the client. Without providing reasons or arguments about quantitative and transparent data, the business development manager could obtain an estimate according to his will, but, in the long run, he will undermine the confidence of the team that made the estimate. If the team invests precious time and applies their best skills in creating an estimate, then sees it questioned for no apparent reason, they will normally react with skepticism, mistrust, and lack of commitment, and this will occur every time the circumstances are repeated. Thus, after a few repetitions, the estimation exercise will become a mere ceremony. From the perspective of the team, estimating will become a necessary but insignificant step, which simply provides a basis for adjustments by the project manager or business development manager.

Conversely, we can envisage circumstances under which an erroneous estimation of effort might cause the project to be underestimated, with an undersized scope, size, or level of difficulty.

The result will be a project budget that is below what might be expected, and this will most likely not be questioned. Instead, it will be considered a "pleasant surprise," and there will be no further analysis that might help identify the estimation error. This can happen even when the error is a simple arithmetic error in the sum of the different items comprising the budget. It is also not unusual for a client to accept figures from the service provider even when the client sees that the figures are significantly lower than reasonably expected. In some cases, the client views the supplier's bid as one that requires the supplier to take financial risks. Therefore, the client assumes the supplier will have a budget surplus available, and, if things go wrong, it is to the detriment of the supplier. Of course, if things do go wrong, this can trigger a contentious relationship that never ends well for either the supplier or the client.

Intentional underestimation on bids may lead to apparent commercial success, with contract awards for the supplier, which might provide short-term growth in sales and hiring related to the new projects. There might also be a period of competitive improvement for the supplier based on contract awards arising from pricing below that of the competition. However, this commercial success will likely diminish as projects eventually reach points where there are limited funds to carry out the required work.

There are some circumstances in which an apparent underestimation is validated by the efficiency and effectiveness of the supplier's organization. Here are a few examples of how low estimates from suppliers can be justified:

- A methodology is used that is perceived as more effective than processes used by competitors.
- More efficient technologies than those of competitors are used.
- Production approaches are applied that substantially improve productivity.
- A previous solution might be reused, such as a development platform that solves a significant part of the project.
- A "software factory" might be used, contributing to increased productivity, reduced inefficiencies, and the availability of architectural and common component solutions, precluding the need to develop each integral part of the solution, and avoiding the major burden of testing each element (which might already have passed a validation process).
- The professional staff might have a higher level of education, training, preparation, or commitment.
- The professional staff might be more highly qualified, experienced, and credentialed.
- The level of remuneration to technical staff, or cost of supervision resulting from corporate location, size, or any other consideration that can represent a lower cost.
- A risk management process might be effectively used to review bids and determine those that will be released and those that will be withheld or canceled.

However, if we have no well-founded reason to justify the difference between our lower estimates and those of other competitors, then we have a problem because it means we are underestimating the project without a proper understanding of its scope, difficulty, and complexity.

## Problem Definition and Methodology Applicability

Planning and estimating must start from a credible and realistic point in the early stages of the project. Otherwise, the project plan becomes a work of fiction that could have disastrous results for the project and adverse impacts on the parties involved in the project. To that end, I want to emphasize the importance of completing the problem definition phase, regardless of the name given to it (e.g., system analysis phase, feasibility study phase, or any other name found in the methodology that is used). This problem definition phase is critical to the overall project. If we do not examine the problem in an effective manner, then we will design, build, and try to implement a system that, despite its best qualities, may be ineffective in resolving the problem or simply provide a suboptimal solution.

Clients tend to be impatient and nervous when anticipating the implementation date of their new information system. Some clients may even suffer anxiety and stress that, in turn, causes them to place undue pressure on the project manager and project team. They want the technical staff to pass through the problem definition effort with a certain lightness in order to enter into the construction of the system as soon as possible. Personally, I have found this type of client on more than one occasion, and it is very difficult to resist the temptation to move quickly across the project planning to calm the anxiety of those clients. They usually offer very convincing and well-intentioned arguments to expedite the process, but experience tells us that taking shortcuts and skipping stages can be detrimental to the overall project success.

The particular arguments that clients usually offer revolve around two axes that can be called the problem definition axis and the methodology applicability axis. These two aspects are considered in the discussion presented below.

Clients may argue that the problem definition effort can be reduced, or even bypassed, because they can supply all the information needed on this subject and we can therefore move forward without additional efforts and avoid repeating a process that does not contribute added value. A variation of this client argument emerges when the client believes that the problem to be solved is much simpler than it seems. This variation is illustrated when the client tries to dismiss the need to conduct interviews and other fact-finding activities that normally facilitate problem definition, and instead encourages moving on to the next phase of development. This argument is expanded when clients cite the proposal stage, indicating that considerable time was spent on explaining the problem, and, therefore, "take and use that information to define the problem and do not waste more time repeating work already done."

An extreme case of client influence on the problem definition phase can be found with the client who tells us that they have hired us because of our experience and expertise on this kind of project. They say that, by virtue of our status as experts, we must define the problem without their participation and then submit the solution to them for validation.

Another collection of client arguments will often appear when the project team prepares a work plan based on strict, step-by-step adherence to methodology guidance. The arguments are usually preceded by the client showing respect for the supplier's experience, qualities, and skills and, of course, greater respect for the methodological approach. Too often, these points are raised by the client and serve to soften the messages that immediately follow. Clients will express a variety of concerns related to methodology use, such as the following:

- The methodology proposed is too rigid for the size of the current project and that will hinder project progress.
- The methodology requires redundant tasks and activities that do not add value and only serve to slow down the development process.
- The methodology is too narrow and too generic, and that prevents adaptation in response to the unique contingencies that may arise in a real project.
- The methodology is very useful when a team is inexperienced or lacking in knowledge, guiding them step by step, but it contributes nothing to "experienced professionals like us." (The client seeks to establish a level of complicity with the supplier to facilitate a concession regarding the methodology use.)

These client concerns represent the kind of pressure brought to bear on the project manager and project team. They create a circumstance which must be taken into account by those responsible for the project, but they also must be addressed from a management perspective. Caution must be used to avoid giving in to pressure in a simplistic way. If the project team gives in to pressure from the client, this concession will not end the problem, but will probably be a source of major problems to follow. Of course, any subsequent problems will be viewed by the client as the responsibility of the project team, and the team will find little to no understanding from the client when such problems arise.

## Client Obsession with Final Product Delivery

Sometimes, the perception of the client is that the originally scheduled date at which the information system is to be in place is closer than anyone acknowledges, and, although the project may still be in its early stages, perhaps awaiting contract execution and project team formation, the client begins to show concern about meeting internal deadlines, sensing that the project is already delayed. The client's anxiety begins to build in anticipation of the need for timely project completion, and ways to expedite the development process are already being discussed.

This situation and other more subtle conditions indicate a lack of absolute faith in the usefulness and need to follow a methodology to ensure timely delivery of a quality product. When the client begins to express thoughts like, "Here we do things like that," this provides some indication that the client may be taking an informal path, with improvisation used as a way to achieve the project outcomes. When anxiety affects the client, there is a tendency to introduce a series of shortcuts that reduces the effort prescribed by the methodology, and which could also impact the project outcome and sacrifice product quality.

Another common feature in these organizations is that they only give value to the final product delivered by the project—the implemented information system. They do not always recognize that the development effort is normally separated into phases, such as analysis, design, construction, and implementation. Perhaps this occurs because they did not give value to the first phases oriented to the analysis of the problem and design of the solution.

Some companies are not accustomed to working with independent consultancies that manage the systems development process using methods prescribed by their project engineering department, and this represents another feature that some clients do not value. After signing the contract, the client usually perceives responsibility for the development effort to be in the hands of the supplier. However, the client maintains continuous control and pressure to achieve the development and implementation deadlines. This leaves no room for collaboration to ensure that the benefits and advantages of the new system will be achieved, which, at times, can appear to be of little interest to the client, who is consumed with meeting the implementation date.

Clients who are obsessed with meeting the original implementation date will sometimes try to avoid or unnecessarily rush portions of the development effort. They often forget why the project was started in the first place, and they refocus on achieving an implemented system rather than on the purpose it will serve. This can occur particularly when the client's bid and supplier selection process takes so long that when the project finally starts it is already weeks or months behind the established schedule. Needless to say, in these circumstances, the client fails to recognize their formal procurement process as the time-consuming cause of delays that can effectively penalize or influence the project schedule.

The client's focus on the original system delivery date is also affected when the client begins to have new thoughts and different perspectives of the outcome of the project during the development effort. The client will tend to lose overall perspective for the project and fall into a one-dimensional view that considers the different factors that define the project as independent variables. Therefore, the client treats each perspective as if it has nothing to do with any other project perspective.

For example, we might find clients who ask to extend the scope of a particular project while they demand the cost of the project and its delivery date remain unchanged. In another common situation, the client presents a condition or circumstance in which the system is needed before the originally planned implementation date. However, the client does not accept trimming the scope in order to achieve the new delivery date, or splitting the project into two parts for initial delivery of the essential system functions followed later by full information system implementation.

The fundamental premise of project management warrants restatement here: that project plans are created as a means to manage the project. Project management occurs when the project manager manages the effort according to established plans, which may be modified. To that end, it is very important to understand that the only basis for the effective management of any project is to have a good work plan that breaks down work into homogeneous and elementary work units, and to incorporate project estimates for cost, schedule, and resource management into the phases, activities, and tasks of the associated work breakdown structure. There should be no changes to the project that are not reflected in the project work plan. Changes that are considered should be thoroughly examined for impact on cost, schedule, and resource utilization.

All stakeholders with an interest related to a project must be aware that the calendar is not the result of the whim of the project leader; rather, it is a result of the project planning effort. Stakeholders should also know that one plan element, such as the project schedule, cannot be changed without affecting the cost and resource utilization of the project. This considered, it is insane how often project schedules are modified without consideration of other elements.

Project planning elements may have some tolerance to change, and may even have a range in which their values can change without necessarily impacting on the rest of the project. However, any change will likely have some effect on margins and losses for the supplier, and time and cost for the client. However, these gaps are neither infinite nor so high as to admit any change without making a detailed examination and verification of the state that remains after the changes are introduced.

## Issues Arising from Project Management

One problem that arises in many projects is related to team attitude, when the team, for various reasons, maintains strict adherence to the established process rather than bowing to the pressures presented to them. Sometimes this pressure originates on the client side as a result of the causes listed in the previous section, and sometimes pressure comes from the direction of the supplier's management, who try to leapfrog and eliminate essential activities in an attempt to find a shortcut to project completion. Such shortcuts are considered as the means to expedite project work, to reduce project costs, and often to influence and increase a supplier's profit margin.

Taking shortcuts can sometimes be a dangerous and irresponsible endeavor. If the project was properly planned, then each activity and task presented in the work plan was included because of its contributions to the successful delivery of the product. In fact, if an activity is dispensable, and can be bypassed without having a negative impact on the project deliverables or product quality, then it should never have been included in the project plan in the first place.

## Change Management Issues

There could be circumstances when a valid reason exists to remove certain tasks. For example, it could be determined that user documentation that was originally planned for publication in several languages (e.g., English, French, and Spanish) is now only needed in English. This might occur when designers decide to provide contextual help within the application rather than in a separate published document. As a matter of record, the user documentation will still be published in English, but other language versions are no longer needed. Therefore, this task, or series of tasks, can be considered for removal from the project work plan. Of course, appropriate adjustments to the project's cost and schedule will also be needed when such tasks are eliminated.

Project changes are an inevitable reality for every project, and an inherent part of an effective project management process. This process provides for the timely consideration of change requests and allows a managed approach for the continuous adaptation of projects to authorized changes that occur in the environment from conception to implementation. Of significance is the fact that the change management process enables changes to be made, but with an awareness of the impact and disruption caused. Although some changes may be necessary, they are not necessarily desirable or good for the progress of the project. Therefore, change management is inherently a strict and restrictive process.

## Issues Resulting from Project Control

There are also many occasions where in the phase previous to hiring we prepare a project plan that offers an inspired vision and brilliant planning of the project that includes all key aspects, but which is condemned to fall into oblivion as soon as the project commences.

For various reasons, some already mentioned above and many others that can be justified or not, the project manager abandons the initial planning and starts the project without a clear reference to the basic plan as guidance for the actions, activities, and work of the team, and as a result loses all effectiveness and results orientation. The plans become just a sterile planning exercise, because they are not used at all, and there is always the question of whether the plan was an empty exercise or whether the indolence of the team hampered its capitalization and use.

In other cases, the projects fall into a spiral of confusion, and as work is carried out, everything becomes tangled into an intricate web that seems impossible to unravel, so much so that the team may be tempted to think they can do it well in a particular way and simply surrender complying with interim milestones of the plan in order to reach the final goal of the project more quickly. This is an error that sometimes clients can accept, appreciate, and even support if they do not value the intermediate products as necessary in finding the best way to the final product. This occurs with some frequency.

This mistake is inexcusable and ends with a project that is out of control, with no one knowing where the project is going or how far it is to be completed because, in most cases, the team ultimately loses perception of the horizon, the destination, and the ultimate goal of the project. Instead, the aim is very often replaced by the simple completion of the project itself as a business fact agreed on between the client and the provider, at any price and on any terms, and the grounds and reasons that inspired the project are forgotten.

## Supplier–Client Balance of Power Issues

A project represents a contract between two parties, the service provider and the client. This establishes a business relationship on a balanced plane that matches their respective power to the balance of goods and services to be exchanged in the transaction. However, this balance may be broken, in dramatic fashion, in favor of one of the two parties as a result of the circumstances surrounding the project. In general, however, any imbalance will likely be negligible or minor, and will not cause any adversity for either party.

It is possible for the supplier to experience some form of "injury" relative to its business interests. This might occur, for example, when there is an extension of scope for which the cost was not billed to the customer. The particular circumstances will dictate whether this situation favors the supplier or the client. It could favor the supplier if it facilitates subsequent work, and perhaps spares subsequent cost overruns. It could favor the client if it provides some added value without additional cost. These matters are not uncommon, are normally minor, and do not usually affect the relative balance of power of each party.

However, in some cases, this balance of power can be upset dramatically, making one party beholden or "hostage" to the other party, with the creation of a position of influence that enables the more powerful party to determine the future of the weaker party, and possibly their freedom of choice regarding obligations established in the associated contract.

I have known some cases in recent months in which a supplier, notwithstanding its multinational dimension and proven solvency, was trapped in flawed relationships in which it had to meet the demands of the customers. Some clients might be considered abusive, as they threaten to sever a relationship while owing a significant amount of debt to the supplier in relation to unpaid bills. Although the sum owed may be relatively small compared to the overall value of services specified in the contract, the supplier is placed in a risky position as it waits to see the true intentions of the client.

In one case, the client was a regional administration that 2 years previously had brought in a services company to conduct a project for a half-million dollars and with a time horizon of 6 months. The project was for the construction of a new management system to support the implementation of a new law enacted by the national government. In parallel, the client wanted to orchestrate a temporary system that would permit a temporary response to the demands of citizens affected by the introduction of new rules. The same services company was asked to do this development effort without the support of any separate or distinct contract, where it would provide some technical support to the client's information systems department in the modification of legacy systems to support basic operations in the transition period until the new information system was introduced.

The supplier assigned the technical resources without having a clear idea of the extent of the collaboration, or how or when an appropriate contract would be established. The client postponed the contract based on the premise that this preliminary effort was something that was necessarily small and easily resolved, although the size was difficult to estimate in advance. Again, in parallel, there was an additional requirement on the original, larger project to create a website. This would be a web portal through which citizens would find information about the new rule, its provisions, benefits, and the details necessary for a preliminary assessment of its potential impact on each citizen. As the client did not have the resources for developing and hosting this portal, it requested additional support from the supplier, and that too was arranged informally and without a specific contract.

This gave rise to a need to give support to citizens, who, after being informed by the web page, could contact the agency via a telephone call to complete or confirm their understanding and personalize the guidance that was provided. The client requested the supplier develop this service. Once implemented, this support service would be transferred to the corresponding department of the public institution. However, delays on more than one occasion caused system operations to remain in the hands of the supplier. As the awareness of benefits associated with this citizens' program grew, interest was aroused, prompting an increase in demand that gradually increased the number of agents needed to maintain an adequate level of service quality. This burden fell upon the supplier, who was still working without a formal contract.

Meanwhile, the original system development project that was needed in response to the new law took some turns. The client faced the effort with an inexperienced staff that was responsible for the organization's involvement in developing the new features for citizen use. It was a challenge, and it was delaying the project's progress. The regional administrator decided to adapt the rules of the national law in order to enable them to implement the system within their area of responsibility. These "new rules" effected some changes that suggested the new system might become obsolete before its implementation. Moreover, the accelerated evolution of the temporary solution had already included some essential operations that were intended for the new system. Having this interim capability discouraged the client from expending the effort that would provide for the migration of the temporary system and further implementation of a new system.

One year after the start of the project, it was decided to direct the primary efforts to adapt the new system relative to the implementation of the new rules, with imminent publication of those rules expected, but the temporary solution was to be maintained for the duration of the current rules. By this time, the additional services that the supplier had provided to the government represented over $400,000. At this point, the contract extension to support the adaptation of the new system to address the new rules was issued, and a draft was presented to the supplier for evaluation. The supplier was already under strong pressure from the administration, and it was suggested that if no agreement could be reached in the short term, then the client might break relations with the supplier, who was already facing the potential loss of the amounts outstanding. Agreement was reached to provide $700,000 to the supplier. This amount would cover all the planned changes needed to adapt the new information system to the new rules, of which publication was announced as imminent, and to settle all obligations to date.

However, just as the negotiations concluded, the client included a new request to create a data warehouse and a business intelligence tool to be used for the purposes of compiling and reporting balanced scorecard information. This action again attempted to break the recently recovered balance of power, and the supplier had no choice but to accept the request without additional cost because of its apparent simplicity (e.g., a couple of reports). However, the truth about the complexity of this effort would turn out to be very different.

A year following the previous negotiation and more than 2 years after the start of the initial project (which was expected to take only 6 months), the system is still not implemented and contracting for the expansion of the project is still pending. The costs being discussed do not consider the new requirements introduced after reaching the last agreement. Furthermore, the new rules are still unpublished. It is uncertain when they will be published, and there is some uncertainty if they will even correspond with the draft that was forwarded to the supplier as a basis for adapting the information system to the new needs and requirements.

In this case, the regional administration took advantage of the power imbalance to mark the walk permanently to the company, which had been forced into an ongoing situation in which its only options were to accept the demands and requirements of the client and assume the corresponding losses or accept the possibility that the relationship had broken down and lose the whole amount invested in advance to date.

## Issues Resulting from Project Delays

Projects will often experience small delays and date postponements, and these are usually minor and justified if we consider them individually. However, when these delays are aggregated, this broader view could tell us that the project cannot withstand any additional delays and remain on track for a timely completion.

One effect of this situation is the absorption of any time buffer that the planner may have included in the project work plan. In other words, extra time was allotted in the work plan, but now that time has been consumed by the series of small delays that have occurred. With this time buffer reduced or eliminated, all remaining project activities become critical and time-constrained in order to achieve final product delivery in a timely manner. When time becomes critical, the rigor of intermediate product reviews also suffers. Reviews too often become less demanding as the project team tries to expedite the development process in an effort to achieve product delivery dates. Unfortunately, when rigor is reduced, it can sometimes result in a product prone to errors and defects. This problem is exacerbated when various project stakeholders demonstrate an attitude that accepts such reduced rigor and lack of attention to the product, and that may be the essential root of the problem.

So, if those stakeholders interested in the project have attitudes and excuses that serve to avoid adequate reviews, then the supplier needs to make an effort to explain the importance and implications of each of the intermediate products. If the supplier fails to do so, it is ignoring its responsibility to effectively manage the system development process.

## Issues Arising from Poor Communication

Every project aims to produce a product that will introduce changes that transform the way things are done and the business processes in the organization. As such, the product is characterized by many features that are developed according to a sequence of activities specified in the project work plan. The work plan is developed by the project team with the input of specialists from various departments. The participation of staff from different departments should bring into play their skills and abilities as contributions needed to achieve the project objectives. It is essential to have effective communication and interaction among the various participants. However, we too often find that team and stakeholder communication is very poor.

There have always been cases of projects in which certain members are isolated to some extent from other team members. Generally, when this situation is detected it will be resolved to make team members more inclusive in the development effort. This situation is intensified when any lack of communication becomes the norm rather than the exception, particularly when project managers begin to accept that situation as normal, because then no action is taken to resolve it, mitigate it, or control it in any way.

Approximately 3 years ago, I was invited to participate in a project where this very situation occurred with a clarity that allows me to illustrate this point. The client was a local government agency in a nearby capital city, a city with prominent tourism. The agency decided to launch a project for the implementation of a public service that allowed it to respond to queries and issues related to municipal management raised by citizens, visitors, and tourists. The service would address general interest items such as tourist facility locations and timetables, information on employment at these facilities, and access times and conditions related to certain tourist services (e.g., temporary fishing permits, and fishing and diving excursions to a nearby sea nature preserve).

The technicians representing the interests of the municipal council had split the overall project into two separate contracts, taking into account the different orientation and scope of each project and the parties concerned, which were different but complementary to one another. This division was made with similar budgets of about $400K for each project.

In the bidding process, contracts were awarded to two different services companies that were subsequently combined in a merger with a third services company. The municipal organization saw the new situation as an opportunity to exploit synergies between the two respective teams.

As an additional safeguard, the agency sought the appointment of an inter-projects coordinator. This role had no executive authority over either of the two projects, but provided facilitation and mediation between the two teams to minimize the potential difficulties of communication and coordination between the project managers and their respective teams. This coordinator role was assigned to me, and in the ensuing months I supported both projects.

I found that there were many situations where there were difficulties of communication and, to my surprise, on many occasions, the problems were not so much between the projects, but within the teams for each project.

The orientation of both projects was common, and based on providing public services to citizens and visitors. This included developing a capability for the public to contact the agency in person at municipal offices, by calling a special toll-free number, or by mail, email, or other means deemed appropriate. It was planned that patrons should be able to receive complete information regardless of the channel they used to contact the agency. The service should also ask patrons only for information necessary to provide the most suitable response to the queries raised.

Each project was initiated with an in-depth analysis that was intended to examine the problem from two perspectives: (i) globally, considering together common aspects of the public services system development effort for both projects, and (ii) individually, considering the specific aspects of the public services that each project must define and accomplish to achieve the best solution for that portion of the effort (to include verifying consistency between the respective solutions for each project to ensure that the final integration would result in a solution suited to the client's needs).

The requirement for this cross-project collaboration was included in specifications for both projects, as presented in the accompanying request for proposals (RFP) for each project. In fact, the contract award was based on the offers of collaboration, along with the experience and knowledge that each team brought to the development effort. The client appreciated these fundamentals, which tipped the client's decision in favor of the tenders submitted by the two companies (and later formed as one company following their acquisition by a third company).

After the start of the project, it became clear that there were problems of communication. For example, meetings were very long and unproductive. They would include several hours of discussion, and conclude with no apparent agreement or resolution on any aspect of the project. Subsequent meetings were often a repetition of the same discussions, as if the last meeting had not taken place at all.

It was observed that these meetings lacked common practices that would provide the necessary rigor for effective meeting planning. Although the meetings were planned in advance, they were conducted with a preset frequency and with the same predefined content for each meeting. This preset agenda did not elicit the desired participation and response needed to evaluate project progress or to discuss the next steps in the work effort. Furthermore, meeting minutes did not accurately reflect the discussions held and the commitments made in earlier meetings.

Over the weeks, one of the two projects gradually approached an understanding of the customer's needs, with the client's engineering department wanting to conduct the design, development, and modeling analysis of the problem based on a set of interaction scenarios that reflected system operations quite well. Meanwhile, the other project still had not found a suitable level of understanding, and this mismatch resulted in ongoing discussions and protests about the products that they would offer. However, one day, the head of this project, tired of criticisms received at discussions with the technical staff of the municipality, recognized that he did not have a complete understanding when he saw no use or value in the efforts being made to define the interaction scenarios. As a result, he asked for and received guidance from his superiors. The project manager admitted that some of his distress was removed when he finally acknowledged his limitations and shared his thoughts. This discrepancy between what was proposed in the offer and agreed to at the initial meetings and what the project manager was willing to do, or could do, was the primary cause of the tensions and difficulties that affected the project's progress.

Meanwhile, the supplier independently acquired licenses for a product that was to be used in modeling and creating the prototype. This was done instead of acquiring a tool that the client believed offered a more suitable and neutral design for the definition of an independent prototype, which would later allow a choice between the alternatives studied to evaluate possible solutions. Despite the protests of the client, this fact conditioned the subsequent selection process, which was now geared more to justifying why the particular modeling tool was chosen over other alternative tools. This lack of communication between the two projects, within each of the projects, and particularly between the client and supplier, were handicaps that consumed an enormous amount of energy, resources, and time in counteracting their effects.

Communication problems can have many causes, and one prominent cause lies in the super specialization of some of the technical staff assigned to the project. These individuals bring significant expertise and privileged knowledge of a particular product or a part of the systems solution. This often prompts them to impose conditions and circumstances on the project, which can provide an artificial focus on the part of the work they know. To that end, these experts will too often unnecessarily disregard consideration of the entire system, or any part of the system or project considered to be secondary or subordinate to their areas of expertise.

Another cause of communication difficulties can be associated with a lack of expertise and experience among team members assigned to the project. This becomes a problem if the deficit is accompanied by a lack of awareness of this limitation, with team members doing nothing to overcome their limitations. Sometimes individuals may try to deflect responsibility for such conditions to other project team members, and they use positions of power, such as project manager or team leader, rather than knowledge or experience to influence their relationships with the client or team members.

In a similar manner, good communication is affected by a progressively more pronounced growth in the shortage of skills, not purely technical, such as speaking skills, reading comprehension skills, and effective writing skills. This calls into question the operational capacity of the professionals who are experiencing personal limitations or difficulties in these communication-related skills. Their technical expertise may be excellent, but they can become technological hermits when communication dysfunctions arise to prevent them from having effective professional interactions and exchanges of information and ideas.

## Issues Arising from the Use of Preferred Resources

In the latter years of the 1990s and into the 2000s, suppliers and services organizations have been trying to overcome management deficiencies and leadership challenges by introducing a new generation of project managers. These new generation managers are still, with some very notable exceptions, somewhat immature and lacking sufficient consistency to maintain the order and discipline required in the projects under their responsibilities.

These new project managers, despite having more training than their predecessors and some form of project management certification that represents completion of a training program, seem to apply what they have learned in an inconsistent and undisciplined manner. Too many of them lack practical experience, and will often start from a more theoretical basis, rather than from an awareness of the impacts of their actions on project and business outcomes.

Suppliers and services companies will adopt this approach to project management for two main reasons. First, the organization wants to achieve the cost-cutting benefits that are highlighted and, perhaps, promised by this approach. However, this neglects addressing the experience of existing managers and the effects of replacing them with new individuals who become qualified by virtue of their theoretical training. Second, the organization recognizes value and relies on the warranties of independent certification as a business benefit. However, this may be done without giving credence to complementary learning factors such as the internalization of knowledge and practical training at work, the transfer of knowledge between old and new managers, or any other similar consideration that requires a slower pace for the substitution and replacement of those on the front line of client and project management.

This can result in an approach to project management where the importance of the project team is diminished, along with the positive values that teams contribute to the organization. Instead, a sense of individuality is imposed, where team members concentrate on their own specialized section of the work, which does not particularly contribute to the common or global interests and constraints. To that end, the project team's collective work may be minimized by the effects of project work being reduced to a simple aggregation of individuals who perform work without effective and consistent coordination and collaboration.

This approach can impose certain restrictions on the formation of the project team, leading to major and urgent problems for the supplier or service company. One problem is the pressing need for each team member to be fully qualified in the specialty to which they are assigned, and to demonstrate the ability to carry responsibility for more or less independent and autonomous work. This may not always be seen as a problem, but as a reasonable condition and desirable situation for those team members capable of performing the work. However, this approach makes it virtually impossible for team members to grow professionally if they always have a limited scope in their work assignments. If strictly adhered to, this approach could also diminish opportunities for entry-level and midcareer professionals who are looking to expand their experience and to improve their positions on the project team and within the company.

Thus, a programmer will program indefinitely, or perhaps become a senior programmer. The analyst will advance in a similar manner, and the same for other project team positions. For every role or profile the professional development process will be slower when individuals stay with the same company rather than going through the disruption of changing companies (as the only way to accomplish reasonable professional development). The introduction of new junior team members will be difficult if not impossible when this approach is applied within the organization.

The movement of knowledge and ideas within the team will be restricted to formal consultations formulated by the project manager. Generally, team members will jealously guard and keep their knowledge to themselves and not share with others in confidence. Such hoarding will be a means to protect them from being replaced by new lower-cost professionals, perpetuating a culture of scarcity.

This approach to project management results in a shortage at all levels when the business creates a structural and cultural position affecting all areas of the organization, including opportunities, training, budget, projects, ideas, and solutions. In this context, companies make an effort to reduce costs by eliminating all traces of downtime in their structures, requiring that all their professionals be assigned to 100% productive projects, reducing training to a minimum or even eliminating the budget for this area, preventing the growth of its professionals, freezing their profiles and qualifications, and conducting salary reviews simply as an exercise for economic update purposes.

The individuals in these companies will become aware of the reduced opportunities for professional advancement within their organizations, and turn their gaze toward the employment market. They are likely to look and find new opportunities with competitors that are establishing similar policies, but with a willingness to pay more for relevant expertise and knowledge. For some individuals, this is done repeatedly in an attempt to increase the wages. Companies acquire these individuals, often creating high-end contracts that do not always correspond to the value of the professional profiles. When this occurs, it can give rise to other dysfunctions within the team, particularly when team members see newcomers with better contracts and hiring conditions than their own. This can then prompt those team members to enter into this festival of job changes. As employees depart, this may cause companies to lose credibility with their remaining employees and their customers.

As a result, business managers end up placing their best projects exclusively in the hands of trusted managers, who have their origin on the same professional path within the company or with whom they have developed a trusted personal relationship. The managers do the same when choosing project leaders to take charge of the projects. This, in turn, generates some impoverishing effects on the company's intellectual capital.

First, the effective size of the company, in terms of the available skills, knowledge, and experience for each project, will be reduced to the scope of knowledge of each manager, at their respective level within the company. This denies any use of or reference to the skills and experience of individuals who are not a part of the manager's "inner circle" of friends and colleagues. In general, it reduces the number of professionals available to each project. This reduction impoverishes the intellectual capital of the company. Even though a company may have hundreds or thousands of employees, the staff size is reduced to a relatively small group of people equivalent to the staff of a smaller company. This places the company at a real disadvantage by a consequential imbalance in the availability of intellectual resources.

Second, there is the apparent creation of two types of affiliations within the organization, and each offers different levels of opportunity and recognition that are impervious to each other, and that transcend all layers and levels of the organization. The upper "caste" consists of those individuals who have the confidence of a manager or responsible team leader and are invariably chosen for new project assignments, especially if they have visibility and offer possibilities for promotion. The end result is a potential for individuals in this group to suffer an over-demand from being assigned to different projects, including part-time work. Working at full capacity can hamper their performance and focus, and can sometimes cause exhaustion and stress, reducing their efficiency even more.

In addition to this "select group" are all other professionals in the organization—those who do not have personal relationships with any director or manager, who do not have a long-term affiliation with the company, and who have possibly been hired only for a specific project and face potential dismissal when the project is completed. These professionals will be assigned to projects of visibility with the possibility of internal promotion only when they can show requisite experience and when positions cannot be fulfilled by the "select group" of professionals. Otherwise, they are likely to be assigned to low-visibility projects with a low level of attention from management.

Naturally, when the relative performance of each of the two groups is reviewed, managers can verify empirically that the two groups have different results. This helps them justify the wisdom used and management decisions made, albeit in a somewhat discriminatory and shortsighted manner, as reasonable and prudent. Sometimes, when preferred resources continuously work together on successive project assignments, these "trusted" resources, because they are human, can produce conflicts and problems that affect the project. In such circumstances, managers will bring in professionals who can finish the development effort. The "trusted" individuals who are removed will be considered again for a future project.

## Issues Arising from the Supplier's Orientation to the Client

This section presents an array of various thoughts and considerations based on the supplier's orientation to the client and the client's interests. This discussion inherently also deals with other stakeholders in the project management environment.

A problem that appears with some frequency is the loss of attention to the client's perspective, and it can produce a series of negative consequences that can have adverse impacts on the project. One negative consequence is the increasing failure of the project to address the expectations and interests of the client and the various stakeholders. This failure can be total, but will usually only be partial as long as timely consideration is given to the interests of the client and other project stakeholders.

The systems development effort requires a climate of trust; this is a precious commodity and should be a concern of all involved parties, especially the supplier, who has the final responsibility for project success. If the necessary trust between the client and the supplier is seriously injured, it will produce a dramatic, adverse effect on the project and for all stakeholders involved.

In a mature and competitive information technology market, it is sometimes difficult to acquire new clients. In many cases, the ability to overcome this difficulty is the difference between generating a profit or loss in the annual financial report. To that end, the supplier selection process is usually very demanding, with a multitude of competing service providers offering a solution to the same problem—a problem that the client has defined in such detail that little space is left for supplier innovation. Therefore, offers and estimates are sent to the client with very competitive prices, so margins that are applied in the evaluations are very narrow. Because clients give special importance to the pricing, it normally represents more than 50% in the weighting of the supplier selection decision. So, each competitor should make a firm cost commitment, based on a cost evaluation exercise, when they seek a contract that is awarded on a competitive basis.

When a client awards a contract to a services firm, the client will also normally demonstrate a sense of confidence in their selection. This creates a climate of trust that will facilitate the exchange of information in an effective manner among team members. It will also support growth in the business relationship between the client and the supplier. When properly managed, the relationship begun in a temporary and finite project effort can grow to proportions beyond the current project, and with significant benefits to both the client and the supplier.

When a strong client–supplier business relationship is established, the client will build trust in the supplier and show more reliance on the supplier's technical capability. For example, the client may start to define projects and project work with a lower level of formalization that gives the supplier a greater capacity to respond to the changing environment. When a trusted supplier participates in an environment of attenuated competition, the established client relationship may help the supplier achieve a favored position, thereby avoiding marketing costs, which presumably will provide better margins for the supplier's business.

Trust can diminish rapidly when the client perceives or otherwise believes that the supplier is not showing the required level of consideration or attention to client issues and interests. When that occurs, the business relationship deteriorates and all the benefits of client trust immediately disappear. It will be very difficult to restore mutual trust unless one party (usually the supplier) takes a strong and courageous step to rectify the situation and regain the client's confidence.

Sometimes the source of a problem is rooted in a project that is immature and not yet ready for execution. This can occur as a result of various internal and external conditions that influence the project. In some cases, laws and industry regulations may change to affect the system design. Also, valid midcourse changes in project scope may occur to change the project outcome. Sometimes, as a project nears completion, new technology is introduced to make the product obsolete. Any one of these situations can create disagreements and disputes, particularly with regard to who will pay the costs for the necessary changes. The supplier will need to be prepared to address such disputes in a business-like manner and without causing major damage to the client–supplier relationship.

One of the most common problems, and probably the most difficult to resolve, is the failure of the supplier to obtain adequate knowledge of the client's business, its nature, essence, and operations. This limited knowledge and awareness can cause significant delays in the progress of projects throughout their duration. Initially, analysts will have greater difficulty in understanding the problem to be solved by not knowing or understanding the context in which the client has framed the effort. In the design phase, any lack of knowledge about the client's business could result in a dubious design process, and questioning by the client's technical staff of how well the design will satisfy the client's business needs. The client's technical staff could also develop a devalued perception about the supplier's analysts and designers. Although the supplier may try to explain their work as one using a standard approach, the client does not understand how the supplier's team can claim to be specialists on solutions if they are unaware of the variety of problems to be solved and the business environment in which they operate.

## Chapter 15

# Creating a Methods Approach to Work

The development and implementation of information systems that incorporate new information technologies and communications represents a considerable effort for any public or private organization. It involves significant budgets and significant cost to explore opportunities, which requires evaluating and choosing from different potential investments. Those investments could include other similar projects, new facilities, new business lines, or product development.

Before nonselected opportunities are dismissed, we must be sure that the expected benefits of the chosen project are realistic and attainable. If the chosen opportunity fails to produce the desired results, then the wrong opportunity was selected and the investment will be lost. To that end, the project selection aspect of project management is critically important to ensure that investments are selected with a commitment to produce the expected results and to allow the company to realize the desired competitive advantage.

The evaluation of alternative investments that leads to the subsequent selection of a particular development project represents the intent to implement a change in the organization. The project effort will introduce an extraordinary work effort that is above, beyond, and separate from routine operations. Irrespective of the extent of the changes to be implemented, the project will be defined by certain characteristics that show it as a separate and distinct work effort.

The following are a few of the key characteristics of every project:

- A project has a specific purpose that justifies its existence. The extent to which that purpose is achieved will represent a measure of project success or failure for the project stakeholders and the rest of the organization.

**167**

- The project life is finite. Every project has a beginning and an end that defines a time limit in which project work is performed. Beyond that time, the project ceases to exist and the project team will be dissolved and reassigned to their respective business units.
- Each project has deliverables that result from the project work effort. Project deliverables include one or more products and subproducts that are presented to a client who has specified the constraints of quality for those products and the deadlines for their delivery.
- A project represents commitment to a unique work effort (in contrast to recurring routine operations). It is planned and performed by the project team, a collection of qualified individuals who are brought together for the sole purpose of completing project work.
- Resources allocated to the project are organized in a project-specific manner, which may represent alterations of the normal organizational hierarchy; positions and roles of the assigned project team members may also be adjusted to facilitate their project participation.

Projects are conducted for the purpose of achieving specified objectives, and, in turn, to realize benefits from achieving those objectives. Each project has criteria and metrics that are used to manage progress and to verify the accomplishment of project objectives. As each project is unique, with unique objectives, we start the project effort with an understanding that the project is a unique event that is not aligned with routine operations, and that it does not answer to the same operational criteria used by the rest of the organization. In fact, project dynamics will be more intense, more flexible, and faster than most work efforts in other areas of the organization.

The team assigned to the project will often require frequent collaboration of specialists from different areas, departments, or organizational units. Thus, in different stages we find specialists in information technology, programmers, and analysts working with marketing specialists, graphic designers, management controllers, and customer service representatives. Each of these individuals will contribute to the project based on their personal and professional history and experience. This multidisciplinary collaboration will present challenges related to internal communication and mutual understanding among team members, and this will require additional efforts by all participants to explain, from their respective expertise, the key concepts to other team members and stakeholders. Although some team members may be neophytes relative to system development projects, they are real authorities in their respective technical and professional fields of endeavor.

## Project Team Dynamics

Creating an effective project team climate, where each team member gives up their individuality in recognition of the team's collective goals and interests, represents a significant challenge that will encounter some difficulties. Effective team performance ultimately relies on creating a cohesive project team that is characterized by work efforts and interactions that are empathetic, synergistic, and cooperative. Mutual encouragement and individual courage on the part of team members who are committed to the project goal will reduce detrimental team member behavior and promote success that can be shared among colleagues. Moreover, project team composition, when it consists of multidisciplinary experts, should be devoid of undesirable vices and routines that may be tolerated in other parts of the organization where employees are more tolerant of these behaviors, either by loyalty to the organization or by the routine nature of activities and work performed.

Management should remember that if the project has the best available team, its members will be highly competent professionals, and these individuals will readily identify the lack of necessary management commitment. In turn, their performance will likely be consistent with the support that they observe on the part of management. On the other hand, if management has not allocated the best team available, this might raise issues of management negligence because of the potential adverse impacts on the project. It might also have some career consequences for the well-qualified members of the team, who are placed at risk when assigned with lesser qualified or even unqualified team members.

The projects and the teams that perform work on each project need the full commitment of the organization. This commitment must be present at the highest management levels, and must be real, continuous, and even notorious. This commitment must be more than a simple statement of support that is cordial, but distant. Rather, it should be demonstrated by managers at all levels as a reflection of organizational interests and organizational standards.

## Management Communication

Effective, sincere, and transparent communication by management is an essential prerequisite for a smooth-running project. Management must convey the intended project goal, the primary and secondary objectives to be achieved, the expectations of stakeholders, and any relevant data and information that may exist about the project. This must be provided to the project team to facilitate their identification and access to all stakeholders. The initial transfer of knowledge and information at the onset of the project will be the first step toward effective communication between project teams and management.

Depending on the project size and the makeup of the assigned work team, different project control mechanisms and management approaches may be required. If the project is small, perhaps involving a one-man team, this individual will likely have all the initial information needed to start the project. However, management must avoid neglecting this person in terms of the need for communication, verification, and project control between management and the team, even though the team is a single person. However, a project team will normally consist of several members who will perform in different roles to accomplish the different tasks and activities for which they are particularly qualified. This creates a peculiar situation in which the project manager is responsible for managing the project, but project success depends entirely on the team members to carry out the project work in a coherent way.

## Project Team Expertise and Evaluation

The project manager, sometimes with the help of a specialist, prepares an initial estimate of the project at the beginning of the effort. This estimate must be reviewed on several occasions during the project to confirm that it remains valid, and to adapt it to new events occurring and new information being received. This need for revision of the estimates reflects the interdependence evolving between the project manager and other members of the project team, and it brings together the respective areas of expertise of the active members of the project who know the project, its tasks and activities, and the effort required in their respective areas of competence.

Management will also want to monitor the progress of the tasks assigned to each member. Ideally, such project oversight is based on quantifiable and objective measurement of the project. However, it is normal that the project uses the subjective evaluation of progress from the team specialists in many activities and jobs that have no objective measure. This lack of objective metric poses a serious problem for the management of projects, because it makes subjective project assessments compulsory. This subjective assessment can be done by the project manager when there is sufficient information to do so. However, the subjective assessment can include the opinions of team members responsible for particular components in the development effort.

Involving team members should not be interpreted as a sign of weakness or a lack of knowledge, skills or leadership by the project manager, but as the best way to achieve some benefits, as suggested in the following.

First, a more accurate estimate results from interactions of the project manager and team members that are mutually reinforcing. When the professionals who know the project work first hand become involved in evaluation activities, this does not constitute a waiver of responsibility by the project manager. Rather, it considers the experience and knowledge of qualified professionals to obtain valuable feedback.

The project manager's authority is not reduced at all by requesting the opinions of specialists on the project. It should be understood that the responsibility of the project continues to reside with the project manager. Collaboration with project team members simply serves to facilitate the final estimate by harmonizing the different estimates obtained from team members. This exercise allows us to compare and contrast the different sources, which invariably improves the outcome of the estimate.

The second benefit is that team members who participate in the assessment of the project estimate and subsequent planning will be more inclined to achieve the project objectives and make every effort to achieve compliance with the forecasts made. This involvement in the process of project management control and monitoring will facilitate the commitment of all team members and provide reliable communications within the project. So, every time you report the progress of the project, each member will offer their assessment of progress with full transparency, in the confidence that individual input is valued and taken into consideration.

If team members are given an appropriate level of authorization to carry out responsibilities independently with the support of their direct supervisors and project manager, we will be setting up a team for above-average performance. Team members will then direct their capacity and effort to achieving common goals as they grow professionally to learn new skills through an intensive exchange of experiences and lessons learned that raises the preparedness of each participant.

## Principles for Team Cohesion

The practices carried out within the work environment should be based on a set of positive principles that strengthen team cohesion and lead them to achieve project goals. To that end, positive values should be defined and set forth clearly and specifically, without any possibility of confusion or misinterpretation, and it is unacceptable to specify any value that could be interpreted as discriminatory, arbitrary, or simply negative. After all, the value of these principles lies in the motivation and cohesion that will be influenced by their positive status and concreteness. Everyone needs to understand them clearly, in the same way, without confusion or uncertainty of any kind. Here then are two principles that should be considered as candidates for any project and inspiring cultural elements shared by the members of any team.

The first is a principle of transparency. Sharing information with transparency does not mean that everyone knows all the information, but that each team member has all the information needed to accomplish assigned work. Similarly, it does not promote "assembly-management" or groupthink where each team member has the same opinions and values. Rather, team members participate together in a way that establishes responsibilities, hierarchies, and dependencies, ranges of tolerance and a multitude of mechanisms that seek to make its operation more effective. All team members must be aware of their responsibilities on the project, their working relationships on the project, and their contribution to achieving the objectives of the project. This information should be clear and shared in a transparent way, and there cannot be different versions that change depending on individual perspectives or individual interpretations.

The second principle that should be considered in every project is the tolerance for error. Tolerating errors does not mean establishing a low level of demand, or accepting any relaxation in this respect. It means creating a work environment that promotes continuous improvement and innovation, giving the team confidence and appropriate support to consider what they do from a critical perspective and to dare to identify, propose, and implement improvements that facilitate progress and design optimization. This does not authorize individuals to do what they want. Rather, it enables improvements to be proposed and assessed according to procedures that will ensure avoidance of unnecessary risks. However, each team member should know that some mistakes are acceptable if their proposals have been properly considered and evaluated.

To that end, the project is manageable and amenable to control because each team member will keep track of tasks and estimates assigned to them. In turn, team members will monitor any changes or corrections that need to be applied to the plan. They will also report on progress for the tasks under their responsibility, noting any deviations that may occur, analyzing the causes and proposing corrective actions, and improving confidence that corrective actions will be addressed.

## Guidelines for Work Plan Preparation

There are some general guidelines that should be considered when preparing the project work plan. These guidelines will influence whether or not work plan control is simple or complicated.

The most important guideline may be the first step in creating the work plan to define a work breakdown structure (WBS). The WBS is a decomposition of the work effort from the whole project at phase level, with further decomposition of phases into activities, and activities into tasks, and so on. The WBS will continue to decompose work elements until the basic tasks and subtasks of the project are reached. In this process, planners should take into account considerations such as not starting decomposition of the following task-level activities until completion of the next higher level. However, that does not mean that all work elements require decomposition to the same depth, or to the same number of levels of decomposition.

We all know that we have reached a sufficient level of detail in the decomposition when activities or tasks can be estimated with a reasonable degree of certainty. Work elements with a duration of 80 h (or 2 weeks) are generally considered to be reasonable and easily controlled. Once the WBS is prepared, we can identify, in parallel, (i) those responsible for the execution of each activity or task and (ii) the outputs expected as a result of the project work performed. We can also appoint technical leaders and prepare necessary estimates for the lowest-level work elements. These estimates are then aggregated at successively higher levels in the WBS. This approach is known as bottom-up estimating because it proceeds from work elements at the lowest level to the highest to calculate the project estimates.

The use of a reference methodology ensures that we will define a proper and complete WBS, avoiding the inclusion of tasks that do not add value to the project and including tasks that are essential to effective project management. There are several methodological approaches that can be used to help plan the project, each with its own features and characteristics. In some cases, methodology selection is influenced by its suitability for management oversight and control. In other cases, it is selected for its focus on the accomplishment of technical aspects of the project. Among the many existing methodologies, we can distinguish a number of types according to their orientation and approach, as described in the following sections.

## Methodologies for Software Production

Methodologies used for the production of software have a direct focus on the effort needed to create and implement information system applications. To that end, this type of methodology will deploy a tasks map that specifies activities related to the technical work. This orientation has led to the emergence of methodologies as a way to guide the way toward information systems development that responds to the needs of organizations. It is a valuable asset for new or less experienced professionals, and it provides a valuable reference for more experienced individuals.

These methodologies are primarily aimed at bringing efficiency to the process of designing, building, and deploying solutions using emerging technology and tools. A methodology of this type provides a very specific approach, which seeks to ignore or isolate the inherent difficulties in the use of technologies or tools for the customer, particularly those involved in information system development and implementation for the first time. It will often provide a series of guides and shortcuts that will influence project work in an optimal way, avoiding errors and problems identified previously in other companies. Most methodologies incorporate presumptive best practices, which can contribute to the proper implementation of technology and tools that influence the system design and development effort. Therefore, we can say that methodologies for software production have a limited scope, based on the technology or tool that motivates their definition.

Such methodologies are often promoted by institutions of all kinds, from governments, such as the methodology METRICA, which is property of the Ministry of Public Administration of the Government of Spain, or ASAP, developed by the SAP organization and especially designed for the implementation of their enterprise resources planning (ERP). In some instances, methodologies such as METRICA offer two versions, one for projects in which technologies are based on structured languages, and another for technologies whose tools are object oriented.

Methodologies having a specific purpose can be found in the marketplace, with a great variety offered by the multitude of companies and organizations that have made laudable efforts to translate their experience into a viable methodology product. Thus, we could find methodologies for application development under different environments, to include structured languages like COBOL, object-oriented languages such as C++, and Java. The methodology approach can be used on traditional projects, agile development projects, and extreme programming efforts. It may be based on the work approaches developed by software factories or other delocalized work processes. Methodologies can be used to implement business management software solutions like ERP, along with business intelligence solutions and data warehousing. In any case, the approach of all these methodologies is very technical, focused on facilitating the implementation of tasks and activities directly related to the implementation of technologies and the use of the tools by work teams to facilitate system development and implementation.

Themes that fall outside this type of methodology approach will generally include anything that is not in the area of technology. This includes aspects of project management, change management, acceptance of new system users into the organization and other stakeholders affiliated with the project, management of customer–supplier relationships, and the resolution of problems that are not considered relevant to the technical perspective of the work performed.

## Methodologies Oriented to Business Process Management

A second type of methodology approach is that oriented to business process management (BPM) or BP. This approach has emerged more recently, during the 1990s and into the 2000s, and is used for the optimization of operations related to business processes. Although it may be useful in other situations, it is primarily used when a company is outsourcing one of its business processes.

In the latter years of the twentieth century, with the emerging globalization of markets and the resulting increased competition, many companies made strategic choices to gain business benefits from being "leaders" and "early adopters" in business process analysis. These companies examined their business based on the business processes involved, and cataloged them into three basic categories: (i) strategic, (ii) major, and (iii) key processes and support.

From this classification, they aimed to remain competitive by concentrating their efforts, talent, and resources in areas of strategic management and key processes. The development of this approach helped companies trust in the service companies to which they yielded the management of support processes that were necessary for the business, but whose contribution was of incidental value and secondary in importance to the strategy business objectives of the company. This methodology approach helped maintain or place companies in business leadership positions in the new global context.

Outsourcers appeared on the scene; service companies assumed the management of business processes for its customers. This released the managers from the attention that was previously devoted to this part of the business, and allowed them to concentrate on core processes.

At first, the outsourced processes were related to technology, but then diversified rapidly, including invoice printing processes for large consumption enterprises and utilities (e.g., electricity, water distribution) that had been significant activities of information systems departments. The maintenance of applications and information systems were also addressed by outsourcing, and ultimately outsourcing of the entire information systems function (with assets transmission) was achieved.

This outsourcing was solidified in strategic partnerships in the middle and long terms, perhaps 3 to 5 years, but sometimes 10 years, and renewable after that. Often the agreements involved the transfer of assets, primarily hardware, facilities, and buildings, and almost always related to operations. However, the customer's manager would always remain in the process to act as coordinator and verifier of the services rendered.

There was no fixed or universal pattern for outsourcing support. Each company defined the model that best fit its needs and best served its purpose in improving competitiveness in the marketplace. Soon it was found that outsourcing could generate significant savings opportunities that customers demanded to share with their suppliers, thereby increasing the benefits to be obtained.

When a company outsources the management of such processes, it is taking a chance that concentrating on the management of key processes in the company will create a strong competitive business advantage. Benefits are also achieved by making cost reductions, which are incorporated into business results, or are used to finance the technological renovation of the information systems of the company.

The realization of these advantages encouraged larger companies to extend outsourcing to other processes that shared support processes with information technology. So began the outsourcing of accounting processes for some larger oil companies, which rapidly introduced similar processes into other companies. Post-sale support to customers and users by means of a contact center or help desk was one of the most commonly outsourced services, along with other services that provided shared infrastructure development and contributed to more reduced costs and greater benefits to client companies.

The increasing pressure to achieve lower costs for customers, along with the logic that the service provider also improves its contribution margins, led to the emergence of a number of practices aimed at optimizing processes and reducing unit costs. These were soon collected in the form of methodologies for the management of business processes. These methodologies facilitated systematic support for the assumption of processes and functions in outsourcing, a practice for which they had been designed, but they also offered opportunities for improvement in other environments.

These methodologies are much less known, although some of their tools are widely used and applied to other areas of business management because of the usefulness and benefits provided. This may be due to the fact that the proponents of organized and systematic development were private companies engaged in providing business process outsourcing for large customers.

BPM methodologies are strictly focused on process efficiency, and therefore provide a framework of tools, techniques, and activities aimed at better understanding the processes utilized. This includes identifying their basic activities as a means to optimize a systematic process re-engineering effort. In particular, process steps will be identified and measured to assess their contribution to the value delivered to customers.

Re-engineering techniques can be applied with tools such as activity-based costing (ABC) and its derivative activity-based management (ABM). These tools help in the redesign of business processes based on the cost and value that every transaction represents and on the criticality of the transaction relative to the whole process. The result will be more efficient processes that are simplified, more robust, and less risky, which provides greater customer value and superior performance for the entire company.

BPM process outsourcing used within the framework of larger business operations normally produces very substantial advantages that enable the company to pay less to the outsourcer than for the same service supported by the internal management. The outsourcing service provider also transfers knowledge and operational capability as additional benefits of the business relationship. In fact, there are companies that implement outsourcing as a way to optimize these processes, and then take back process responsibility after improvements designed and introduced by the outsourcer have been achieved. In many cases, the customer organization will internalize the benefits obtained in this way, and they will often last for years after the outsourcer business relationship expires. There have also been some instances where the customer acquires the process development tools for at least some of its techniques and tools in process re-engineering, or in the design and implementation of new capabilities that facilitate the expansion of the scope of business of the company.

The focus of these methodologies is very technical and aimed in a particular way to the tasks and activities developed in the process. This leaves little for customers and stakeholders to consider in relation to the relationship, management, and control of the project or the value delivered by the project to customers. Likewise, it ignores considerations that are uniquely aligned with information technology and communications. The methodologies will often regard this matter as support tools necessary to manage the processes but incidental and marginal to the aim pursued by the management of business processes. When it identifies a substantial need in the field of information systems that may require a distinct and separate effort, it is assumed to generate a project for the creation of the new functionality.

## Methodologies for the Management of Client and Supplier Relationships

The plethora of methodologies developed by technology service providers were targeted for specific use. It soon became difficult for customers to maintain effective control of projects with any rigor. When customers worked with one supplier, project solutions were more or less homogeneous and were developed using the same technology. It was possible to train internal project managers to use the methodology of the supplier, and to maintain a standard dialog based on the common and specialized knowledge of the methodology being used.

However, when more than one supplier was involved, with each supplier using its own methodology to organize their business and projects, this made it difficult to coordinate across projects. If there were more than two or three providers, the inconsistent dialog imposed by different methodologies caused serious difficulties for customers' project managers. Each methodology started from different premises when organizing tasks and activities to create work plans, and the terminology related to project deliverables was different. Although different suppliers usually retained the name of the product, the systems development and implementation effort often varied in composition or structure.

These differences produced an environment of confusion, making it difficult to maintain control over projects and their progress, or to know the project status with any certainty, and making it difficult to validate the products delivered because there was a continuous need to verify accomplishments according to the criteria of each of the specific methodologies applied to the project. The presence of multiple methodologies caused the benefits of any one methodology to be reduced or lost.

For this reason, and to overcome these problems, there was a need to create a guide to facilitate the relationship with these suppliers and to standardize the work effort and its results. This was particularly needed by public organizations, which were suffering from this problem more acutely because of their method of contracting technology services through an open bidding process.

Such guides soon evolved into a level of specification and detail as methodology tools aimed at simplifying the relationship between customers and suppliers. This type of methodology considers three key objectives:

■ The first objective is to facilitate in the precontractual phase the choice of the best offer suitable for the client. This is intended to resolve the gaps and differences between the different methodologies of providers by adopting an approach geared to the production of software. In this way, the products to be developed, including their structure and composition, are specified and released to the suppliers who can use the methodology of their choice to deliver products with the defined attributes. This approach does not force suppliers to use either public methods that are freely distributed or methodologies that are private and restricted for use by the companies that own them. Instead, suppliers can use the methodology of their choice that is best suited to their work, and in which they are presumably most proficient.

■ The second objective is to reduce or eliminate the difficulties arising from having multiple methodologies and terminologies in use by different suppliers, which are usually internalized in their corporate culture, making it difficult to maintain a transparent relationship with customers who have multiple vendors. The client establishes the list of products that the project must deliver, while relying on the supplier to provide the definition and organization with respect to the deadlines for the delivery of defined products.

- The third objective is to resolve conflicts that could appear at the end of projects when the products are delivered and verified. These conflicts arise when it is clear that deliverables come from different understandings of the client and supplier. Likewise, inconsistent use of document names needs to be rectified. These methodologies help to eliminate the ambiguity spreading among customers and suppliers, which were making it difficult to achieve the benefits sought from the design and development of the information systems.

One of the methodologies that gained some distribution among European public administrations was called EUROMETHOD. Its implementation was partial, and today it is more of a memory, having been replaced by a more ambitious approach. All these methodologies had a primary focus on efficiency, trying to simplify the relationship between the client and the supplier. Of course, these approaches only had meaning and application within a framework of a customer–supplier relationship. In this context, the methodology offered a standardized framework, unique and neutral to all providers, and this permitted clarification of the products to be delivered in a way that avoided any ambiguity.

These methods were limited or restricted to providing a scope that identified the products but did not define the tasks or task dependencies required for the product design and development effort. This definition was left in the hands of the supplier, who applied the methodology approach of their choice and experience to organize and manage team performance.

These methods also represent a significant milestone in opening up competition to the institutional clients and many other companies that, until now, lacked their own methodologies. However, with the security of these methods and the adoption of emerging methodologies published for the construction of information systems, suppliers gained access to markets, customers, and projects that were previously blocked to them. Of course, such methods are specific and focused, so they leave out other nontechnical processes that may be needed.

## Methodologies Oriented to Project Management

With the passage of time, professionals in IT gradually became aware that a technology project was not so different from other types of projects such as constructing a new house or factory, developing a new road or transportation hub, or creating a new manufacturing production line. This insight allowed IT project professionals to examine how construction, engineering, and other professional disciplines were addressing project management solutions within their frame of reference. In turn, they adapted their findings about project management processes and practices for use by project managers specializing in information technology and communications.

This comparison of IT projects with other types of projects showed project management as an independent discipline common to all types of projects; for IT professionals, aspects of information technology and communications represent the project technical objectives. This comparison allowed them to distinguish a methodology designed specifically for project management that would serve the business needs and interests of any organization regardless of the technical nature of the work.

The project management methodology is indifferent to the project purpose, scope, technology, duration, or any other dimension you want to consider. Management should follow this methodology using the same criteria for every project in an organization, regardless of the technical orientation, if they want to ensure business success. Project management methodologies have been promoted by independent practitioners affiliated with both governmental agencies and with private companies. Some have been linked with universities and institutions of higher learning.

We can cite the Project Management Institute (PMI) as a globally recognized and prestigious source for project management standards, as contained in its publication, *A Guide to the Project Management Body of Knowledge (PMBOK®)*. This standard defines a set of management processes that focus on rigorous project oversight and control during the entire project life cycle. This standard is frequently used as a basis for creating project management methodologies deployed around the world. PMI also promotes several certification programs for project managers and other professionals in the project management environment. In particular, PMI's Project Management Professional (PMP®) certification is based on demonstrating knowledge and experience using the principles prescribed in PMBOK®, and this certification is a highly regarded professional achievement.

Another source of project management guidance deserves mention: the PRINCE2 Methodology. PRINCE2 was created by the Office of Government Commerce (OGC), a British government agency, which released it under license to the APM Group for promotion. This methodology, unlike the previous one, focuses on the rigorous definition of the main products of the project. From this definition, the project is divided into a series of iterations that will deliver the different products required by users. It progressively refines the project definition to reduce uncertainty as the project proceeds. It is a different approach that is very suitable for projects that start from a low level of formalization, whether from the dimensions of the project or from the inexperience of the users on the project team.

A common feature of project management methodologies lies in the promoting entities having a sufficiently large structure to promote methodology use. This ensures quality and rigor in its application, along with the training of users to ensure their understanding of the methodology. It may also provide for testing and certification to guarantee that professional work will be accomplished for the employer and for the customer. This practice implies a differential contribution of value added over other methodologies, which allows the sponsoring organization to keep in touch with the market and with professionals, making successive versions of the methodologies incorporate improvements that meet ever-present new challenges.

Project management methodologies focus on the effective management of projects and on ensuring the project will achieve the established objectives. It gives project managers a framework for independent management of a technology problem, with specific techniques and tools oriented to tackling the technology aspects of any project. However, this is done without jeopardizing the application of broader project management practices and techniques. Of course, this does not mean that the circumstances of each project are not considered; on the contrary, projects should always be adapted to the particular circumstances in which they operate, and project management is not an exception.

As suggested above, the scope of these methodologies is specialized and limited to the management of projects that could marginalize the development of the technical work that must be planned, monitored, and verified. Despite the advantages of an independent system of certification that ensures the preparation of professionals that pass training and relevant tests, methodology use is not an automatic guarantee of success. These professionals must also show an aptitude to adapt principles and practices for customized use on each new project.

Project management methodologies apply different approaches, but they all focus on the problems of project management, leaving the technical details to technical methodologies, which presumably will be used to plan and control the technical work. These methodologies permit and even require the use of technical methodologies to solve the technological aspects of building information systems. Each methodology must be focused on solving the problem for which it has been designed as a means to ensure proper control of the entire project.

## Methodologies Oriented to Systems Integration

In the latter years of the 1990s, companies with claims to leadership in the marketplace for new technologies gave credence and value to methodologies as a source of competitive advantage. After becoming aware of the limitations associated with previously described methods, the need to respond with an integrated methodology solution was identified. The desired solution was to develop an integrated set of tools and methodologies that were owned as intellectual capital.

Some of these companies, including leading international consultants, made a significant effort to provide a coherent response to this need for an integrated approach under a single methodological paradigm. This could be used for all types of projects, including the development of new information systems, the maintenance of computer applications, the selection of software, and the implementation of business management solutions such as ERP, Data Warehouse, or client relationship management (CRM). The solution would integrate the two aspects of the project, and then separately address the technical work and management of the project itself.

These methodologies have been promoted by private entities, usually large consulting firms or service providers that use technology as a weapon to gain advantage over competitors. In turn, they share this integrated solution with their customers as a form of establishing differentiation in the marketplace and as a means to build higher loyalty from their customers.

The scope of this integrated approach is global because, by definition, its precise purpose is to cover and provide a common framework to organize, prioritize, and coordinate all projects and initiatives under a single high-level process. The disadvantage of these methods is that the approach is applied with more ambition than is necessary, resulting in oversized work plans that can be very appropriate for projects with high complexity, but may prove too intense for simple or smaller-scale projects. The advantage of such methods is that they provide a multifaceted and multidisciplinary approach that considers, in an integrated way, different aspects of project management and technical work.

The successful implementation of such methodologies requires trained professionals who have internalized the structure to ensure that they can successfully implement complex and large projects. In some cases, it may also require specialized software and equipment.

## Current Conditions in Project Management

There are now many organizations involved in change management on a global scale, with thousands of users affected in different countries and continents and in different cultures with different languages. These changes can affect one or more lines of business, or they can represent the creation of new business units for these companies. They can present serious problems for those organizations that do not know how to deal with these situations, with the complexity and difficulty overwhelming their comprehension and capabilities. Faced with such situations, the answer is to implement a next-generation approach, an appropriate integration methodology. This should be done with methodology specialists who are experienced and prepared for the rigors of deployment and implementation.

If a situation is more straightforward, then the solution to be adopted can be a simpler, less ambitious one. However, it should still consider the two basic perspectives of any project:

■ For the project management aspect, a complete and comprehensive project management methodology solution should be selected. This includes such methodologies as those based on the PMBOK® standard or other methods such as PRINCE2 from the OGC.

■ For the technical aspect, a methodology that addresses the particular technology or technical work should be selected. This can include appropriate tools for the technical nature of the project, such as the production of software, process engineering, agile development, or other technical process used.

Organizations need to ensure that projects are under control at all times considering the two aspects mentioned. This implies a certain complexity of project management, but this will result in higher proportions of success that provide the greatest benefit to the performing organization and to the project's customer.

## Chapter 16

# The Role of Information Systems in Generating Business Value

Information systems have experienced a dizzying transformation, with their role gaining a growing importance since their entry into the business world in recent years. This transformation has radically changed all aspects of information systems, including the hardware and equipment used by companies, the basic software and applications, and the technical training provided to system users. It is also represented by new attention to increasingly large development teams, including specialists from varied disciplines, which has introduced complexity into the business environment. The companies themselves have undergone a steady metamorphosis over the years, learning to shift on the fly, while venturing into a future full of unknowns, and this places questions and doubts into the minds of managers concerned about the evolution of their business.

We have witnessed a dynamic situation over the years in which every organization, company, and government agency has been moving toward a more or less common level of maturity and internalization of the contributions associated with information systems. However, the level of maturity achieved in these organizations differs depending on such things as the starting position of each organization, the market or industry in which business is conducted, and the prevailing business culture and its receptiveness to technology-based solutions. These and other conditions have influenced the business value obtained from the introduction of information technology and communications solutions, and, consequently, this has influenced the confidence that the institutions have placed in the information systems deployed within those organizations.

## Information Systems Maturity Development

The move toward a common state of maturity can be examined in relation to a number of developing stages. These are observed from a historical perspective, and it is possible that some organizations have not yet experienced full development, sometimes because they are immature organizations and tend to remain in an intermediate state of information system maturity. In other cases, the introduction of new technologies in the organization has been facilitated by experienced managers who bring previous experience and lessons learned from their use of information systems in other organizations, and not as an internalized action within the current organization.

This pattern for introducing information technology and communications has been led from a subordinate position, with a reliance on the departments whose objectives, priorities, and development goals and initiatives are dependent on technology use. In particular, information systems have traditionally focused on the interests and needs of administration and finance departments as a basis for their introduction. These departments use technologies as tools for accomplishing their services. Systems have been introduced regardless of alternative approaches that might have allowed the resolution of broader organizational needs and interests, and which could have achieved greater benefits within the organization.

Guidance given to the placement of these technologies invariably originated in administrative departments, where there was a need to automate repetitive tasks in order to reduce the burden of a heavy administrative staff workload, which would otherwise require many resources that contributed only small value to the organization. The role entrusted to the new technology was to provide administrative support to employees performing certain operations and administrative processes. The efficiency objectives pursued by administrative departments with the introduction of the first information systems were clear, obvious, and very commendable.

Computers and related applications were introduced, usually in a context of significant corporate growth and rapid business expansion. This provided an opportunity to achieve economies of scale, where the computers and software were expensive and tailored to each company, but enabled organizations to assume an increased workload with minimum marginal costs. In particular, information systems reduced the need for more staff, and the costs associated with staff education, training, and supervision. At other times, information systems have had a more dramatic entry into the business scene as the prelude to a reduction in the workforce. In many cases, this caused the introduction of information technology to have a bad reputation as it was used to reduce the number of employees and replace them with the functionality of the new technologies.

In these early stages, increased efficiency obtained by the introduction of computers could take the following different forms, among others, depending on the organization:

- Increased production capacity (with regard to administrative tasks)
- Reduced costs associated with administrative work
- Increased responsiveness in terms of time and quality management
- Improved collaboration, coordination, reporting, and information sharing across departments

However, there were also some disadvantages which, to the introduction and implementation of information systems in the business environment, include the following:

- A narrow focus on automation was limited to simple machine-based transactions that were often isolated and unconnected within the administrative process.
- Old procedures were replicated in a step-by-step fashion conceived and designed for the previous, handmade working conditions, and were now outdated and overtaken by new circumstances.
- Processes and operations were designed for use by the same people who made it previously and who would not reap benefits with these new tools in the business environment.

Accordingly, some pioneers realized that they had to adapt the way they introduced new technologies in order to deliver the greatest benefits from their implementation. To that end, a new focus was placed on implementation projects that introduced information systems into the organization.

Another stage of maturity emerged as project goals were no longer just the simple automation of administrative processes. Organizations began to rethink the whole process, looking for greater efficiencies and higher profits from the implementation of information systems. New technologies leveraged a redesign and simplification of the work flow, and information systems began to take on a different, more central role reflecting the importance of automating processes simplified by the elimination of unnecessary steps.

Projects geared toward the reorganization of activities in this maturity stage were driven by administrative departments that still saw the computer as an office machine, and had not yet made the leap to information system use at the factory level or in other enterprise environments. The orientation of these projects was still focused on the optimization of administrative processes, but from a more global perspective. Of course, in this stage, organizations had still not yet discovered the full potential that information technologies and communications could provide to user organizations.

The project objectives remained basically identical, but were tailored to the new vision and expansion of scope. As well as improving efficiency in operations, increasing the processing capacity of administrative units, and reducing bureaucratic costs, other objectives more in line with the new vision surfaced. This included interest in the simplification of administrative processes and work procedures and in improving capacity management and control. The consequence of this new vision was the adaptation of many classic administrative structures to new processes designed specifically for computer management and which made certain positions and jobs unnecessary.

When this trend finished maturing it would move into the next stage of industrial operations where it would lead to a complete understanding of business management. In turn, this would spread to the entire company in the name of process management. With the introduction of process management in the business environment, information systems became emancipated from administrative departments as they spread to other areas of organizations.

## Process Management

The following are some pertinent impacts and outcomes associated with process management:

- Companies increased their size significantly to acquire global dimensions in order to enjoy the benefits associated with size, while gaining economies of scale. However, the growth occurred in unmanageable proportions, and that increased the difficulty resulting from changing needs within the organization.
- Hierarchical structures were difficult to manage before mutating to multidimensional, matrix structures. Now, information systems implementation is the ideal solution to providing support for operations across core business units.
- Information systems have facilitated the automation of a variety of activities to extend the scope of support across an entire organization, and this support is also gradually shifting toward the customer, both internally and externally, to help generate additional value for customers.
- Information systems have become comprehensive and pervasive, and that has prompted the need for optimization of resources used relative to information system performance. This threat on resources extends to the whole company, without any department or process area being exempt.

These impacts occurred with the advent of process management as a method for designing and re-engineering business processes, and for optimizing performance by implementing new business capabilities. Process reengineering provides a systematic, comprehensive, and intuitive approach that encourages effective delegation, empowerment, and transparent and consistent accountability at all levels of an organization. Its application to the design of business processes optimizes the use of company resources by the identification of activities and the streamlining of processes that add little or no value.

The transparency that process re-engineering provides helps reduce the time needed for diagnosis and preparation of appropriate action plans for any corrective activity. In addition, process management also allows organizations to design more flexible and dynamic results, and is key to changing and transforming old hierarchical structures that have become obsolete. To that end, it facilitates the introduction of lighter, flatter, and less hierarchical structures that work well in organizations with multidimensional matrix structures.

The use of process management in organizations today allows people to work together to achieve common goals, despite belonging to different departments. It facilitates the establishment of work teams as a way to overcome the limitations that were previously represented by isolated work that ignored the common goal and offered a fragmented vision of the process that created a barrier to customer satisfaction. In this context, the team concept extends beyond the traditional boundaries of each separate department to encompass the entire organization. This approach also elevates the importance of management information systems and their contribution to business interests to previously unknown limits.

Information technologies and communications in this new paradigm become vitally important as a tool for structuring an organization and the processes that require performance that would be impossible to achieve without the assistance of effective technologies. Work is transformed, and it is producing in all departments a progressive reduction on the use of paper. Physical files are transferred to computerized management systems, where information can flow at almost instantaneous speeds among the various participants in a process. For example, it can now be determined in a matter of seconds who has yet to review or approve a document, without interfering with anyone's work. Furthermore, it has become easier to enter business rules to allow the generation of automated alerts when a predetermined period has passed, and this can be done without management involvement, and will not be missed when someone leaves the organization, falls ill, or is on vacation or absent for an extended period of time.

This maturity can create a cultural shift in the organization that results in a change of attitude among employees, allowing them to develop a customer orientation that is much clearer and more responsive in managing old problems and difficulties. Before this stage was reached, many organizations had vertical departments with each focused on achieving its own goals, and this was sometimes in opposition to those of other departments in the organization. Sometimes, we lose the global reference, that the ultimate purpose is for everyone to share in achieving the customer satisfaction.

When business process re-engineering is properly applied, organizations begin sharing information about processes and general operations across business units, and this reduces unnecessary redundancies. It also lowers the likelihood of difficulties reaching customers, who may choose to leave the business relationship because of frustration and inconvenience.

## Today's Information Systems Maturity

The approach to information systems implementation today is one in which each department maintains its identity, but each knows more about its contribution to the processes involved. This rectifies the short-sightedness of earlier business unit participation and involvement. This change of perspective will bring most benefits resulting from the implementation of process management. Thus, operations are performed more efficiently, planned based on the achievement of specific targets, and are transparently shared by all in an unequivocal manner related to requirements, customer demands and expectations, and greater optimization of resource utilization. This results in higher profitability and a sustainable improvement in business operations within the organization.

Moreover, thanks to the support provided by information systems operating around this model, managers have recognized the obligation to delegate some of the information system functions to process owners, and they, in turn, must define the responsibilities for the involvement of their people in the development of the process. The roles of people involved in the processes in different departments must be stated in clear terms.

The role that each individual plays in the process, their scope of responsibility and contribution, must be written in a transparent manner. The definition of the function of every worker in the process can increase their degree of involvement and motivation. If people have more information about the results of their work, and how their work affects the final results of the company and customer satisfaction, they work with more motivation.

In this new framework, the employee is not limited to performing tasks without knowing the relationship to project objectives and how the result of their work will affect other participants and other tasks. Now, they are given an understanding of this in a clear and precise manner, and they gain an appreciation of their function within the organization because they know the purpose and importance of their work. This improves overall performance as employees start to feel responsible for accomplishing assigned duties, with the knowledge that the quality of their work is a factor in the next successive step in the development process. As this occurs, everyone involved contributes to a more effective and cohesive work team.

Guidance for process management allows managers and work team members to achieve additional benefits that contribute to the improved performance of the organization. These benefits include, for example, an increased ability to identify opportunities for improvement by the managers and participants in the process. Thanks to the global view of component operations, recommendations can be made regardless of who initially carried out the process. This helps to identify and remove the duplication of effort, and it streamlines the steps and activities to overcome the difficulties previously associated with limited vision and limited responsibility.

The new perspective provided by process management creates a climate of mutual commitment to improvement that recognizes the contributions made by all involved. This creates positive feedback for the system and facilitates the beginnings of a virtuous circle in which all stakeholders will be involved. In short, this new process management approach to systematize the business activities will contribute to the use of processes, information, and ideas in an integrated manner, and increase the involvement and commitment of staff regardless of their relative position with respect to the process.

Through personal involvement, I served in process management to facilitate the achievement of role commitment by all participants in the process, to increase their association with the objectives established for process activities, and to improve their motivation toward understanding the purpose of the tasks they perform and how they interact with those performed by others.

This approach is diametrically opposed to a model that was widely implemented for many years in our hierarchical organizations. It started from the assumption of limited competition and a major reduction in people. To a large extent, employees were seen merely as cogs and mechanisms who performed simple and elementary operations that could be repeated an endless number of times during a day's work. This model is known as the Pygmalion effect, and it promotes the premise that employees ultimately behave as mere automatons, without their own thoughts, opinions, or ideas, endlessly repeating the operation for which they were trained.

Instead, our new approach defines a transparent process, the outputs to be achieved, and the constraints that affect the implementation of each process step. This approach streamlines the whole process, and can be critical in some environments. It also provides a solution through the chain of command, and improves the quality of decisions, using a higher level of information and knowledge about the specific circumstances facing the decision maker. Thus, higher-level managers can act on normal operations only in exceptional cases, when circumstances surpass the authority of lower-level managers.

This approach releases a significant amount of time and energy that was previously devoted to tasks, by effective delegation of authority to decision makers. This time is made available by allowing managers closer to the business operations to address issues, with the creation and exercise of thoughtful and carefully prepared corporate policies.

# Chapter 17

# Value Chain and Process Management

Value chain and process management are inextricably linked as a means to serve the business interests of an organization. Together they provide for both the design and implementation of business processes. They also enable organizations to evaluate the processes for effectiveness and efficiency. Details regarding their application in the business environment are considered in this chapter.

## Process Mapping

Process management begins with the development of a complete and comprehensive process map that lists all relevant processes, shows their relationship to one another, and indicates their purpose in the global business process. Preparation of this process map involves several aspects and considerations that must be taken into account, including those discussed below:

- *Process purpose.* The purpose of the process should be clearly identified and defined in a reliable way. If you have difficulty in determining the process purpose, then that process should be considered for elimination from the process re-engineering effort. It should be understood that this aspect is fundamental to process management. The purpose represents the reason the process will be performed, and if we cannot define it clearly, it is very possible that we are in an activity that is done for historical reasons, by custom, or perhaps on a whim. Regardless of the reason, a process without a specified purpose is most likely an activity that is not needed to achieve the results required by the business.

■ *Process customers (and input/output recipients).* Similarly, customers and suppliers involved in the process should be identified with absolute precision. Knowing what interests are served, who provides process input products, and who receives the results or outcome of the process is absolutely necessary. If you do not clearly identify these participants, they will not have reliable information in response to the triggering events (e.g., actions, transactions, or circumstances) that prompt each process to be started. In particular, if we cannot clearly identify the customer (or output recipient) in the process, we will be faced with a process that consumes resources to produce a product of doubtful utility and value. That makes the process a candidate to be suppressed or at least reconsidered.

■ *Process owner.* Another essential aspect of process management that must be uniquely identified is the person responsible for the process, or the process owner. This individual must have sufficient authority within their organization, or by delegation, to effectively manage the resources needed for the process, and these people will often belong to differents departments of the organization, becoming involved at different stages of the process.

■ *Process description.* It is also crucial to identify with sufficient clarity and detail the activities that make up the process. This includes its scope and a description of where the process begins and ends. It is not enough to identify the constituent activities; the process must also be properly placed in context, detailing the operations performed, workflows, flow of materials, and the kinds of resources that will be involved within the organization. The process description should provide an express reference to the limits or boundaries of the process and the sequence in which all operations must be performed to achieve its purpose.

■ *Process participants.* When specifying the details of the process, the persons involved in the process should also be identified. The persons involved, in one way or another, are part of the process, and their roles and responsibilities should be described. In particular, it is very important to define who is responsible for overseeing process work, and the methods that will be used to accomplish that oversight.

This process mapping should be done at various levels to enable the process to be considered, from elementary activities to global operations.

The process definition provides a detailed description that is comprehensive, with starting content in terms of the work to be performed and the responsibilities to be fulfilled by different individuals at various levels in the organization. It should be noted that in this new paradigm of the business organization, responsibilities and dependencies are no longer linear; rather, they are often more complex, with multiple business unit heads having varied responsibilities. This concept is summarized in Figure 17.1. We should also consider checks and safety measures, both preventive and corrective, that will be applied to the process and to each of the constituent activities. This could include identifying the environmental conditions necessary for the process tasks to be performed.

Training needed for process implementation should also be identified. This includes specifying the training and education required by those who will be involved in process execution and management. Such training can examine relevant processes, and promote the effective discharge of responsibilities and tasks entrusted to each individual and to the team overall.

A detailed monitoring scheme is also needed to allow different individuals and teams to monitor progress in achieving objectives, and to identify any deviations and problems early. This allows corrective measures to be applied for the renewal of the process toward its target, and for process maintenance to re-establish the expected parameters of performance. This monitoring scheme will normally include a collection of appropriate process indicators, oriented to verify if the circumstances allow the process to start, how well the process was performed, and the quality of the results obtained by the process.

Each of these indicators must meet specific control objectives that will enable process owners to validate the relevance and utility of processes, and to eliminate mechanisms that contribute little or nothing to control and process improvement. The monitoring scheme should identify the methods to be used for process measurement, any instrumentation required, the frequency of controls and inspections applied to the process, and the details of the rigor applied to ensure that quality monitoring and measurement are achieved in a reliable way.

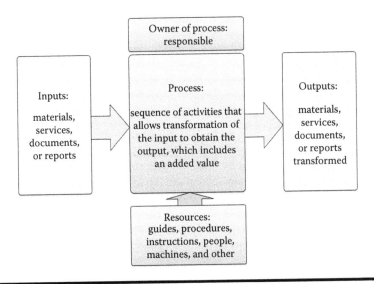

**Figure 17.1   Process definition diagram.**

It is very useful to prepare an organized and understandable depiction of all information related to each process step using a flow chart to illustrate an intuitive approach for process performance. In this way, we can see the different routes that track the materials, resources, and information used during the various stages of the process. Thus, it becomes easier to visualize the process as a clear sequence of key actions that will generate value for the organization. This depiction can also highlight the critical path of the process or value chain that constitutes the "core activities" of the total business process.

Core activities should be given adequate attention to build and maintain the competitive advantages of the organization. These core activities should be reviewed carefully to see if they have differences with the actual sequence of tasks performed, and to try to locate the causes of any deviations and identify areas for potential improvement. It should be noted that while other tasks in the process can have a limited impact on process outcomes and the business results of the company, the performance of tasks that make up the critical path of the process may have very significant effects on these parameters. The management of core activities should therefore be the primary object of attention for management, who must devote a significant part of their time to the control, management, and improvement of these processes.

Process diagrams provide a simplified and intuitive overview of the process, which helps identify problem areas, duplications of effort, bottlenecks, and points where it is possible to influence process improvement. At the same time, these flow charts can also display the interrelationships between different stages of the process or between processes. This will facilitate communication between different business units and departments involved in the different phases of the business process.

## Key Processes

In a process management environment, managers should prioritize devoting attention to the key processes that make up the value chain and critical path of the global business process. Management should engage in defining the process or processes that are part of such a critical path to generating value for customers. They should participate at all levels in the definition of the purpose, scope, control objectives, workflows, process functions, resource roles, and operations to be implemented in achieving the business objectives. It must be remembered that these processes constitute the core business and are the pillars that form the basis for setting the corporate identity and competitive position in the market.

Naturally, this should include the systematic collection of all the information needed to properly define the process. This information will enable managers to define the purpose of the process and the process owner to establish the control objectives and indicators needed to achieve the targets. With this systematic information, key factors can be defined according to their relative importance in achieving the objectives of the process. Process indicators that will facilitate the capture of all relevant information should be defined to help determine the capacity and efficiency of the process. Process standards and measurements should be set to check whether the process meets the specified objectives set by management, and measurement results should be used for continuous monitoring of processes, maintenance, adaptation, and improvement.

The control levels of each part of the process will be defined taking into account the importance of each stage of the process and its impact on the results, to include specifying the control techniques, methods, and measurement equipment to be used. The specification and design of control techniques should take into account the cost of establishing checkpoints, the features to be tested, and acceptance criteria and types of inspections, ensuring that the cost of prevention is not greater than the cost of potential adverse effects to be avoided.

All these considerations must be incorporated into the process map, to include a means to detect and correct any duplication in the collection of monitoring data. These process maps can have additional utilities such as education for improvement, or initial training for new employees or for those that change their responsibility within the organization. They also help visualize the advantages that could result from the automation of certain tasks to reduce cycle time and the effect on business risks of all kinds.

The management team will be responsible for managing team participation, which includes responsibility for adapting the process, if necessary, to optimize and implement improvements and changes that the owner has determined must be implemented. The process owner, meanwhile, will follow up with team meetings to review the process, to ensure the necessary revisions have been accomplished, and to implement the improvements that have been deemed necessary based on data collected in monitoring process indicators and process measures.

It is also a responsibility of the process owner to monitor process execution and to ensure that the people involved in executing the tasks that are part of the process know their responsibilities and conduct the process in a proper manner. If any process problems are detected (e.g., conflicts of interest, lack of necessary involvement by the responsible department, or workers who have uncertain allegiances), the management team should take action, first through dialog, and then, if that is not enough, by requesting sufficient authority to manage the problem or conflict.

Process execution includes activities that show proper attention to the systematic management of the process. This is usually accomplished with frequent follow-up meetings that are used to review relevant data collected for each process, to define process indicators, controls, and measurements, and to provide objective data that will enable proper management of the process. Attention should also be paid on an ongoing basis to optimize the performance of the available resources used to implement the process. In particular, if data collection is appropriate and the selected process indicators are set correctly to track their progress, they can identify weaknesses and areas for improvement. If an abnormality or a source of instability is detected in the process, this part of the process must be examined to identify and eliminate the causes of faults.

The values of process indicators and their evolution over time will allow the detection of possible areas of improvement and allow decisions to be made to act on the control variables. Therefore, it is important to correctly choose the process indicators that will be used to assess the process and to help the decision making based on performance parameters. Process indicators should be of proper magnitude, sensible, cost-effective, reliable, and comparable over time to allow the process to show evolution and trends. For each of the indicators used, there should be an objective outcome that allows a comparison of actual results with those set as target values. When a process fails to achieve its objectives, improvement plans should be developed and corrective actions implemented to act on the control variables to achieve the desired results. Once areas for improvement are identified, corrective measures must be implemented or process modifications made in order to change or improve the process. Actions implemented to change the behavior of the process should be evaluated again with the development of new process indicators to check whether or not the actions taken have provided the expected improvements.

The performance indicators of key processes must be updated periodically to ensure consistency with the objectives of the process. Monthly indicators for monitoring the process are included in the report of monthly management control of the process, which is presented to management.

The following are among the key processes that can be considered within any organization:

- All commercial activities related to capturing demand or obtaining customer orders that will result in sales and revenue for the organization
- All actions related to the customer service organization that will result in greater satisfaction with products and services delivered
- The development of commercial offers to the consumer to try to get their orders and contracts, and related income if actual sales are achieved
- The sale of products and services to customers and the receipt of associated revenue for the organization
- Production planning and operations that are required to deliver products and services consistent with the terms of customer orders and contracts, or the redesign of a production process to improve performance or resolve difficulties affecting normal operations
- Assessment and analysis of supplier prequalification to ensure the best sources of supply according to the criteria of quality and the tolerances established in the production process
- Customer service for public markets and consumption
- Delivery of products or service to the customer as a "moment of truth" transaction, with regard to ensuring quality perceptions that the customer associates

with the purchase experience, and with regard to achieving customer willingness to re-sign or otherwise examine alternatives with the organization

## Strategic Processes

In addition to the key processes of the core business, organizations will also attend to strategic processes. Strategic processes are related to the future development of the organization, including the preparation of strategic objectives and corporate policies that will guide the direction of the organization, like using a compass.

The preparation and dissemination of corporate policies goes beyond the operational scope of management oversight, and involves gathering and using information and knowledge to facilitate the strategic alignment of all layers of management within the organization. Such policies can replace or otherwise save significant efforts to correct inadequate courses of action to new conditions and to avoid difficulties due to lack of a synchronous approach by management within the organization.

There are many sources of information used by management to establish strategic direction and to ascertain the conditions of the organization's market and industry. Some are internal and can result from the upward flow of information from the business network and employees. There are also a number of excellent sources of strategic information.

An important information source may be found in after-sales service and customer care, which provides valuable indicators regarding customer perception, particularly customer dissatisfaction with the company or its products and services. To that end, conducting periodic surveys of customer satisfaction allows for invaluable feedback to detect problems with the service or products offered to customers. That feedback can also be used to improve the company's image, and, when properly studied, may allow for the design of new products suited for customers. This enables the organization to increase its competitive advantage against other providers who are not actively listening to their customers.

However, management needs additional information that can only be achieved through actions such as market research and market assessments to identify emerging trends and opportunities. Also, close examination of invention and design (I&D) and project research and development can be performed to gain a better understanding of strategic business perspectives. Proper interpretation of this information enables the organization to anticipate customer needs, to examine the supply capability and offerings of its competitors, and to exploit emerging market niches that can be highly profitable for the organization. In turn, this information can be translated and incorporated for use in strategic business plans.

Internal and external business communication is another strategic process that too often does not receive adequate attention. Effective business communication is key to generating a strong corporate culture and distinct business presence in the marketplace. Critical communication processes should be included in the strategic objectives of the organization, and developed and practiced in the course of strategic business management.

## Support Processes

Support processes are largely related to managing human resources, recruiting candidates, selecting staff, and performing the administration of personnel functions, including the calculation and payment of payroll, fulfillment of social security requirements, and compliance with tax obligations. Another process directly related to personnel actions may be internal communication, which we have previously considered as strategic but which can also be seen as support, depending on the context.

Staff training can also be considered a process of support or assistance. This considers aspects such as the creation of a knowledge map of the organization. It particularly includes identifying the needs and planning training for employees, to include developing and disseminating a calendar of the training schedule, the course material, and the quality of the training.

Another aspect generally regarded as a support process includes activities related to the management and maintenance of facilities, resources and general machinery, and materials and services not directly related to key business processes. This can include oversight of vendor evaluations, and purchasing, procuring, and monitoring related to domestic consumer products and supplies.

Other processes that can be categorized as supportive are related to aspects of product sales and customer services, planning and development of promotions and advertising, the distribution of product and service catalogs to customers, the development and distribution of customer gifts and event invitations, and other similar actions.

## Information Systems as a Corporate Process

The role of information systems in the context of a process deserves special mention. It has evolved in recent years to influence many public and private organizations and institutions of varying size and across various industries. Until recently, information systems were associated with the administrative practices of the company, largely considered to be among the supporting processes in areas of accounting and finance, human resources, personnel management, or sales management. We have since seen the progressive emancipation of information systems away from traditional administrative departments.

Information systems have evolved to show increased value to the organization through their role as a means to display and distribute the image of the company as a products and services provider. In turn, customers have recognized the value that information systems acquired for innovation have provided when redesigning products, services, and benefits, or to illuminate new products and services that complement the company's current customer offerings. In this way, companies have become more aware of their value to customer information and have given more attention to the use of information systems in developing and maintaining customer relationships. Therefore, the processes associated with information use have given an added advantage to the organization and its customers.

Thus, information systems in many organizations are recognized as support processes. They can also be considered as strategic processes for their role in making business decisions or, in other cases, as key processes integrated into the critical paths of core corporate business processes. In the role in the core business, information systems can leverage competitive differentiation and provide substantial added value. In particular, differentiation is made between the leaders, who have a vision for implementing effective strategies and policies, and followers, who merely imitate practices of successful leaders in information system design and implementation. Maintaining constant innovation is the real source of competitive advantage, and this differentiation will grow more and more as leaders enjoy the results of working with the opportunities that lie in day-to-day business realities, while leaving the followers, rooted in traditional practices aimed at the repetition of obsolete models, to venture only on safe paths.

## Chapter 18

# Opportunities to Create Value through Information Systems

Information systems managers in any organization now have the opportunity to move to the forefront of leadership in their respective businesses. Will they step forward and assume the new role being offered to them or will they prefer to stay quietly in the background in a functional business support role?

## A New Paradigm for Business Value

Professionals in information technology and communications are in a position to provide significant value to companies and organizations that have sufficient vision to integrate the possibilities they offer. For years, technology leaders have invested considerable effort in explaining their roles to the entire organization and to the departments and administrative areas that are usually framed within the organization. Now they have the opportunity to help the organization differentiate from competitors and to provide higher value to its customers through the use of modern information systems.

Those responsible for information systems have historically blamed management areas or finance management because they were unable to explain in any depth the value that technology could contribute to the business. This limited the ability to justify the investment needed for effective use of information technology in business. Fortunately, the situation has changed significantly, and those responsible for information technology positions are starting to be placed on the first level of management, including membership on steering committees, in many organizations. However, relatively few organizations fully understand these technologies, and too many organizations continue to see information technology as a "lesser evil," or as a way to save on human resources, but without capturing the business benefits from emerging opportunities in the information technology field.

The entrepreneurs, business owners, and professional managers in information technology continue to face difficulties in providing justifications for information systems. Regardless of the purpose for the investment (e.g., a new packaging line, a new distribution process, or a new store), any investment that has a tangible result will always repress investing in information systems. The contributions of information systems to a business are hard to justify, in part because they have intangible results. Also, there is a chronic problem in the nature of communication between those responsible for information systems and enterprise management.

On the one hand, specialists in new technologies rely on a self-justification paradigm in which the technology itself is reason enough to undertake system implementation projects, and to maintain the potential that technology upgrades represent. This paradigm, which is evident to the initiated, but cryptic and incomprehensible to others, is a problem in communication between those responsible for new technologies and the rest of the management team. This condition can hinder productive interactions and even contribute, in many cases, to misunderstandings and resentment toward the leadership team for its reluctance in funding proposed projects from the technological perspective.

Consequently, technology professionals try to convince the management team of the need for a technology by presenting tedious and convoluted explanations and all sorts of very technical reasons why more systems projects are needed, without explaining why this should even be considered. Thus, a mixed message, overloaded with jargon and technical terminology, is provided in a vain attempt to convince management of needs based on a professional discipline perspective. This can prevent executives from gaining a comprehensive understanding of the need, and this can cause rejection and mistrust of the proposed systems development efforts.

The strategic direction of the organization calls for projects that can be justified based on profitability for the organization, and not on technical advantage arguments. Executive managers will examine information system projects in a manner comparable to projects proposed by nontechnical managers in areas such as production, sales, and distribution, which are justified in a quantitative manner with budgets and income projections. These proposals are expressed in terms that are perfectly aligned with the strategic direction of the organization, which allows comparison with other projects and investment alternatives based on priority, expected performance, repayment terms, or any other business criteria.

This chasm between the paradigms of management and those of information systems professionals makes communication difficult between the two groups, and appears to be a penalty factor for technology projects. Technology project proposals are too often presented without sufficient business justification (in terms that management can accept and understand), as a matter of conformance to standard practices in the business world.

The idea that information systems can play a decisive role in the future of a company has not been sufficiently considered and appreciated within many organizations. They have yet to realize that when they learn how to use information systems properly, they gain a competitive tool that provides differential value over the competition. Many business managers still see the costs of introducing new technologies as an expense and not as an investment. Accordingly, they focus on reducing cost impacts to a minimum in order to achieve savings that can be used to finance other investments, investments that they value as more productive or more efficient for performance improvement.

Information systems, or more precisely, information and knowledge management, represent a potential business value that makes the difference between organizations that define the market and its rules, creating opportunities for success, and companies that are satisfied to merely follow in the footsteps of those who are leading the effort.

# Defining Information Technology Value

Information technology and communication provides an efficient and effective means to work with information and knowledge. Technology professionals will likely agree that there are certain sets of data that offer business value. Consider the following short list:

- Customer organization
- Customer preferences, habits, and valuation of products and services
- Organization elasticity of consumption relative to changes in price, demand, or any other aspect of the market
- Organization costs, including variable costs, budgets, or any other aspect of internal data used by management to make decisions on a rational basis and in a timely manner

Having this type of information defines the difference between a company that gets exceptional business results on a routine basis and a company that struggles to simply survive, living with anxiety every time they have to make a key business decision without reliable information, and having to rely on the intuition of responsible individuals in lieu of factual information.

An effective data collection process is necessary to obtain this information, validate it, and then make it available to the right people at the right time. This is the inherent responsibility of information systems; it is the reason for having an information system, the mission and purpose of every information system. However, new technologies are often associated more with business attributes of the company, to improve decision making, expand knowledge management or incorporate functions and features that support the strategic direction and operational needs of the organization.

Meanwhile, those responsible for information systems have still not found a way to achieve consistent and reliable business advantages and benefits to the organization. Without these achievements, technology projects will continue to be seen as lacking business justification and they will have no way to elevate the discourse to the level of business.

Arguments to justify system development projects are met with skepticism and, sometimes, with rejection. They are received with uncertainty and suspicion in light of repeated failures to meet expectations. Moreover, the benefits promised by information systems projects are not accompanied by a reasoned business justification of how they are going to achieve desired business results, so they get minimal recognition.

From a conceptual level, it is obvious that information systems implementation projects provide unquestionable value to organizations from an operational perspective. Departments and business units within the organization probably could not survive and fulfill their normal operations if they dispensed with the applications and information systems that support the performance and management of those operations. We can therefore say that new technologies bring positive value that produces significant advantages and benefits for organizations that employ them. Those advantages and benefits have two types of foundations that we can differentiate according to the level of development that they require. First, there is the effect of transforming the way the organization conducts its daily operations by incorporating these technologies, thereby acquiring a work capacity and responsiveness to customers. Second, there is a less direct effect but an equally valid business advantage that lies in having superior knowledge to guide the strategic direction in response to activities of the market or industry in which the organization operates. This knowledge helps identify and evaluate circumstances and trends in the marketplace that, when properly treated and considered, allow early detection of changes and a necessary early response to those changes. This can be a critical advantage in today's competitive business world.

The systematic use of information technology can also provide the basis for continuous quality improvement and operational safety, creating the foundation of a trusting relationship with both internal and external customers. This leads to increased customer loyalty, and improvements in the customer relationship. In turn, this ensures some continuity in the relationship, and enables an increase in revenue, without added promotional costs, when the organization retains the business of existing customers.

Although we may agree on the generic assumptions discussed above, we still find it difficult to justify this kind of input when we are dealing with a specific project. Why does this happen? Is it just a kind of mental block that besets us with anxiety when starting a new project and that hinders a thorough, orderly, and rigorous analysis? Perhaps the problem is that we try to find answers without a procedure to guide us, or we just do not know where to find the answers?

Personally, I am of the opinion that we are facing a reality that, as in many other areas, we can see clearly at the conceptual level, but find it hard to pinpoint, contrast, and provide detail for a specific project. Therefore, I believe that if we have an orderly system with which to find what might be called the "deposits of value," it will be easier or at least possible to irrefutably justify the value contributed by any particular information systems project at any point in time.

To begin, we must think of different ways by which information systems can create value for the organization. The remaining subsections of this chapter will consider some prominent options that can be applied to justify information systems projects.

## Information Systems Can Help Reduce Costs

Since information technology and communications began to be applied to the world of business and administration, they have offered clear advantages in terms of efficiency and productivity.

Their contributions are manifested in various forms and have varied effects. Information technology has been able to absorb increased workloads without increasing the staff resources dedicated to the tasks, saving on labor costs, as well as the associated supervision and control. This has allowed companies and businesses to experience exceptional profit margins thanks to the almost direct conversion of marginal revenue resulting from the negligible cost associated with additional operations.

In a similar manner, the contribution of information technology has helped resolve conditions of deteriorating profitability or similar financial difficulties through enhanced work efficiency and the elimination of jobs and their associated costs. This practice has been observed primarily in administrative positions as a result of the automation of many operations, which has reduced the need for the specialized staff who carried out these tasks. The application of information technology to industrial processes and automation has sharply reduced the labor necessary to perform the operations that once required a large staff. In extreme cases, factory workers have been replaced by a legion of robot-like devices that are controlled by more or less powerful centralized servers that coordinate and control their actions. This is the case in sectors such as the automotive industry, but it also occurs with varying degrees of intensity in other business sectors.

Thus, information technology has improved processes to make them faster and more effective, delivering products and services in less time. This makes them more responsive to customer needs and avoids maintaining costly inventories of unproductive finished products, only to offer a satisfactory customer response time to customers with largely obsolete products, with the resulting cost to the company to be borne somewhat stoically. Moreover, the processes have improved to be more effective, giving customers what they demand and at the moment that they need it. This level of customer service is essentially impossible to achieve, at reasonable cost, without the contribution of information technology.

Information technology offers customers an extraordinary level of customer service that distinguishes the suppliers that have such capability. This is achieved by the savings to customers that results from the reduction or even elimination of their inventory, because they trust their suppliers to avoid stock-outs. In the most extreme cases, some companies have integrated their information systems with suppliers, and they have developed their operations without keeping inventory. This minimizes current assets, and it improves profitability exponentially.

Information technology offers possibilities for optimized processes that can operate the business of organizations with minimal resources and can virtualize a lot of resources that previously required significant investments. This includes, for example, the possibility of telecommuting employees doing their work from home, without requiring a physical space and associated facilities such as power, lighting, furniture, computer, or air conditioning. Adoption of this type of approach allows the company to save by avoiding the costs of facilities and equipment that would otherwise have to be provided to employees. This approach also favors a positive balance between personal life and work for employees, who can avoid discomfort and congestion in the tedious and long commutes to work and back home that are inevitable in many of our cities.

Using this approach, companies can also relocate to further reduce their costs without compromising their operational effectiveness. I am not talking about the type of relocation caused by globalization, which may sound like something more applicable to large corporations. Rather, I am referring to a more domestic type of affordable relocation for any company, which by its nature has no need to maintain a public image based on its facilities, and can dispense with its central location in favor of other operational considerations. For example, an organization may want to maintain a sales office and a representative in a central location, but on a smaller operational scale. Likewise, the organization may no longer need to have an extensive and expensive corporate headquarters, but may move to where most of its employees are located, or to a peripheral industrial area where the costs will be much more reasonable for the space and facilities needed.

These changes can be considered to transform the way transactions are handled in the development of business in today's organizations. They provide significant savings that enable organizations to provide superior business results never achieved before. This improved performance allows new projects of modernization and improvement to create a positive dynamic that can lead to a virtuous cycle of innovation and sustained progress.

The implementation of these technologies provides access to a wide variety of advantages and benefits, along with the others already mentioned, allowing the achievement of significant savings for organizations.

# Information Systems Can Facilitate Process Improvements

This review provides an opportunity to apply systematic techniques to conduct re-engineering to improve and optimize the business operations. Process re-engineering should be systematically and rigorously applied, according to the different steps established by the process used. Process re-engineering can be performed by considering the automated role of relevant information systems in the organization. In particular, it is desirable to incorporate information systems capability in the creation or revision of business processes.

We must identify the different actors, departments, individuals, or players involved, along with the sequence of actions, activities, and constraints to be carried out. If done from an analytical perspective, with appropriate attention applied to each step, we can identify and implement opportunities for process and operational improvement.

When performing this process, the focus is placed on the value of the product or service, and how it can be successfully delivered to the customer at a greater value but with a lower cost. When this is achieved, there will be associated opportunities to gain market share, to reach new customers and new market segments, and to find business opportunities that were not previously accessible. These opportunities will introduce advantages related to obtaining economies of scale, which should facilitate increased profitability and commercial success for the organization.

At the same time, the re-engineering process should identify operations that can be resolved or otherwise handled by information systems with minimal or no manual intervention. This allows the mechanization of relevant operational processes within the information system, and that has consequential benefits for the organization in terms of cost, time, and resource utilization.

Moreover, by deploying a powerful communications infrastructure, computing resources can be concentrated or distributed across business units according to the desires of the organization. This avoids any easements associated with the physical distribution of employees, facilities, or any other factor of production. If we add the ability to virtualize servers on shared infrastructure and possible off-site hosting, we can allow processing capabilities to evolve according to business needs and without expensive migration processes or suspension of service. This can be done at a reasonable cost and with an administrative staff that does not require extensive technical training.

If business circumstances allow, the infrastructure can be set up with information system components that provide a service that incurs costs only when it is used. In this way, the cost of infrastructure and its maintenance can be drastically reduced without detriment to the benefits to be achieved. Quite the contrary, in addition to providing a standard level of service, the infrastructure can also include a premium level of service, which supports adaptation to changing organizational needs and responsiveness in a dynamic market. Infrastructure possibilities are very flexible, and this is just one added point of awareness that can be considered among the solutions that best suit organizational needs.

Another contribution that information systems provide is the ability to automate many business operations, including subjective, logical decisions that are based upon clear rules and a well-defined process. Information technology has been applied for some time to control simple operations of all kinds. This automation has allowed many companies to achieve significant advantages and benefits that have allowed them to move ahead of competitors, opening a gap that is becoming increasingly larger. With the advancement of technologies such as machine vision and many others that allow inspection of products without manual intervention, this closes the circle and facilitates the entry of information systems into process areas that were previously the bastion of human operators.

The cost of such components and tools is still significantly high and their application is still limited to industries and areas where, because of the volume of production, the hazard, or the cost of products, manual inspection by agents is becoming prohibitively expensive. So, a decision to acquire and implement information technology tools may be an investment that needs to recover business costs in a more reasonable time.

However, before going too far, it should be recognized that many administrative processes where decisions can be defined with precision can be supported by many of today's information systems. Even if only partially incorporated into an automated process that ultimately leaves the decision to a human agent, the lead-up actions are supported by the system, thus reducing workload and increasing the minimum management requirements of those responsible.

Information system decision support provides two prominent advantages: (i) by improving the productive capacity of the process for use across the organization, and (ii) by improving the quality of decisions made within the process. When a particular case presents a situation that has attributes that make automated decisions difficult, the information system can separate it from the general flow and redirect the matter to a human agent, together with the presentation of all relevant and available information. Thus, human intervention disappears and changes the behavior of information output in the overall system, leaving a more productive gear mechanism to move to action by exception. The human agent can therefore focus on more complex cases that require specific and specialized attention, where personal knowledge and experience are applied.

## Information Systems Can Assist in Meeting Customer Demands

The introduction of information systems in areas such as sales and presales functions can provide benefits that may be essential for developing a competitive position. This includes such things as dissemination of offers and promotional campaigns, customer order management, shipping and product delivery, and customer billing. It may also include postsales support such as customer claims or customer service, among other possible automated functions.

Each occasion of customer interaction provides an opportunity to demonstrate high-quality service, and to build a sense of loyalty that causes customers to return to buy new products or services. In turn, satisfied customers will often share their experience with friends and acquaintances in other organizations, thereby providing the potential to acquire new customers.

These reasons should be enough to ensure that customer contacts are consistently treated as if each one is a "critical moment" in which customer retention is positively influenced.

Therefore, any investment made in creating specialized structures that enables individuals to facilitate customer service and support is a valid approach to customer relationship management. This includes such things as providing individual training and awareness on the importance of their role in customer relationships, equipping individuals with the tools that help them to work more efficiently and effectively, and enabling them to provide clear and concrete answers in response to customer questions and inquiries and even to claims and complaints. Ultimately, customer satisfaction should pay off in customer loyalty and provide expanded awareness of the organization when each customer touts the products and services to others in the marketplace.

In addition to employees placing importance on their roles as agents of good will, these individuals can also facilitate information gathering relative to each customer encounter. It is important for them to be aware that each customer contact represents an opportunity to gather, record, and refine vital customer information about their perceptions of the products and services, and their concerns, needs, and desires related to our business transactions. This information becomes an input to the continuous improvement of design and development of new products and contributes to a database of business intelligence that can have considerable business value.

In this effort to capture customer information as a means to improve ourselves, our products and services, and the production processes that we use, it is inevitable that new technologies will play a role in capturing all of this information in a systematic and structured way. Thanks to the information technology tools available to us, it is now possible to "associate a face with the name" of each customer.

The customer is the central focus of our business center, and, by using information technology tools, is no longer merely an abstract or impersonal transaction. Rather, as a means to better service and improve customer satisfaction, we can align personal attributes with defined and explainable behaviors to manage the customer relationship with growing personalization. Individuals representing the customer's organization become known by name, and they respond to professional interactions that are viewed as a long-term business relationship.

This personal knowledge about customers can include the grouping and segmentation of customers according to attributes that facilitate the business relationship and awareness of customer needs. The business relationships can then be examined to identify customer trends, making it possible to anticipate emerging customer business needs for which solutions will be required. This effort includes collecting and contrasting customer needs and interests across different customers. Therefore, when certain trends are indicated for one customer, other customers of the same type (or within the same grouping) can be examined for that same business tendency and interest. This approach can change the way business originates, breaking the usual sequence of sales to define parallels of what needs and interests a particular customer grouping may have in common.

## Information Systems Can Optimize Data Management

Information systems are implemented to improve operational efficiency. From the onset of this technology, this trend has continued. In the early days, information systems tried to resolve simple and isolated business operations that required intensive calculations. By virtue of volume and repetition, these systems were gradually advanced to consider the resolution of more sophisticated operations that addressed such matters as safety and quality management by simplifying human–computer interactions. Thus, the design and construction of any current system has a requirement for "data only" as a condition for efficient information system operation. This ensures that each piece of data enters the system only once and is stored in one single location of the system for later use by the processes, calculations, and utilities that need a particular data element. This provides maximum value to every individual effort by users.

Initially, a full-time staff was required for such data entry. This staff was then replaced by a handful of data entry specialists, allowing us to significantly increase the working capacity of the system. Later, this dependence was also eliminated, shifting the burden of responsibility for data entry to the employees producing the data, either directly or indirectly as a function of system capability. This remains a trend that continues today and one that tries to optimize data handling for the information system as a whole. It offers an advantage by providing immediacy between data generation and its introduction into the system that ensures data continuity and accuracy. The result is a greater reliance on the information system by users, particularly in efforts where responsibility for the quality of the information entered and maintained is shared, and for continuous monitoring of output accuracy, quality, and suitability.

In line with this trend, we see the emergence of the integrated enterprise resources planning (ERP) system. This system is integrated on a single database with global deployment, which can be used to consider and resolve information management problems and issues in all areas of business of any organization. In this way, the added advantage is achieved of a consistent user interface in any business area of the company. This saves time and effort in training users, and allows extraordinary ease of reallocation of responsibilities and internal mobility of the workforce, without the restrictions that normally occur when different applications are used in different business units of an organization.

New technologies, in an effort to expand access to information systems to new employees and transfers within the organization, are still being considered in different ways for optimization of data management. There is a tendency to decentralize and customize access to information systems, opening them to all devices, personal computers (PCs), point-of-sale (POS) devices, laptops or notebooks, and netbooks. All of these terminals are connected to corporate servers by means of a ubiquitous WAN using encryption technology and other security assurances for network access that is transparent to the respective users, but safe and inaccessible to intruders.

On the other hand, there are also trends to building capacity to process data in large centralized servers, which are housed in server farms that are hosted and managed by communications operators. This concentration of computing capacity is done with the intention of facilitating "anywhere access," optimizing the time of service and system availability, and all done while maintaining reasonable costs.

There is also an extraordinary development that has occurred with the introduction of digital communications, and the associated evolution toward integration of computing on a single portable device that is smaller, more personal, more ubiquitous, and more powerful in processing capabilities. This trend is highlighted by the introduction of personal digital assistants (PDAs) and smart phones that integrate voice and data communications with email and SMS messaging applications, and often include a host of powerful and useful tools, such as word processing, spreadsheets, presentation managers, digital audio playback, digital video playback, image and photo managers, Web browsing, photography, and sophisticated solutions for personal management such as note taking and calendar management.

These devices are integrated at the same time to the two vital aspects of leisure and work, thus becoming absolutely essential devices that act as a true record of the individual. This breaks the separation between work time and personal time as they simultaneously address personal and work matters. They embody the "always connected" model, and you get a marginal commitment and immediate response from employees when such devices are provided by an organization as a business tool.

In the same vein, routed multichannel integration is being realized in many areas of economic activity where faxes, emails, SMS, or voice messages recorded by sophisticated interactive voice response (IVR) systems are intertwined and integrated to provide a coherent and comprehensive response to customers.

As already suggested, the purpose of all these measures, technologies, technical solutions, and resources of all kinds is to achieve a transparent, effective, and value-added solution for the customer, without requiring a prohibitive number of resources to do so.

# Information Systems Can Increase Revenues

Information technology can multiply the reach of our business operations to achieve a superior customer base that can be accessed by traditional methods or by automated methods that have added efficiency and lower marginal costs. Relevant information is obtained by processing data related to routine business operations, where data attributes are identified for the purposes of managing our products and services and to customize the supply available to each customer and situation. This provides benefits that include a significant reduction in unit costs per transaction. This makes it possible either to improve our margins per transaction, or to transfer savings to the marketplace by reducing the price of products and services.

The potential for sales growth from the transfer of the savings to the market-place will be determined by the elasticity of demand pricing, which is based on decision-making information that can also be made available from information systems. Transferring the advantages of cost reduction to the marketplace can prompt increased sales of our products and services, and this expands the size of our market, providing a new competitive advantage arising from increased sales volume, with its attendant economies of scale, increased revenues, and improved margins.

The evolving popularity and effects of expanding our customer base will also prompt improved perceptions of our products and services by customers and potential customers. This provides a positive reinforcement or reaffirmation of each customer's decision to choose our product or service when they feel we can be trusted. Their decision to use our products and services is strengthened when they see others in the marketplace doing so. This also results in new sales and higher business revenue.

Moreover, the systematic use of information systems to support customer relationships, popularly known as customer relationship management (CRM), facilitates the management and use of all information needed to provide an adequate response to any customer needs, whether by means of direct and personal attention in person or by phone, or by some form of technology-based online support and assistance. The CRM system also helps the organization to reverse the traditional role of the customer as initiator of contact, as it enables the organization to take the initiative to contact the customer in the business relationship. Such contact can be made to provide products or services that may be interesting to the customer in light of the information that is compiled regarding their needs and their consumption habits. These tools let you increase the number of times that customers are contacted, and therefore increase the number of opportunities to offer products and services to each customer. This can potentially lead to a greater number of sales transactions and higher business revenues.

When business intelligence systems are used in combination with information systems, the benefits and advantages for the organization can multiply. Business intelligence systems such as Data Warehouse, Datamarts, and other analytical databases can produce multidimensional analyses of information on customers, products, and transactions conducted over a period of time. Different perspectives of analysis can be used to add or exclude relevant business information, allowing the identification of behavioral patterns that help us establish customer profiles as a basis for suggesting products and services that may be of interest to our customers. These analyses can be conducted using a multitude of segmentation parameters:

- The history of the customer business relationship thus far, their frequency of purchase, products, and services purchased, and the level of expenditure in each transaction or over a period of time
- The identification of the customer representatives according to their gender, age, salary level, education, occupation, residence, family status, or any other parameter of a personal nature that may have been included in the analysis
- The detection of latent relationships between products and services that complement each other, as determined by what is observed in a significant proportion of transactions for different customer segments
- The identification of opportunities to suggest new products and services that may be of interest to customers based on the factors above, and to trigger customers, particularly compulsive buying customers, to consider the need before buying the solution elsewhere

In any case, the likely result is increased sales, improved business results, and a positive net contribution of information systems that can be reported to management as benefits that are achieved with the investment projects pursued.

# Information Systems Can Help Design New Products and Services

Business information systems can provide extremely valuable information that is the difference between the success and failure of a company. Business management systems tend to have limited scope that is focused on managing the business transactions that occur. However, this information can provide valuable feedback that enables you to ascertain the level of customer satisfaction and the customer's perception of the quality of products and services of the organization. The volume of issues that arise from customer inquiries will provide sufficient opportunities to use support tools such as automated IVR tools, and frequently asked questions (FAQs), which facilitate self-service by customers and provide mechanisms for improving customer care.

However, if we stay at this automated level, we lose opportunities to advance essential business value. We give up the extraordinary value that is available through customer interactions that inform us about unmet needs from our products and services, about features that do not operate properly or as smoothly they should, and about simply unintelligible conditions faced by the average user. These interactions represent business opportunities that provide ideas and insight to improve our products, even to define new products that take advantage of emerging market niches that no competitor has yet identified. This treasure trove of information can be uncovered if you can listen to customers, understand their needs, and offer an agile response and a sincere commitment to resolving their needs.

Customers, through their interactions with officials who provide customer service and care in the business relationship, offer valuable information that can be used to improve products and services. This customer information can be handled in the following ways:

- Identification of features and benefits that add nothing particular to the product from a customer perspective, but technically represent a significant part of the cost.
- Identification of features and benefits that the customer misses and would appreciate being built, distinguishing our product from the competitors. This information, in one way or another, can be used to trigger a re-engineering the product or service to be provided, including the possible generation of new or complementary products that provide certain features and benefits as options.
- Identification of effective use and design problems that require specialized attention, based on receipt of reliable information from users who have experienced the difficulties, assessed their criticality, and provided information on the circumstances and conditions under which problems occur. This customer input has potentially significant cost savings when the information is treated like product research.

Simple interactions with customers can identify new business opportunities that take advantage of seemingly inconsequential ideas and aspirations, along with learning about unmet customer needs that help define new products and services that can create entirely new markets.

## Information Systems Can Create Demand

Despite the traditional role of information systems in support of business operations and automated processes, new technologies can generate new business for themselves that can be exploited either by both traditional companies as well as new technology-prominent companies. These companies can point, for example, to new business in digital media content such as videos, movies, games, and music in MP3 format, among others. These information system capabilities can be developed to exploit the possibilities and potential of the Internet and widespread access to communications networks. This type of business transaction takes place entirely in the digital environment; you can view the catalog of the distributor, listen to previews or view content of those items in which we are interested, choose items that result from our indicated preferences, and electronically purchase an item. This series of activities can complete a business transaction without any direct contact from outside the network and without human intervention in the item selection and sales process.

However, in many cases, information systems do not have to completely replace the traditional transaction by electronic means. Instead, they offer customers an option to make purchases in a tradition manner (e.g., in person or by phone) or by electronic means. This helps organizations to reach new customers and markets, and to create product and service demands they would otherwise have been unlikely to obtain. Consider the case for travel and tourism, whether the purchase is for airline, train, or bus tickets, rental cars, hotel reservations, or integrated vacation packages. Each of these items can be purchased and paid for over the Internet thanks to information systems specifically designed for this type of sale.

Another example involving the expansion of demand may be found with the providers or suppliers of books, music discs, toys, perfumes, and many other consumer goods, who have seized the opportunities that information technology offers to expand their markets globally. Today, companies like Amazon.com are distributing products worldwide through information systems that reach any country and location with consumer demand. This even includes a network of associated entrepreneurs who set up access to the Amazon.com information system through an array of sophisticated information subsystems.

The idea is that information systems can add business value to companies in many ways, but the approach to achieving this value should be planned and verified in order to properly position the effort within the organization, and to properly receive the advantages and benefits that they offer. However, this value must be explained and proven in a transparent and reliable way, so that senior enterprise managers can recognize the strategic role that information technology can have in their organizations.

In the near future, information systems projects will not continue to be justified solely by technological criteria. Rather, a direction must be taken to maintain a strategic perspective that is clearly defined and aligned in a way such that the information system will provide distinct contributions in terms of business results. This approach will be needed in order to obtain the necessary resources to develop information system projects for business value, in contrast and competition with traditional information system production efforts.

# Chapter 19

# Managing the Return on Investment

Organizations of all kinds, whether public or private, government or nongovernmental, always have limited resources when trying to maximize the performance and the utility derived from resource utilization. Moreover, the number of projects as investments that can be addressed is usually higher than the available financing. For this reason, management must always be involved in choosing which projects or initiatives will receive the available investment funding. Of course, this is always to the detriment of other opportunities that remain unfunded and possibly discarded.

In this context, understanding how organizations approach decisions on the selection and prioritization of projects and initiatives provides an indication of the strategic considerations and business conditions that may be taken into account. The potential success or failure of a project or initiative will be evaluated by the performing organization.

The first thing to be explained and understood is the conceptual project framework. From the perspective of a corporate director who has responsibility for managing economic and financial matters in order to achieve desired business outcomes, a project is nothing more than an investment opportunity. It requires resources of various kinds to design and develop a product for internal use. This means that the project deliverable will not be directly converted into revenue from the sale of the resulting product, but its value will be seen in its contributions to the overall business effort of the organization.

In contrast, some projects will fall outside this definition. Service providers and suppliers, such as engineering firms or service companies that perform custom projects for external customers in exchange for a fee, will normally have revenue resulting from the project effort. This type of project effort may or may not have a dedicated investment evaluation or distinct selection process. However, it will more often undergo a sales review that considers capability and readiness (financial and otherwise) to perform work for an external paying customer.

I consider both approaches to be critical and fundamental in terms of creating business value. The prospect that interests me is how all this work is defined, with particular attention placed on how a return on investment will be achieved in each case.

A project makes business sense if the customer is willing to pay a price to offset all costs associated with the work effort, with a profit margin that is determined independently by the performing organization according to its size and position in the marketplace. From the perspective of these companies, project costs and profit margins will be recovered through the sale of the end-product to the customer for an established price. That price may be a standard and common cost if the project is conducted as a gated or "turnkey" operation, where costs, schedule, and resource utilization are known as a result of a repetitive work effort. A standard project will have a standard investment, and it will likely return a standard profit margin. However, if the project is based on variable fees or fees plus expenses incurred, as needed, then this usually indicates a customized project work effort; in this case a standard or common approach cannot reasonably be assigned, and a standard investment of cost, schedule, and resource utilization cannot be planned.

This approach, strictly speaking, does not necessarily specify that the project will produce any measurable value to the customer, although product functionality and capability will be known and emphasized. Rather, the performing organization usually maintains a short-term perspective and focus on the margin that will be produced by the project. This is because the performing organization depends on projects performed for customers to generate revenue that allows it to bear the costs of meeting the payroll for its employees, specialists, and vendors, in addition to meeting their various business obligations.

I maintain the idea that any organization approaches its investments encouraged by the prospect that some revenue will be obtained to compensate for the time and resources devoted to each project. Also, a portion of that revenue should represent compensation for the risks incurred and managed during project performance. The performing organization can agree to consider a project when management (i) recognizes it as a productive and profitable investment, (ii) shows that it fits into the business strategy, (iii) provides the financial funding and resource capability necessary to perform the project, and (iv) determines that investment funding does not conflict with other similar and more profitable investments.

# Investment Decision Factors

In the process of investment analysis, decision makers must take into account many factors that have varying degrees of influence on the investment outcome of the project. Several of these factors are considered below.

## *Project Cost Factors*

First, we must consider the economic aspects intrinsically related to each project, as represented by the various costs and revenues of each project. This can be done by preparing a project estimate that provides sufficient detail to consider both the anticipated revenues and expenses that will occur at various points in time as a means to assess the project outcome.

Typically, this approach is used to identify a more or less extensive series of cost values associated with the project schedule, which can be considered in terms of years, months, or any interim period that may be appropriate to planning effort. Often the project costs are represented according to financial quarters or semesters. It should be noted that the shorter the duration of the period considered, the more effort is required to accomplish more detailed planning. For a longer period, the planning exercise will be easier, but this may be difficult to control later. An ideal approach would be to seek a balance between the two levels of detail that allows us to prepare estimates with a certain ease and some certainty, as a means to provide planning, monitoring, and control of the plan without requiring an extraordinary or excessive planning effort. This will allow us to track the progress and outcomes of the project to ensure financial and economic factors are properly managed.

## *Project Duration Factors*

When establishing the number of periods to consider for project planning and subsequent monitoring and control, the period or duration of the project life cycle needs to be clearly distinguished. The duration of the project normally represents the period from inception to completion, and includes system implementation and delivery to the users.

It may be difficult to define when a project starts. So, we might consider a project starting any time between when you first identify the purpose of the project, or problem to be solved, and the formal launch of the project. However, for the purposes of project planning, the corresponding cost–benefit analysis will usually indicate the beginning of the project to be the moment when the project manager responsible for its management begins work. There may or may not be a formal kick-off meeting before or after this appointment.

Furthermore, completion of the project must be established as the time when the project deliverables are transferred to users and stakeholders in the customer's business environment. This is represented by actions of the users who have received, reviewed, and accepted the project deliverables, by closure of all open project issues to the satisfaction of stakeholders, by receipt of any required payments for services rendered and products produced, and, subsequently, by the project leader taking action to dissolve or otherwise reassign members of the project team.

## Cost–Benefit Accounting Factors

In the process of project financial planning, it will normally be seen that the project period just prior to project closure is a period when more intense investment expenditures could be required. At this point in time, expenses are still needed for resources and supplies, but full remuneration from the customer has not yet been achieved. However, in association with project closure, the performing organization will begin to receive payments and remuneration from the delivery and commissioning of the project results, and accounting for project expenses should be achieved at this time.

Some projects will not have a customer that pays for a particular work effort. These are often seen as internal projects that provide some form of efficiency or other business value in which a return on investment or business benefit is not immediately recognized. Therefore, in the analysis of costs and benefits for the project, we can add the anticipated period of realization of benefits, which will usually be a more extensive and prolonged period that follows after completion of the project.

In preparing this financial assessment, we must be particularly rigorous, responsible, and very aware that the data we develop will likely serve as a basis for subsequent decision making by management. For this reason, we must take full account of basic accounting principles and axioms in order to provide accurate numbers that can be used for precise decision making. Among the principles that I believe must be applied, the most important is the principle of prudence.

The precautionary principle asks us, in any accounting year, to apply a double rule as to the nature of accounting that is performed. In this way, costs, expenses, or adverse events to the detriment of the organization must register as soon as they are known, while revenues and favorable results are recorded only when realized. Naturally, the principle stated in this way is also applicable to the routine operations of most companies. Of course, a financial projection prepared for any project that cannot record any revenue or profits should not be done.

We must avoid triumphant feelings that lead to overestimates of the potential positive outcomes of the project and underestimates of the risks and costs necessary to achieve them. For this reason, we must maintain a responsible attitude, even to the point of pessimism, to make us reflect on all the economic projections of the project, including costs that are viewed as insignificant or unlikely to affect revenue and expenses at the time of planning.

## Project Risk Factors

When a project is first considered, the financial valuation of the project includes provisional figures that are prepared in anticipation of the project. However, the project itself will take place in an uncertain environment in which conditions will be subject to contingencies that are needed in response to a variety of circumstances. This may cause actual figures to fluctuate upward, downward, or in disparate ways, and that requires us to take certain precautions.

Every project has inevitable risks that must be duly considered in conjunction with financial planning of the project. Thus, for projects performed in a stable business environment, we should always give the risk condition a longer period of time and attention than we might normally consider. Similarly, for projects performed in an unstable business environment, the shorter the term in which risks have to be managed, the greater the assurance we will have in meeting the project valuation figures reflected in the planning.

## Project Benefit Factors

The project completion date should be considered as a crucial decision in the planning process. The most important reason for this, in my opinion, is that an appropriate project completion date can mean the difference between achieving all of the benefits that are needed to justify the investment, and not reaching the threshold of profitability or realization of benefits required by management based on the investment. In this sense, there is no fixed rule to determine the time needed for cost–benefit analyses on each project, but sufficient time is needed to accurately identify benefit and profitability.

Some project investments can be justified in a short period of time after the development and delivery of products to users and customers, the benefits of which are realized in renewed operational stability. This stability can be seen early following project completion, and it may last for considerable periods of time, even much longer than necessary to justify the investment required. Other project investments produce benefits that are obtained later in the course of subsequent product maintenance.

There are also opportunistic projects whose benefits are considerable in the first moments after launch, but disappear or are greatly reduced under changing market conditions. We can also find projects that offer initial high yields at first, but benefits then reduce gradually over long periods of time. In contrast, there are some project investments that initially produce small benefits, but which grow over time as the product is widely used within the organization.

## Technology Project Factors

Projects with significant implications based in technology will have applicability to Moore's Law, already mentioned at an earlier point in this work. This law specifies that the capabilities of the microprocessors incorporated into current computers are advancing at an accelerated rate to offer higher speeds at reduced costs. This behavior must be carefully taken into account when planning technology investments, otherwise we could end up with a plethora of computers that become obsolete before their acquisition becomes truly necessary. This accelerated obsolescence, based essentially on economics, but also on technological drivers, generally occurs on all computers that incorporate microprocessors, including servers and workstations, desktops and laptops, PDAs and Smartphone devices, routers and switches, and all types of control equipment. This factor should be taken into account when planning projects and related supplies, as a slight delay in the acquisition of equipment can allow more computing power at a better price.

To accomplish this cost–benefit analysis, we conduct an exercise to define the stage at which we plan to develop the product for subsequent use. In principle, we are free to define this as we want, assuming that conditions will remain unchanged based on our experience and available information. To that end, it is essential to properly document the assumptions made and the basis of our forecasts and, if necessary, reconsider such assumptions throughout the project.

## *Opportunity Cost Factors*

In the context of relatively scarce resources or, alternately in view of the abundance of investment opportunities for the same resources, when an organization chooses a destination for investment funds, other opportunities are automatically waived. So we must establish the means to examine the value and the potential yield of the chosen investment against the value and the potential yield of other available investments.

Opportunity costs can take different forms depending on the circumstances. First, if the project is an alternative to a financial investment, either by deposit-bearing accounts having a certain rate of return or by acquisition of assets such as bonds, debentures or other fixed financial assets, the opportunity cost can be determined with certainty because both investments are based on the distribution of financial value offered by each asset. In contrast, if the investment alternatives to the project are other projects, we will then determine opportunity costs based on the expected financial performance and associated cost-effectiveness of each alternative project that is under consideration.

In this environment, it is imperative to have a strict, systematic, and rigorous method to measure the expected financial return from selected projects based on a fair comparison among all possible investment opportunities. We must take care to avoid contamination of the process and its criteria with subjectivity that is likely to hamper the process. At the end of this process, a substantive assessment of the various projects will be placed in our portfolio, with corresponding objective metrics that allow us to compare each project with one another and against other possible investments that the company may be considering.

# Introduction to Return on Investment

Among the methods that can be applied to assessing investment projects is return on investment (ROI), which is particularly well suited in its flexibility for projects such as those involving the analysis, design, development, and implementation of information systems. ROI is a ratio calculated for a given project or investment that is obtained using a comparable measure of the expected profitability. This ratio is only a tool to provide guidance on calculating the expected performance of the project, and it does not replace the discretion of the manager who must make the relevant selection decision. ROI contributes to a more informed decision, and therefore one that has more objectivity and better quality.

ROI is a measure that should not be taken as a guarantee of performance. Rather, it is an indication of the results that can be achieved from successful project performance. It should be understood that the ratio, along with many of the values used in its calculation, is not an objective value obtained by actual measurements, but a subjective elaboration based on a number of assumptions for different parameters in the form of estimates and projections that define a future financial scenario. It has considerable subjectivity that reflects the business attitude and perspectives of the evaluator, where factors such as risk aversion and phobias can play a role.

To the extent that ROI is developed as a forecast of a future financial outcome, it is subject to certain conditions that could affect changes in the parameters used in calculating it. First, it may occur that some of the key parameters used to predict the future outcome end up with a different behavior than expected. This will impact the expected ROI values, and the project manager will likely have to recalculate ROI based on the new measured values and in light of new information.

A second possible cause of ROI deviation occurs when one of the parameters used in calculations is not considered key, either because its potential impact is deemed negligible or it was assumed to not influence the planning horizon of the project. The project outcome then shows an ROI that is different than expected, with that difference being due to the parameter that was minimized during ROI calculations. Nevertheless, the cause should be reviewed and managed to avoid this problem in the future. In this case, we should examine the assessment model as a whole, making note of how the parameters affected the accuracy of ROI calculations.

Finally, The ROI may be inaccurate because of simple errors made in calculating it, or in estimating values used in the calculation. In this case, we must simply correct any input errors made and recalculate the correct ROI value.

Despite the difficulties associated with ROI calculations, this approach is a great tool for supporting the decision-making process on projects and investments. It introduces a level of professional rigor into project management in a manner similar to that done for the selection of financial investments in the world of economic and financial management.

## ROI Concepts

ROI is a simple measure of the expected profit or loss result of a particular investment, which may take the form of returns, receipts, revenue, interest, or capital, and represents an increase or decrease in the assets of the investor. This metric is systematically used for making investment decisions based on predictive economic and financial indicators of value resulting from an investment's performance and behavior.

ROI enables a uniform framework for financial comparisons, such as:

■ Selection of financial investments of any kind
■ Selection of alternative investment projects
■ Comparison of financial results of companies and industries

ROI use requires the adoption of certain precautions to ensure the homogeneity of the data obtained. Among the precautions that can be taken into account, we should pay particular attention to the following:

■ We must determine how local and national tax laws will affect the investment project. In principle, if we are comparing investments or projects that will all be influenced by the same tax laws and rates of taxation, then the contrast should be negligible and the effect of taxation can generally be ignored, simplifying the ROI calculations. However, if the investments comparison involves different countries, different tax regimes, or different tax reporting timeframes, it then becomes desirable to provide tax details in the ROI calculations. Otherwise, any subsequent decisions made could be suboptimal when the effects of different tax structures are not properly accounted for.
■ We should take into account the various macroeconomic variables that influence the financial outcomes of investments. Among the most obvious of these variables may be the rate of inflation. The inflation rate represents the rate at which money depreciates in the territory, country, or region where you are or where the funds of the company are located. It is the extent to which prices rise and fall as an indicator of the purchasing power in a given geographical area. This value is important when considering investments. Any revenue received from the investment that is lower than this rate represents a loss of value. When using ROI calculations to predict the ROI, we should make an effort to find the most profitable investments that ensure at least a minimal return in the value of investment performance.
■ The interest rate is another macroeconomic variable that influences financial investment outcomes and warrants consideration. Interest rates represent the compensation that you can get for the money if deposited in a financial institution without taking risks or making investments with uncertain outcomes. Since an investment project will always be associated with some level of risk,

however small, the outcome should still produce financial results that are greater than those achieved through mere financial deposits. Interest rates can also affect project investments in terms of paying back any monies borrowed or financial considerations given to perform the project. In particular, interest rates will fluctuate over time, so the interest rates applicable to the payback period need to be predicted and applied to calculations with some level of accuracy.

## Calculating the ROI

ROI is an original ratio of the financial world often used to measure and determine the financial benefits that will be realized from investments. When ROI is calculated for multiple potential investment opportunities, it allows those opportunities to be compared and contrasted as a means to select the opportunity that provides the greatest return on investment.

In essence, the ROI calculation compares the net return on investment for the project against the investment required for performing that project. This reduces the overall financial yield obtained in a manner that represents the profit on each dollar invested. In this process of reduction of investment performance, some precautions that have been mentioned earlier should be taken, and they will be repeated in our discussion on ROI calculations as points of emphasis.

The effects of inflation should be included in ROI calculations relative to the devaluation of income over time; between two equal investments, it will always be preferable to select the one whose yields are obtained earlier. For example, consider the opportunity to invest in two projects, each of which requires allocating the same amount of $400,000 to provide a return of $425,000. In these circumstances, we may not think about the timing or the effect of inflation. We might therefore be indifferent as to whether we should invest in one or the other as they both produce the same yield. However, if the first investment produces the result in 12 months, but the second requires 3 years to accomplish the same result, you will not need any special financial training to recognize that obtaining $25,000 in 1 year is a better deal than $25,000 in 3 years. In an inflationary market situation, with steady increases in the price of goods and services, we can buy more products and services with $25,000 in our investment account this year than we can next year.

ROI calculations should reflect consideration of investment risks. As risks increase, this incurs increased investments that should be compensated to offset the risks taken by the investor. This factor is very important and should be carefully documented. In some circumstances, risks may prompt a refusal to invest in certain projects and investments that exceed the investor's risk tolerance. This can occur despite expectations of extraordinary yields and brilliant performance when the investor believes that the risks of the investment outweigh the financial investment that the investor is willing to bear. The use of weighting in ROI calculations will systematically compare investments, considering various kinds and levels of risk.

Similarly, the opportunity cost of the project or investment should be examined. In this respect, it is important to compare the expected returns on investments from other projects under consideration, and take into account the interest rates that will affect those returns. We can always consider what could be achieved if we select none of the projects under consideration and just place the money in an interest-bearing bank account, or if we buy financial assets of equivalent value, without risk of any kind. Thus, any investment project that aims to increase the overall return on investment for the organization should offer a better opportunity cost than other potential investments, and to an extent that offsets the associated investment risk.

To calculate ROI, we can consider several formulas of increasing complexity. In the simplest case, we have a formula in the form of a percentage that relates the investment required and the results as follows:

$$\text{ROI} = 100 \times \frac{\text{Benefits obtained}}{\text{Capital invested}}$$

Another possible expression of ROI can be used when benefits cannot clearly be enumerated, and we can use an arithmetic expression with the following basic formula:

$$\text{ROI}_{\text{Arit}} = \frac{\text{Value}_{\text{final}} - \text{Value}_{\text{initial}}}{\text{Value}_{\text{initial}}} = \frac{\text{Value}_{\text{final}}}{\text{Value}_{\text{initial}}} - 1$$

These formulas and expressions are used with other financial ratios such as net present value (NPV) to calculate the respective values used as input data in the above formulas. In general, NPV can be calculated for the respective "Value" variables and inserted into the equation.

NPV is a standard term that represents a calculation of the present value of an investment adjusted according to the expected future cash flows associated with the investment or project. The method is somewhat simple and represents discounting the present value by applying a suitable correction rate for all future cash flows of the investment or project. The value obtained by this formula is the project's net present value, that is, the benefit we hope to achieve from the investment. The advantage of this procedure is that it provides a corrected value that takes into account the value of money at different points in time in the project; it considers the different yields, and the effect of inflation, at the moment in time that returns are obtained.

The formula that allows us to obtain the NPV is

$$\text{NPV} = \sum_{\text{period}=1}^{n} \frac{\text{Value}_{\text{period}}}{(1+k)^{\text{period}}} - \text{Initial\_Investment}$$

In this formula, $k$ represents the rate of correction. This is generally the inflation rate, provided for each period in the duration of the investment or project. It may also include a correction factor related to the opportunity cost. Thus, for a risk-free project, we could include the inflation rate based on a fixed income, so that the NPV obtained is positive if the investment has performed better than expected. Otherwise, we can add a coefficient representing the opportunity cost.

The resulting NPV value can be interpreted according to the following general guidelines:

- When the NPV is a positive value or >0, the investment will produce results above the required return, and the decision to take on the project is deemed reasonable because the project will produce value for the company.
- When the NPV is a negative value or <0, the investment will produce results that do not achieve the required return, and the more reasonable decision is to not take on such a project because it would create reduced value for the company, where the investment is greater than the return.
- When the NPV is 0, the investment will produce no gain or loss with respect to the required return, and therefore does not add a monetary value that is any greater than depositing the funds in other reduced-risk, interest-bearing investments.

Usually the investment alternative with the highest NPV is the one that offers a more favorable outcome in economic terms for the organization. However, this does not mean it is always chosen, because in many cases business organizations decide to follow a different course of action. In some instances, organizations will consider criteria other than return on investment. While obtaining a return on investment and showing profit from investments is highly desirable, there may be reasons other than financial for conducting investment projects. In particular, there may be interest in obtaining other business benefits such as market position, increased production capacity, improved image, increased responsiveness to customers, and reduced time for the delivery of goods or services. These are reasons that can contribute to improved business outcomes in the future, but they do not represent the certainty of revenue generation at this time.

When the NPV takes on a value equal to 0, then the variable $k$ is renamed *IRR*, which is the internal rate of return. IRR represents the return that we are providing by conducting the project or investment under consideration. The IRR value is used to determine acceptance or rejection of a proposed investment project. The decision process involves comparing the IRR value with a minimum rate or shear rate, the opportunity cost of investment set by the corporation to accept the risks inherent to their business. If the calculation of IRR exceeds the minimum rate, the investment project is accepted; otherwise the opportunity is rejected.

In this context, the general guidelines for using IRR calculations in decision making should be as follows:

- If IRR is greater than or equal to the required minimum return or opportunity cost, the project should be accepted because it represents a potential opportunity to improve business outcomes.
- If IRR is less than the minimum return or opportunity cost, the project should be rejected because it does not reach the level of profitability that can be obtained without assuming any risk.

When using IRR in investment decisions for project selection, certain considerations need to be taken into account, as discussed below.

Using IRR as a criterion for acceptance or rejection of investments must take into account the nature of the investment. The general approach outlined above is only true if the project represents such an investment. The dynamics of the project might be such that at the beginning there are negative cash flows, representing costs incurred or payments, but then positive cash flows, which represent revenues, profits, or income of any kind as result of materialization of benefits, derived from project, as business improvements. If, however, the opposite occurs, with positive cash flow at first followed by negative cash flow, then we should consider the guidelines in reverse and the decision to accept or reject the investment or the project should apply exactly the reverse.

IRR can also be used to compare mutually exclusive projects. The preferred investment option will present a higher IRR, provided that the projects have an identical risk level, the same duration, and require the same initial investment. If these considerations are different, a deeper analysis will be required to take into consideration the circumstances.

IRR also has its limitations, one of which is found in the appraisal of "special projects" in which there is a problem of inconsistency in IRR due to mathematical sign changes associated with cash flows. This occurs when the project requires an input of funds at different times during the life cycle to meet specific needs, while at other periods in the life cycle it offers returns. In this situation, the project will be represented by multiple IRR values according to the number of mathematical sign changes that occur in the cash flow. This complicates the decision on acceptance or rejection of the investment and requires the use of more complex formulas that include IRR calculations that are corrected or adjusted to resolve this problem.

# Chapter 20

# Project Analysis and the Business Case

When we decided to use return on investment (ROI) and other financial ratios examined in the previous chapter to analyze and select investment projects in our organization, we integrated purely economic criteria and reasoning that corporate management knows and commonly uses in their work. We can now also express projects in terms of business and in a language that is closer to how management thinks. We do this as a means to facilitate understanding and to allow us to antici-pate conclusions and reasoning coming from management to justify the decisions.

To use this language of management, we may have to use indexes such as ROI, net present value (NPV), and internal rate of return (IRR). This should not repre-sent a great difficulty for most, as we can perform the necessary calculations using a simple financial calculator or electronic spreadsheet. Some devices may have these specific functions incorporated. However, beyond the use of financial calculations, we must have basic information that enables us to perform the necessary delibera-tions for project selection. To do this, we will require an orderly process of reflection, as suggested in the content below.

## Concepts Applied to Project Planning

The first step is to define the investment horizon; in this case, we will use the time-frame of the project life cycle. Consideration of this horizon expands our vision from the usual perspective on project planning. Typically, when a project manager is planning the project, consideration will be made relative to the project's timeframe, which ends at the time of delivery of project outputs and their implementation. However, this does not normally take into account what happens after that time. In particular, it does not take into account the realization and management of resulting benefits for consideration by project managers.

As result, the benefits to be provided by the project deliverables and how to achieve them will likely be vague and not exceed a few lines in the project planning document, perhaps briefly in the introduction to the project. However, it is difficult to find the justification of need and the desirability of undertaking a project that is described in generic and superficial ways, without providing any objective insight into the benefits to be achieved.

In technology projects, as a general rule, the benefits will start to appear after implementation of the information system and completion of the project. As a result, as the planning of projects is limited to the time frame of the project itself, the project plans do not include the measure of value, benefits, or results obtained from the implementation of the project deliverable. Therefore, benefits such as recovery of the investment are not readily apparent.

Once the overall project time frame is defined, we then proceed to divide the total time into periods of control, which may be annual, monthly, or another time-frame that is best suited to the nature and constraints of the project. On this calendar, we will define the points in time when we will measure the financial status of the project, either in the form of added revenue or in the form of savings achieved by the project. The associated procedure will reflect the checklists to be used, the measurements to be taken, the expected values, and the individual responsible for carrying out such controls.

The project budget will also be defined to include an estimate of the projected costs and expected monetary returns resulting from each project period. This information will be presented in terms of cash flows, with positive values for revenues, income, and profits, and negative values for costs incurred, outgoing payments and expenses, and losses.

We must then estimate the value of benefits that we expect to acquire in each of the calendar periods. This includes using variables that define the investment environment, such as interest rates and macroeconomic variables (e.g., inflation). This information is routinely published, and can be obtained from institutions such as central banks, finance departments, local and national governments, and international organizations. These variables and a reliable estimate are essential for performing a comparison between different investment alternatives.

Once we have supporting information from the various sources, we are ready to perform the necessary calculations of the various ratios to justify the value of the investment project. In preparing our justification, we must explain how we have calculated the different indicators, the information sources used, and the basis of our assumptions. We should also present the costs and revenues that we have associated with the project for each of the periods, and explain the reasons why we believe that such estimates will materialize and evolve as predicted.

# The Cost–Benefit Analysis

We can find a multitude of methods to accomplish the difficult process of project evaluation and selection. Each has its own characteristics and constraints. The most basic approach is a technical analysis of investments and projects, and its application is widespread in financial and economic environments where the main consideration is the economic return on investment. This procedure involves the application of financial criteria to assess the economic performance of the investment projects considered to be the most profitable, which are expected to achieve the greatest possible returns using available capital.

Among the tools and approaches that have been designed to overcome the limitations of technical analysis, which was useful and necessary but insufficient to capture the complexity of the current business environment, is the cost–benefit analysis for investment projects. This approach is used to formulate and evaluate projects with consideration of the costs and benefits that the project represents. The intention remains that the benefits or returns that the project provides to the organization will exceed the costs it must bear to conduct the project. The difference from a technical analysis is that it not only considers the cash flows and monetary concepts, but also includes consideration of social and environmental factors arising directly or indirectly from the project.

The cost–benefit analysis is a systematic tool that is used to study, analyze, evaluate, and compare projects, and it provides no value to investment cases in respect of technical analyses. Rather, it considers costs and benefits based on the project plan, allowing us to quantify and assign value to both monetary aspects of the project and to other areas such as social or environmental implications, whether arising directly or indirectly from the project.

For comparison purposes, cost–benefit analyses can still use analytical methods such as IRR, NPV, or cost-efficiency, but those calculations include some values that represent the impact of externalities. As such, they tend to improve the quality of decisions, because they consider the global effects and not just short-term perspectives restricted to domestic or in-company inputs and outputs. Thus, the essential difference between cost–benefit and technical analyses procedures used in the majority of companies and organizations for the analysis of investments and associated decision making lies in the emphasis placed to expand the field of research and analysis to social and environmental surroundings. This enables an understanding of the project's impact on the whole, as it provides an exercise in corporate social responsibility and commitment to sustainability of the society and its economic activity.

# The Business Case

When the cost–benefit analysis is systematized and acquires a strategic dimension, the result is included in a document commonly known as a business case. To build a business case requires meticulous investigation and research relative to the environment in which we will plan and conduct the project under consideration. Several recommended steps for developing the business case are discussed below.

## *Define the Project Objectives*

The first step should always be to identify and understand the effects that the project will have on the business environment. Each project represents the implementation of a change in the form of new or adjusted processes or procedures that will be introduced into the work environment. This change usually takes place within the organization that promotes it, but very often there are effects and consequences that will influence change beyond organizational boundaries, perhaps to affect the environment and society in general. To understand the effects that the project may present in the business environment, we need to understand the essence of the project. Therefore, we need to define the project objectives clearly and precisely, in terms of business, and in relation to the general conditions of the marketplace.

Thus, the objective of a project that would offer to customers the ability to register their orders, knowing the status of their shipments, and receive electronic invoices cannot be stated simply as "To build and set up a commercial system to facilitate customer self-service." Without going into the greater complexities of the project, a more appropriate statement of the project would be, "Implementing a business solution that reduces intermediate commercial transactions and allows customers self-service to improve customer satisfaction."

The first statement is technically oriented, and is typically made by the information systems staff as the objective to be reached with the simple implementation of some type of system for customer use without specifying any additional required action, other than further technical support after the completion and implementation of the information system. Moreover, the statement is conditioning the approach to be used, which limits the range of possible solutions explored and may make it harder to consider higher performance solutions.

In contrast, the second statement has more focus on the essentials and features, and includes the need to achieve improved customer satisfaction as an objective. It also offers the features of self-service and reduced dependence on the intermediate involvement of sales representatives of the company as a means to achieve improved customer satisfaction. This statement could also be adjusted to offer additional advantages in terms of reduced time for implementation, a smaller financial investment, and greater flexibility in defining the solution.

Moreover, with the second statement there are some other sources of competitive advantage that can be achieved:

- A reduction in intermediate commercial transactions facilitates extending the market, because we can now receive orders from customers who have not been visited by our sales representatives, and are possibly not known to them. This expands the possibility of reaching and adding new and different customers to our sales network that we could not previously reach due to physical constraints, distance, trade routes, and other factors that pose an impediment to business growth.
- A reduced dependence on sales staff, combined with self-service features, opens the possibility for sales representatives to redirect customers to these tools, and reconsider their work focus.
- The sales department can be restructured for greater efficiency and effectiveness. Such restructuring may take place in several ways, which depend on market conditions, the nature of products and services, and the overall business strategy. Among them, we may find, for example, a strategy to reduce costs by serving customers who are reluctant to use new tools. We could also adopt another strategy for the segmentation of customers according to their particular product or service interests, their purchasing history, their qualification for personalized service, and their potential for an ongoing business relationship in the future.
- The availability of self-service facilities invites customers to perform the business operations needed, when and where they are needed. This provides a permanent link with the customer, which can facilitate the realization of future purchases and contribute to the expansion of potential presence in national and international markets.
- The realization of other benefits such as the elimination of transcription errors from the efforts of sales representatives, the opportunity to enrich the communications and business relationship with each customer as a means to respond to any adverse circumstances that may occur in the market or in the marketplace, the facilitation of correcting customer orders, to include the selection of another product or reduction in quantity, and the capability of the system to offer suggestions regarding alternative and complementary products that can trigger the customer's needs and interests.

In this way, the statement of the objectives of the project should be reviewed to ensure that it is the best expression of the intended purpose of the project, and to ensure that it maintains a strategic perspective that is conveniently formulated to offer the greatest value, considering the market conditions and alignment with the overall strategic business plan. The statement will adequately convey the need for the features and functions to be included in the project effort, defining what can and what cannot be done to meet the target.

## Evaluate and Select the Appropriate Solution

The next step in the process of defining the business case is the definition of the actions needed to achieve the project's objectives. In this step, a repertoire of alternative solutions that can produce the desired outcome are identified and evaluated to choose the most appropriate solution. Each proposed alternative solution must be studied and analyzed from a strategic perspective, taking into account the overall positioning of the organization, the effects of competition, the impact on customer demand, and the verification of how each project contributes to strengthening the corporate business model.

From this generation of alternatives, we will be able to define the course of action, which is then aligned with the corporate business strategy. To achieve this, we must consider both the internal and external environments of the organization, and take into account the interactions between new projects and other operations under way. This is done because external factors can override and change the expected benefits of many projects, and seemingly inconsequential projects can be affected by interactions with existing operations or by rigorous competition for market leadership position by the organization.

The end result of this step is the selection of a viable project that shows potential for producing the desired benefits and financial returns needed to sustain the business.

## Define Stakeholder Communication

The next step in preparing the business case is to summarize the project so that its dimensions are presented in a clear and concise manner. This summary should include aspects scope, cost and budget, time and duration, required resources, and outputs expected. The summary should also specify the milestones that will help to define project progress, as well as the advantages and benefits to be achieved by the project.

The systematic collection of this information will be very useful in defining the different groups of stakeholders that will be affected by the project outcomes, and methods for communicating with project stakeholders should be included. In this process, a communication strategy should be defined to explain the project, its objectives, and consequences to all stakeholders. We will then have a comprehensive plan that identifies the various stakeholders in the project, along with the relevant information and detailed project actions that should be communicated to each stakeholder group. It should indicate the types of information, in terms of content and format, that should be provided to each stakeholder group, the means and frequency with which information is distributed, and who is responsible for such stakeholder communication activities.

When considering the different stakeholder groups, messages to be delivered should be prepared in a tone, style, and format of communication to achieve the greatest effectiveness, considering the roles and the demographic characteristics of individuals that will receive them.

## *Compile Project Guidance Documents*

The next step in the process is to compile the planning and guidance documents needed to carry out the project as a whole. This will include integrating both the project work plan that will guide the development of key project products, and actions arising from other project support plans.

Project support plans will generally consist of the communication plan used for internal and external communications, the change management plan used to control scope changes, the quality management plan used to manage product testing and acceptance among users of the product, and the risk management plan used to control potential adverse impacts on the project. The project management plan will also be included to address the implications, dependencies, and interactions with other projects, actions, and processes currently under way within the organization. It will contribute to identifying conditions that may help or hinder the progress of the current project.

Although normally accomplished by the project charter, the business case can include that charter or otherwise be used to delegate the necessary project management authority to the project manager or team leader. This authority includes specifying responsibilities for organizing and managing project resources, managing the project work effort, and overseeing the project budget and expenditures, all as a means to achieve the expected project results on schedule.

## *Incorporate the Financial Analysis*

Finally, the business case should provide reliable information to evaluate the expected investment and profitability for the project under consideration. To this end, the project budget should account for each action by every resource that will participate and each material or supply consumption that will take place. Likewise, it should assess the benefits of the resulting products for the life of each product.

This step essentially provides for the inclusion of budgetary considerations and any financial analyses performed on the project. The cost–benefit analysis discussed earlier in this chapter is a prominent analysis found in many business cases. Other types of financial analyses can also be included, usually as dictated by senior management within the organization.

### *Closing Comments on Preparing the Business Case*

The business case provides an advantage over other approaches in that we have a rich source of project information based on all of the considerations previously made and documented. This allows us to reach a higher level of certainty, both in the determination of costs to be expended and potential revenue, when evaluating each project for selection.

In short, the business case provides a comprehensive view of the different components and perspectives that play a role in the project. It gathers and contains all relevant project information in an integrated document that offers insights that can be shared across the entire organization. The result is a document that records all information concerning the project, from its genesis onward. It serves as a basis for making project selection decisions, and it provides a means to document those decisions.

## Tracking Business Interests

To maximize the usefulness of the business case, it must include consideration of project plans, and particularly the project work plan that provides a breakdown of details for each phase, activity, task, and other work element iteration of the project. This consideration includes an examination of cost, schedule, and resource utilization, as well as the products to be delivered by the work effort. Each work element has an intrinsic value in itself, independent of the rest of the project, so each adds a certain value, regardless of whether the product is discontinued after delivery, or if the project is not completed as planned.

Thus, if circumstances change dramatically and the project ceases to be justified by the expected results or by the costs involved, the project could be placed on hold or otherwise terminated. To avoid a total loss of all that has been invested thus far, it is possible to obtain value from interim deliverables and work activities that have already been completed. These products or their associated value can be used (or reused) in other projects or investments that monetize the efforts and resources invested to date. For this reason, the business case and relevant analyses should consider financial outcomes if the project does not reach the final and completed stage as planned.

Project progress, along with pertinent business interests, can be monitored and controlled using a series of project checkpoints located at strategic points in the project life cycle. The configuration of these points of control should enable a review of the project to determine if it is still representing the financial expectations presented in the business case. The project reviews associated with these checkpoints will also contribute to management-level decisions regarding project continuation, project hold, or project termination.

Of course, any interruption or early termination of the project necessarily represents the sacrifice of certain benefits and financial returns that were expected outcomes from project performance, as presented in the business case. Sometimes, project reviews will indicate that the benefits and financial returns identified in the original business case can no longer be achieved, which leads to two options for going forward. On the one hand, the project can be put on hold while project plans are revised and a new cost–benefit analysis is created to determine if the project can still continue to completion. This represents the development of a revised business case. On the other hand, it may be determined that the project cannot be sufficiently fixed, and a termination decision is made as a means to retain any benefits or financial returns that have already been achieved and to avoid any further investment losses.

# Chapter 21

# Project Classifications in the Business Environment

Adopting a strategic perspective in project management requires choosing the right evaluation and control approach for each type of project. This cannot be done without understanding each project in a thorough and transparent manner. The simple recognition that a single approach with universally valid criteria does not exist is a significant indicator of the fact that different projects may require different approaches according to each project's nature and purpose, among other variables that may be considered. Whatever approach is used, whether a single criterion or several, we should be able to classify projects in a consistent manner. This classification would clearly associate projects with their defining characteristics.

We can learn from Heraclitus, an ancient Greek philosopher who conveyed his philosophical thoughts that one could not bathe twice in the same river because the river was constantly flowing and changing (i.e., it was the same river, but not the same water). Similarly, no project has been done before. No matter how many information systems have been built, no matter how many times we have implemented Enterprise Resources Planning (ERP), client relationship management (CRM), or other system solutions in our current companies or in our affiliations with other organizations, and no matter how many projects we have conducted, each one is a new and independent effort. Our "background baggage" serves only to give us the experience and lessons we have learned; otherwise, we are always facing a new and distinctly different project that will require all of our attention, use of our creativity, and a complete understanding of the unique conditions and requirements for project success. Each new project must be defined and classified on its own merits.

Classifications are conceptual definitions that aim to simplify the analysis of projects based on the relevance deduced from the repetition of similar projects over time. They provide generic guidance to supplement the professional opinions of those responsible for project management by specifying a series of standard categories and typologies that can be used to describe each project.

## An Approach to Classifying Different Types of Projects

There are many existing taxonomies or classifications that could be used to define the different types of projects that might be encountered. Each meets a specific purpose that is justified by the needs of the organization. The development of taxonomy requires in-depth knowledge about the subject of classification. However, it is not enough to simply have conceptual knowledge; it also requires extensive experience that enables key aspects of classification to be defined for each case and situation, over a significant number of separate experiences. In our case, it would be desirable to have been involved in a meaningful way in a large variety of projects as a basis for participating in the development of project classificiations used by the organization.

In general, we need to apply elaborate and rigorous procedures to define a project classification scheme that can be tested and used under actual conditions, and that can provide an accurate association of project type for all projects that are encountered in the organization. The classification scheme should be sufficiently defined to allow multiple individuals to arrive at the same classification for the same project.

In my experience in project management, where few things are unchangeable and constant, the time constraints are sometimes extraordinary and leave little time for sufficient reflection. To that end, I believe that the best classification is one that is based on attributes that consider first-sight observation of project characteristics, without having to apply any sophisticated procedures. This should provide reasonable assurance and a high probability that the classification will remain unchanged over time thanks to its simplicity.

Thus, I propose to use a classification system based on two project parameters that should be quite obvious and well-defined before starting the project:

- *Nature of the project.* This parameter represents the type of work effort that will be performed, and is the main orientation of the project. It can be ascertained according to the type of products that are expected to result from the project.

- *Payback period of the project.* This parameter represents the point in time at which payback on the investment is achieved. In my opinion, this consideration of the project's full life cycle is of paramount importance, and perhaps even more important than the estimated time for implementation. Implementation will always be subject to greater uncertainty because of changes in scope, work delays and incidents, and even the impacts of management decisions that can speed up, slow down, or stop a project. In contrast, the payback period is a criterion imposed by the general business strategy of the organization, and will be less variable and more important to management's interests.

A system of project classification is based on these two parameters, which can be combined as two axes of a plane to define up to four types of projects that could be encountered in an organization and managed according to the guidance associated with the resulting classification.

## Classification Based on the Nature of the Project

The first parameter deals with the nature of the project under consideration. The term *nature* may be confusing as it is fairly generic and not very strict, but it is quite intuitive if we clarify that we are refering to the nature of the products delivered by the project. From this fundamental consideration, we will examine three factors or characteristics that are essential to understanding how the nature of projects can be represented in today's business environment.

- *Commitment.* For an action or activity to be considered as a project, a commitment should exist between two parties: (i) the customer, understood to be a person, unit, or organization who provides funding needed to finance the project, and who receives the products resulting from the project, and (ii) the supplier, understood to be the person, team, or company who is the specialist performing the efforts and activities to generate the product resulting from the project. These roles of customer and supplier may be exercised by two independent companies or organizations, by two departments within the same organization, by two persons of the same department, or by a number of parties that participate in each of these two roles.

  This commitment can be substantiated under a formal contract, in an internal document such as a work specification that is agreed between departments of the same company, or by a simple verbal agreement between two interested parties. The method used is irrelevant; what matters is that this commitment has a content that is known and shared between the parties, and it should be crystal clear that it must be fulfilled by the supplier to meet the expectations of the customer based on some remuneration.

- *Product.* This term refers, in this context, to the object of the transaction or the outcome of the project. Products are simply deliverables produced and transmitted as a result of the project effort from the supplier to the customer. Products do not necessarily have to take a physical form and material substance; rather, a product, as is commonly understood, is the result of production of the project.

Such objects or project deliverables can be physical or logical, or simply services rendered. They include outputs such as the deliverables of projects in the following examples:

- A new network and communications infrastructure of the organization (including cabling, routers, switches and all components necessary for effective operations, along with appropriate documentation and services).
- A new business management system, perhaps based on an ERP model that is suitably adapted, configured, and customized. This may include the development of small satellite applications that meet certain features not adequately covered by the original system, and the associated infrastructure of servers and desktop computers necessary for its operation.
- The expansion of the storage file server that enables the business unit to support the growing needs of corporate document management.
- The provision for a batch of equipment for 40 new positions consisting of a desktop PC, a TFT 14″ screen, and the usual peripheral components for human–computer interaction (i.e., mouse and keyboard).
- The provision for a new version of the corporate database used to manage the company's transactional information.
- Training for 25 current users and several newly hired users of the new version of an office productivity suite.

■ *Restrictions*. Once the products to be produced by the project are known, product restrictions need to be identified. Restrictions serve in a sense as modifiers, and define the conditions under which products should be delivered to the customer for acceptance and use. Products that do not comply with restrictions will likely be rejected by the customer. Under no circumstances are restrictions implied to be an accessory or secondary consideration to the project scope. On the contrary, they are an essential part of the project definition and as such must be properly managed.

To that end, product restrictions can be critical in the success or failure of an organization, or at least some of the initiatives that are undertaken, based on such considerations as

- The time that the organization can dispose of these products
- The range of products supplied to enable users to have the full functionality as required, or as expected, considering possible requirements to maintain operational parts of the legacy systems that are being updated or replaced
- The system being available around-the-clock, 7 days a week, to support online transactions, allowing for normal maintenance without interrupting the service

– Other conditions that can appear, to a greater or lesser extent, in the customer side as requirements to obtaining the benefits sought by the project launch.

In this context, and after defining the project with a sufficient level of detail, we can ascertain the nature of projects according to their characteristics as one of two types:

■ *Hardware projects.* Projects of this nature are focused mainly on hardware, which could be defined by delivery of a global system, or by delivery of products such as components or materials that have material and physical substance and do not require a significant level of customization. Projects of this nature are aimed at providing equipment, computers, electronics, and materials. This may include the provision of software and associated installation services, but the primary focus is associated with the delivery of the material elements.

■ *Application software projects.* Projects of this nature are defined by the delivery of services related to knowledge and the application of knowledge to the problem solving that is to be achieved by the project. Projects of this nature are focused on consulting and the analysis, design, construction, and implementation of information systems. The product generated may be based on creating software or on re-engineering the internal organization for efficient use of developed software. Application software projects may also include physical components, but not as a primary feature of the project effort.

It may be difficult at times to find projects that have pure characteristics of either nature, so separation into one group or another could result from a subtle difference that becomes more evident with practice. Making a distinction of information system projects based on nature is like trying to compartmentalize categories that are based along a continuum. Characteristics of both are likely to be found to some extent on both types of projects.

## Classification Based on the Payback Period of the Project

The second parameter deals with the payback period of the project under consideration. This axis of project classification represents the time period in which the results expected from the project will be obtained. This time period is the life cycle of the project.

As a matter of convenience, we will consider two possible characteristics to distinguish this classification—short and long. Despite the apparent simplicity of this parameter, the condition of short or long is not easy or trivial, and it must be defined in a way that is consistent with the business practices of the organization.

One approach might be a condition that extends the project duration for several years. However, this approach would likely be affected by considerations from other areas such as accounting and tax, where a standardized and normalized process is used for the amortization of products or materials used in the given timeframe. This is based on financial results rather than any strategic time period, where we have interests before the accountable depreciation period.

Another approach might be to consider the useful life of any product resulting from the project. Ideally, this would be considered for primary products. But this approach would likely encounter technical conditions that subject it to considerable variations, because each product will have a different estimated useful life according to manufacturers' criteria, and according to the maintenance to keep it operational.

Moreover, when products do not have physical attributes, such as software, databases, operating systems, and related tools, it becomes difficult to ascertain product life. Should we consider product life for the period of its installation on designated hardware? Does product life extend only until to the release of the next version? Or, as might occur with self-produced, customized software, does product life extend indefinitely? I personally think that all these considerations are inadequate, and we must find another approach to the issue that provides satisfactory answers to all these questions.

However, despite the variety of choices available, what we are really seeking within the specified time period of the project is what benefits are being generated by the products of the project. We defined the project to provide products that simplify processes and otherwise add business value, and this is often quite different from the technical perspective usually provided by suppliers, manufacturers, and distributors of the products. We need to identify those benefits.

The assessment of benefits can be very difficult to accomplish from a technical perspective, so strategic and business models and considerations will often come into play. These considerations sometimes exceed the capacity of the specialists and decision makers associated with information systems development, who are generally focused on the production and delivery of the product, but will be unable to estimate its subsequent useful life. Therefore, to obtain this information we should examine the project's business case. This document will offer important business insights and guidance that should be applied in conjunction with project management practices.

In the absence of prescribed organizational guidance, we can use the following as guidelines for classifying projects as short or long:

- *Short-term projects.* We can classify the general orientation of a project as short-term when the realization of expected benefits takes place in a period of time that is <3 years. This term is obviously arbitrary and can be varied upward or downward, but it is a period of time in which the degree of certainty for achieving the anticipated benefits is reasonable and the risks and uncertainty that threaten them are manageable.

It should be noted that these benefits and advantages are obtained primarily from the products and services delivered by the project under consideration, without the use of additional actions or projects that may be conducted to exploit the conditions and benefits created by this project. When this happens, the new and additional benefits are not considered among the benefits of the current project.

■ *Long-term projects.* We can classify the general orientation of a project as long-term when the realization of expected benefits is a period of 3 years or longer. Once again, this term can be adjusted according to the business needs and interests of the organization. As result, the level of certainty about such benefits and advantages will be significantly influenced by the time that has elapsed between its estimate and actual implementation, which will mean the possibility of incurring additional risk associated with the larger time span.

■ Moreover, long-term projects will have characteristics that in many cases enable the organization to launch other related projects that take advantage of or amplify the effects of conditions created by the first, longer-term project to give the organization extended benefits and advantages. In many cases, the original project's business case will reference the potential impact of these other pending projects as a means to appropriately recognize the contributions made possible by the longer-term project for the achievement of benefits from subsequent projects.

## The Four Types of Consequential Projects

With reference to the two dimensions defined as characteristics used for project classification, we can depict a relationship in which one axis corresponds to the nature of the project and the other represents the payback period for the realization of benefits. The intersection of these dimensions produces a four-quadrant diagram that represents four project classifications that can be used to delineate the types of projects that will be performed within the organization. This diagram is presented in Figure 21.1.

This diagram can be interpreted in a relatively simple manner. First, along one axis, projects related to the supply of hardware and tools, along with any database software or material items that do not require a significant customization effort, can be divided into the following two classifications:

■ *Equipment projects.* In these, the payback period of investment does not exceed the boundary defined as short term, for example 3 years, and this return is produced by the realization of expected project benefits, without the intervention of additional projects.

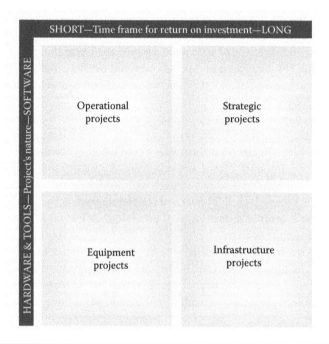

**Figure 21.1   Project types.**

■ *Infrastructure projects,* In these, the period of payback is longer than the specified short term, and the return is produced by the combination of the expected
project benefits along with any benefits provided by additional projects
aligned with the original project.

Along the other axis, projects oriented to the implementation of software and
changes in key components for solving business problems can be divided into two
classifications according to the time required for the return of investment:

■ *Operational projects.* In these, the payback period of investment does not
exceed the threshold for short-term projects, and is produced by the realization of the benefits that its introduction will bring to improved operations.
■ *Strategic projects.* Here, the payback period of investment falls within the
threshold for long-term projects, and it is produced by the combination of the
realization of the benefits directly related to the implementation of the project
and through the benefits provided by other projects that produce benefits
made possible by the original project.

These classifications are described in greater detail in the following subsections.

## Equipment Projects

Equipment projects are projects that will primarily provide physical facilities and materials intended to improve the work efficiency of equipment users in the organization. Equipment projects might typically involve the acquisition and deployment of a defined number of new PCs that are faster or have superior performance to the current computer inventory. This is done to improve user effectiveness through the introduction of improved equipment performance. This could include such improvements as the introduction of barcode readers, the acquisition and implementation of user licenses for new versions of office software, and the acquisition of new TFT 19″ screens to replace old CRT 15″ screens. In general, any project for which the main deliverable is a physical component (i.e., physical property) that provides value directly to users and increases their work contributions will result in the recovery of the investment in the short term (according to the suggested examples above, a period of 3 years).

Equipment projects tend to have high visibility within the organization and, in general, tend to be easily understood because of their immediate and observable effects on the working conditions of affected user groups, who usually welcome such improvements.

## Infrastructure Projects

Infrastructure projects share a common trait with equipment projects in that the products supplied are generally physical goods and equipment introduced as company assets. This shared condition makes project comprehension and justification easier because management is able to see tangible and substantial results. However, infrastructure projects also have important differences. Generally, the resulting project deliverables are much less obvious to the affected users, who can perceive that improvements have been made, but do not always understand the relationship between the investment made and how the associated improvements affect their personal working conditions. The purpose of infrastructure projects is more related to the creation of conditions conducive to developing capability to support current and future business needs, rather than to facilitate an immediate and visible benefit to users.

Projects that have this classification could include, for example, the replacement of network cabling to provide a higher speed in order to absorb the growth of data traffic within the corporate network, replacement of the electronic network to allow wider audience access to the network, and acquisition of a new license for a product that allows single sign-on to resolve the problem of repeated need for application authentication.

These are projects that produce products that, regardless of their visibility and relevance in the short term, will produce long-term benefits, particularly when product features and capabilities are used in subsequent new projects that deliver new possibilities to users and to the organization.

## Operational Projects

Operational projects are those for which the main products, mainly software and services, have a relatively direct and immediate effect on the routine business operations within the organization. Products obtained from this type of project normally have an immediate effect on the work efforts of users.

Projects that have this classification might include a new information system developed to receive and accept orders from customers, a new financial accounting application, a new incident management system that allows the identification and management of existing information systems problems by users, and the implementation of a new client relationship management (CRM) system to give to customer services and support.

Operational projects have products that provide benefits that allow us to recover the investment within a short time, less than the threshold defined for short-term projects, and generate such benefits by simplifying and improving the efficiency of the activities of users or by offering increased profits based on maintaining the same level of effort. These projects also usually provide immediate benefits to users, who will support and accept related new products when they are properly explained, and when they include capability to improve user performance. To that end, users will often be involved in the project and provide collaboration to facilitate development and deployment of the product.

## Strategic Projects

A project is classified as strategic when its transformative effect on the organization represents an opportunity to make a great leap forward or "step change" in business processes. This is in contrast to operational projects that introduce minor changes that facilitate the gradual evolution of business practices in a less dramatic style for the organization.

The deployment and setup of products resulting from strategic projects represents a significant effort to produce higher levels of business performance. However, the projects used to enable future business advantages and benefits do not have to be obvious to affected users. However, they should be informed, when they begin to notice the lack of short-term results, that strategic projects have a long-term perspective. Yet, if this occurs, it is possible that such projects may become subject to resistance and weak acceptance by users in the business environment.

Such projects have a payback period of investment that, by definition, falls within the threshold of long-term projects, over 3 years, so the realization of benefits is likewise mainly long-term. Sometimes, subsequent projects can be leveraged to produce some immediate results with a reasonably low effort, all based on the foundation established by the original strategic project.

We must also recognize that business organizations are subject to changes in the market of information systems, which can have sudden swings in unexpected ways, or which can disable strategic actions when current efforts are overtaken by new developments in the market. On some occasions, new products suddenly become obsolete much earlier than expected; other times, market conditions are misread and the entire corporate strategy must be reconstituted to address the new situation created by the last change that occurred in the marketplace.

# A Case Study for Project Classification

Let us analyze these considerations of project classification by examining a real project performed with a client some time ago. The client was a private institution, but was supported by a foundation of mixed patrons from both public and private sectors. The institution played a major role in the economic revitalization of the region. Among its patrons were representatives from the local city government and the regional government, along with members from the local chamber of commerce and a number of business associations active in the region.

This client managed a facility that was equipped with a most modern means to accommodate commercial fairs, business events and meetings, and political and social appointments. This capability allowed arrangements for specific times and space needed by prominent players in the field of supply and demand. This included such areas as construction and engineering, furniture and wood, ceramic tiles and building materials, fashion, and tourism, among nearly 50 participating trades and disciplines.

The institution managed their operations using an ERP-based solution, which supported the operations of the main business areas and departments of the organization. To complement this solution, they developed a small number of adaptations and extensions designed and constructed to resolve financial and general accounting, business management, sales and distribution, and key aspects related to the maintenance of facilities. These solutions were effectively implemented to allow the marketing department to sell space, stands, and services for exhibitors and visitors.

Customers, especially industry exhibitors, who demanded information about visitors, sought additional value as a return of the investment in their presence and participation in the events that were held at this institution's facilities. They wanted information that would allow them to improve their capability to make decisions based on business strategies. In this context, the institution was asked to install ERP modules to provide business intelligence features to collect detailed information about exhibitors and visitors from each of the events, and to create a data repository that would provide the information requested by various customers.

Thus, when the project definition came to the team that I led at the time, we saw that the project benefits and scope could be much deeper than appeared at first sight. In collaboration with the client, we prepared an extraordinary work plan that offered the building of the requested repository of information. In turn, this provided reports to the sales department responsible for responding to the incessant demands for information from exhibitors, and this cut the number of exhibitors reducing their investments or declining participation in future events.

The information systems department also suffered significant pressure from other internal departments of the institution to generate numerous reports each month. While those reports always revolved around the same themes and content, each business unit asked for minor changes and adaptations for their particular needs and interests, such as for calculations to be made or columns to be included in different reports. Fulfilling these requests always required a considerable added programming and testing effort. This work involved the continued participation of three people, who were dedicated to the effort on a full-time basis. They therefore only had limited time to address other issues such as ongoing maintenance or the development of new features.

We noticed that if we used the business intelligence module to collect the information used in all these reports, we could expand the hub of information originally requested by the sales department to also respond to users in the finance department. That allowed an early release of technicians involved in that effort, and they could now focus on the evolutionary maintenance of all corporate information systems with the consequential advantages of a reduction in associated costs, reduction in dependence on external resources, and increased participation and reinforcement of the team of the institution. This early release also increased their capacity to respond more quickly to changing business needs, leading to a renewal of confidence and improvement in the internal image of the IT department, which had somewhat deteriorated in recent years.

To achieve these benefits, once the data repository was created, technicians were needed to make navigation tools and reports available to all users with access to the information stored in the repository. Now, each user, as needed and according to their level of authority, could access relevant information and generate reports to respond to the specific and concrete needs of the various business interests.

To that end, and with the considerations described below, we believe that we were dealing with a strategic project that had to be managed in a manner befitting that classification. The client understood such considerations and agreed with that description.

The project provided the following additional benefits and value, among others, and as well as those already mentioned:

■ The project provided the implementation of a business intelligence product in a pilot project that would meet current needs, but would enable the organization to respond to future needs in a most effective manner.

■ The project included a specific, value-based approach for business intelligence projects, which would be explained to the technicians of the institution with a dual purpose: they could take over the maintenance of the systems developed, and they could also use it in future projects to define and implement additional information collection and reporting capabilities.

■ The project enabled a team of information systems professionals, which had previously been devoted to the intensive, repetitive, and monotonous production of reports, to be released for work that was more advantageous to the business needs and interests of the institution.

# Chapter 22

---

# Preparing the Project Definition

---

Every time we face a new project, as the project manager responsible for its success, we must ensure that we have a complete understanding of the problem or issue to be resolved in order to provide effective project management. We begin this effort by specifying the type of project or classification that will be used, to provide a very broad understanding of the project. We must then continue to perform a more detailed examination of project requirements and conditions to provide an in-depth understanding of the project. This effort produces a collection of information frequently referred to as the project definition.

## Elements of the Project Definition

Among the considerations to be taken into account in this initial phase of the project, we should pay particular attention to the information available that allows us to determine the main elements of the project definition. At the beginning of the project, only preliminary information is available to construct the project definition. As the project takes form and progresses to formal planning activities, the project definition can be expanded to incorporate more detailed information, or the project definition can serve as a basis for developing details that will be presented in separate project planning documents.

Prominent elements of the project definition include the following:

- *Project requirements.* This refers to all documents that will guide the project work effort, and can include customer interviews, technical specifications, accepted proposals, and any other document or resource that specifies the required approach to work and the expected outcomes.
- *Project work description/approach to work.* This presents the preliminary considerations regarding the nature of work to be accomplished by the project. At a minimum, a description of the project work effort should be prepared initially. However, the project definition can also be used to outline the various phases, activities, and tasks of the project. Ultimately, as accuracy and rigor are applied to the identification of each work element, the preliminary outline contained in the project definition will become a project work breakdown structure (WBS), which establishes a structured and methodological approach to be followed for performing the project work. In turn, all products to be delivered as a result of the project tasks and activities can be aligned with relevant work elements. The preliminary specification of the work effort in the project definition will allow the project team to construct preliminary estimates for cost, schedule, and resource utilization. It will also help them to properly prepare for the imminent product analysis and design activities.
- *Project timescale.* This element comprises a preliminary look at the timescale required for the project, and includes the milestones that must be reached in order to fulfill project requirements. In a sense, a very preliminary project schedule is prepared to illustrate the time constraints that will affect upcoming work. In addition to project requirements, other requirements imposed by external conditions, business commitments, or regulatory dispositions that could be of a legal nature should be specified in the timeline, perhaps as milestones. Knowing these restrictions will ensure that the organization complies with such requirements that if not properly addressed could have negative consequences for the organization.
- *Project resources.* This element represents a very preliminary determination of the resources that will be needed to perform the project. It will provide an indication of who we need to talk with regarding potential roles on the project. It will specify those roles, identify who will be assigned to each of the roles, and define the reporting and work relationships across the various roles. In turn, the project's management structure can be defined, along with communication guidance for both internal project communication and communication between the project and the rest of the organization. This element of the project definition can also be used to identify the project sponsor and the sponsor's position within the organization.
- *Project budget.* This element represents our very preliminary considerations of costs related to the project work effort, according to the timeline and resource constraints that are encountered. This preliminary information will allow us

to establish and evaluate a cost baseline from which we can calculate the benefits and advantages that the project will provide as value that will be received from the project.

# Project Deliverables

As I have already mentioned, all projects represent an extraordinary effort that temporarily disrupts the established order within the organization. Projects presume the appearance of an atypical structure within the organization's operations, and they integrate multidisciplinary resources that perform work in roles that can be very different from those associated with their primary position in the organization. This can include different levels of authority, and different positions and dependencies created for the sole purpose of responding to a special situation that warrants project status. However, of the various professionals and technical specialists are brought together for a purpose, which is to develop and deliver the products and services required by the customer and other project stakeholders.

Therefore, the success of any project, which is normally understood to mean meeting the expectations of stakeholders, relies on the project definition to identify the products to be delivered as a result of the project effort.

Project deliverables can be products and services that are designed and developed for presentation to the relevant customer as each is achieved. There may also be intermediate deliverables that are either presented to the customer or retained for internal use. A discussion on the common types of project deliverables is presented below.

## *The Main Products*

The project definition will include the specification of what constitutes the main product or deliverable of the project. Usually, this will be a fairly generic product that has a superficial definition, but which is further defined by the identification of boundaries that specify what is included and what is excluded. Having a detailed description of what is expected from the project is essential to maximize the chances of success of the project.

For this reason, we take the generic definition of the main product and break it down into its components until the lowest level of the product's structure is reached. Then, we provide added details regarding the characteristics for each component until the description adequately identifies the features and functions of the product to be delivered.

This can be examined further if we consider the business intelligence project mentioned in the previous chapter. In that instance, we find that the products or deliverables to be provided would include, for example, the following:

- Provision of a standard software business intelligence module of the Enterprise Resources Planning (ERP) solution currently deployed by the client, corresponding to the latest version available according to the business agreement currently valid between client and software provider and the corresponding license of use
- Provision of a server with sufficient capacity to accommodate the analytical database and host information for the first 18 months of operation
- Provision of the license for the database software that must store the information in the data repository with enough licenses to serve the anticipated number of users
- Provision of software and licenses for the use of all other products that the above components require to work properly, such as operating system, application server, and web server software

These provisions will require a wide range of services absolutely necessary for product deployment, and to maintain operational capability. This would include such services as

- Installation and integration services in the client environment of the new server provided within the framework of the project
- Installation, configuration, and alignment of the database software, which must support the analytical data model
- Installation, configuration, and alignment of business intelligence software that hosts the data repository presented as a main deliverable for collaboration
- Installation, configuration, and setup of services to connect and use all other components that must be deployed in the client environment

## Technical Documentation

Regarding services related to the definition, construction, and implementation of the data repository and ETL modules (used for the extraction, transformation and loading (ETL) of data required for the effective functioning of information systems), we should try to define the resulting products in a manner consistent with relevant technical documentation. To that end, technical documentation becomes a project deliverable and that documentation can include the following:

- *System analysis document.* This details the various reports and data required for the operation of the system, including data stored in the data repository, axes or dimensions of analysis, and forecast levels of aggregation and partial sums.
- *System design document.* Further described in the data repository to be built, it contains data specifications, dimensional analysis to retrieve the information provided, characteristics of the consultations, presentation of data

management capabilities, and analysis of information and navigation within the data repository. This document will also include information on the sources from which data will be obtained, planned frequency for generating the data to be loaded into the information hub, and the processing load required for the system.

■ *Detailed design documents.* Prepared for each of the systems components, these include the specification required for component construction, taking into account the technical characteristics of the tools that are used in accordance with the customer's technical environment.

■ *Programs and software components documents.* These are a variety of documents that provide guidance for operating the system and for proper integration with the business intelligence software supplied as a standard product that is previously configured and adapted for operation in the customer's environment.

■ *User documentation.* This comprises material for users that includes at least the training material supporting the delivery of training courses for users of the business intelligence system, and material for technical staff members who will receive the information system and maintain its operational capability. These materials allow users to obtain sufficient knowledge about the use and management of the system, and may include screen captures of key system features to illustrate the explanations.

■ *User reference manual.* This contains a detailed explanation of the overall functionality of the new information system from the user's perspective. This manual specifies mandatory user actions in a separate section that can be used as a quick reference for responding to the most common difficulties that a user might face. This includes guidance regarding what to do if something unexpected happens. It provides a resource where users can look for solutions to possible problems that may occur. It can also include a section for frequently asked questions (FAQs), where users can find correct answers to the questions that more commonly arise.

■ *Technical documentation.* This documentation includes all the information that technical staff members from the information systems department may need to maintain proper system operation. Information included in this documentation is oriented to the installation, configuration, and implementation of the system as a whole, with sufficient information provided to support such things as the replacement of the server or the installation of a new version of database software. This enables skilled technicians to install and set up any and all of the system components without outside help. This documentation also provides information and documentation generated during the construction process that is made available to technical systems engineers, who can use it to perform ongoing system maintenance without external support.

■ *Training program delivery.* This is an instructional program that is suitably adapted to the needs of the personnel segments involved in using or managing the new system. This normally includes development of a training plan that describes the training program (i.e., schedule, location, and topical content). In particular, the training plan should consider the training required by two personnel groups:

- *Training aimed at users of the system.* There will be two training sessions directed to basic users of the system. Each session will normally last 3 h and will accommodate up to eight participants. These users should follow up course attendance with on-the-job training that allows them to practice skills learned in the classroom. Among the users who have shown a better proficiency from training, a total of four people can be selected as a reference users group to provide primary support and assistance to their peers. Users in this reference group will receive another special training session, within 30 days of the first and lasting 8 h, where they are able to expand or clarify the explanations about system use, and resolve any unanswered questions they may have about system operations.

- *Technical training oriented at technical personnel in the IT department.* In this group, we will distinguish two types of profiles: the system administrators and maintenance personnel. System administrators will be given a 2 h session in which the instructor will explain the activities required to keep the system operational, the precautions to consider when making a backup of information, and how to perform start/stop services and other frequent maintenance operations. Maintenance personnel will be given an 8 h session in which the instructor will explain all of the technical information generated on the system as a means to learn navigation through all the relevant system documentation. Fifteen days later, this group will attend another 4 h session aimed at resolving questions that have emerged from study of the documentation. It should be understood that the documentation supplied shall comply with the terms of the project's products and any deviation from this will be resolved before the transfer of knowledge within the training provided.

## Specification of Product Details

Product details can be provided in conjunction with the identification of project deliverables. The following items can be included in the specification of product details:

■ *Product characteristics for each product.* For example, product characteristics should include a listing of functions and features to be built into each system component included in main products. If such details are not specified, misunderstandings and conflict can occur to affect the relationship between the project team and their customers and users.

- *Target values for each product.* For example, with regard to the training material: How many pages will it comprise? Will it be printed or placed on electronic media? If it will be delivered on physical media, how many copies will be delivered? If printed, will it be simply stapled or bound? If bound, in what format? Will it be delivered to the customer to allow time for review, or will it be delivered directly to trainees in the classroom?
- *Variation thresholds for each product.* This specification is used to facilitate the adjustment of product characteristics by providing a range or threshold in which the product is deemed acceptable. In contrast, attempts to provide absolute precision would be very difficult and add no value to the project outcome. For example, we can express system response time as having a threshold limit: "The system will have a response time of <1 s." In contrast, we may want to define the approximate size of a document by providing a range of tolerance, which could be expressed as "The manual will have a volume of 80 pages, with a variation of plus or minus 10% allowed." Or we could simply use the expression, "The manual will be developed to have a size that is allowed to range from 72 to 88 pages."

The specification of product details will facilitate the subsequent management of the product delivery. If a product presented for approval is outside expected ranges, it can be directly rejected because it does not meet the specification. However, if the product does meet the specifications, it must be considered at least for review and, unless defects are found, it must be accepted as submitted. To that end, the threshold values become the criteria for acceptance of products with such a specification, and that streamlines project progress.

## Customer Needs and Interests

Information related to customer needs and interests is a vital part of the project definition. This element allows us to understand the underlying motivation and reasoning used by the customer to pursue a particular project. In a sense, this element helps us understand how customer needs have been translated into project requirements, and how project requirements have been translated into product specifications that will address or otherwise resolve the customer's needs. This project definition element also guides us to collect customer business and business relationship information as a means to better understand the customer's organization and to facilitate the customer's involvement in the project.

When starting a new project, we are often entering an unknown territory, where the primary project objectives and main product features may have already been defined by other people. We might be given a predefined project that we must develop with a very little freedom to change anything, because many of the details have been fixed under a contract, which is the prominent document that guides the project.

However, when we enter a project at the beginning, it is important to gain an understanding of customer needs and interests through a comprehensive review of project requirements and product specifications, as they may exist. In turn, we can begin creating project plans, in collaboration with the customer, to respond to those needs and interests. Alternatively, if some or most of the project planning has already been accomplished to give us a predefined project, we can contrast our understanding of the customer needs and interests against relevant project plans. If we detect that the project, as currently planned, does not appear to be the best solution to the problem, then we must attempt to resolve that issue with the customer. This is where our understanding of the customer's business comes into play as a valuable input to the review and collaboration that is needed to make the customer aware of valid concerns about the project solution currently in place.

Projects result from careful analysis and planning before deciding to undertake the work effort. All kinds of reviews and scrutiny are carried out to endorse the suitability of the prescribed solution to resolve the problems facing the customer. Therefore, we must use extreme caution when challenging the effectiveness of the solution. We must be sure that it is sufficiently faulty to warrant the time and effort of a follow-up examination with the customer.

The business case is a business document that is derived from the elements of the project definition to represent the business needs and interests of the performing organization. It will often contain information regarding project value, expected benefits, and the return on investment resulting from the project. If such a business case document already exists, then it should be reviewed to ensure any challenges to the solution do not have an adverse business impact.

This considered, there are a few ways to approach the customer to identify circumstances that may have caused a faulty solution to be accepted, and to present the alternative solutions that have been analyzed for consideration as a replacement solution. The following approaches and reasoning can be considered for use when attempting to open a technical discussion with the customer:

■ Offer a different, but viable solution from among the alternatives that have been examined, and show how it could advantageously resolve the customer's problem. Ideally, this discussion will have some focus on offering greater benefits, lower costs, and perhaps lower risks that could be detrimental to project success.

■ Indicate that the circumstances that warranted the selection of the preferred solution have changed. Therefore, the current project solution will be difficult to fulfill, has more or less become invalid, and little to no value will be achieved if the solution remains intact. This condition may result from the introduction of new and advanced technology, a corporate acquisition and merger that has different standards for information systems projects, or the discontinuation of components slated for the new system. This provides an opportunity to offer the customer a renewed analysis of solutions that can be considered to effectively address business needs and interests.

- In a closely related scenario, indicate that the circumstances that warranted the project have changed, and that the project approach or solution has more or less become obsolete based on original reasoning. Therefore, the project is no longer necessary. This approach may seem strange, but you should consider, for example, that the project plans of most government institutions and public sector organizations are defined and considered complete in the year prior to the start of the project. This is associated with the annual budgeting process, where funding is allocated for projects that will be performed in the subsequent year. In this case, up to 15 months can elapse between the moment that defined the project and its budget, and when the project actually starts. Circumstances like this will often encounter dynamic changes in the needs or conditions that prompted the project, in available technology intended for use on the project, and in strategic or political priorities for performing the project. Therefore, any resemblance between the two time periods is simply coincidental.

- Key managers who occupy relevant positions in the organization to include responsibility for reviewing and approving the system design have changed. They are replaced with individuals who have introduced a different business strategy, and they may even openly support a different approach to information systems development. These circumstances undoubtedly warrant a review of all pending projects, and perhaps a few that are already in progress. The customer can be offered services that facilitate a review of relevant projects, to include the involvement and contributions of the new business leaders in the organization.

All in all, any approach to engage the customer in a meaningful technical dialog will necessarily be based on our knowledge of the customer's organization—size, market, industry, and the like. It will also be based on our awareness of the attitudes and responsibilities of key individuals and managers in the customer's organization—roles, level of participation, level of authority, and the like. Therefore, it is essential that we collect and provide that type of information in the project definition, because the project is ultimately defined by the customer's needs and interests, along with the influence of business strategies, manager ambitions, and prior experience with the performing organization, in general, and the implementation of information systems, in particular.

# Chapter 23

---

# Structural Benefits

---

The project manager must maintain a focus on generating products that provide the greatest possible utility to the organization. This requires keeping a constant eye on the benefits and advantages that the project provides, because it will be through these benefits and advantages that the project achieves its final justification. This is a perspective so clear and obvious that is too often forgotten by project managers and project leaders.

For infrastructure projects, we are essentially acquiring and installing hardware components that have a long-term investment redemption period. These projects can involve such efforts as the renewal of the corporate local area network, the acquisition and installation of the electronics supply network, and the renovation of wiring associated with any hardware installation.

We should consider the ways in which infrastructure projects offer significant benefits that can be measured and evaluated. The remaining subsections of this chapter present several characteristics of infrastructure projects that can be examined in relation to achieving the potential benefits.

## Scalability

Scalability is the property of information systems that indicates the relative ability to assume a greater number of operations than initially assumed without degrading system performance.

A scalable information system can absorb the continuous growth of the organization, whether expressed in number of users, number of transactions, number of customers, or any other dimension under consideration. Scalability assesses the size of the system in a fluid way and in a manner that avoids traumatic intervention that adversely affects current users.

As a general rule, scalability usually requires extensions to the platform that supports the system, and, in most cases, these changes can be made without stopping the service to customers using the system. For example, an organization might implement their information system and then make a subsequent decision to place their files on a Storage Area Network (SAN), with a rack configuration, protected by a RAID-n. This would support the replacement and installation of new releases under a hot-fix formula without shutting down the system. This is in contrast to allocating files on a traditional server with internal storage that would have to be shut down.

Alternately, if the technology architecture had considered this possibility during system design, then the system would already be structured for this scalability. Of course, that would require a somewhat higher cost for initial implementation, but it removes the need to shut down the system at critical points in time. On this point of potential service interruptions, there is no real discussion needed if your business is conducted over the Internet, where continuous 24/7 service is critical. You simply consider a few questions: What would the cost be for each stoppage? How many stops could be made in a year? How many business transactions could be lost with each stop? And, how many customers who suffer service degradation will return again to your site? These questions address data and system management impacts that can affect the business. These impacts can be calculated and deserve consideration, because the answers may warrant paying the extra costs to avoid shutdowns, and it is possible for the cost difference to be recovered in a short time, perhaps only 6 months or less.

Either way, scalability must maintain the right proportions for the expected evolution, with certain safety margins calculated to protect us from an evolution greater than expected. We must maintain a balance and avoid the assumption that we can achieve scalability ad infinitum as a means to avoid costs for an investment that will never be recovered. We must calculate the profits or loss that the lack of this feature will produce for the organization, and find a solution that gives us reasonable scalability with an investment cost that is lower than potential benefits.

## Extensibility

Extensibility is a feature of information systems that can sometimes be confused with scalability, and I would like to clarify the difference. Scalability represents the ability of the information system to absorb more workload units, whatever the metric used (e.g., users, customers, operations, or transactions). These workload units have more or less homogeneous characteristics; each metric used is of the same type, nature, and behavior. The capability of the system may vary according to the installed applications, but the workload units supported by the information system maintain their original form.

In contrast, when we talk about extensibility, we are referring to the information system's capacity to assume additional tasks or expanded task performance. This represents an extension of information system operational capability beyond that originally designed and built. Therefore, extensibility is the capacity for growth of the information system in a different direction than scalability, transverse to it, by which the system expands its focus to make it more widespread throughout the organization.

Extensibility is a system characteristic that can be measured and monitored for potential benefits relative to any changes made to the system. In some cases, extensibility and scalability can be evaluated together as a means to ascertain the mutual benefits that can be achieved.

# Flexibility

Flexibility is a characteristic that represents the ability of an information system to adapt itself to the changes occurring in the environment before its functionality suffers enough to prevent it from providing a satisfactory response to the needs of users in the organization.

Flexibility addresses a quality issue that is essential and critical, because the business environment is constantly changing. The information system needs to be responsive to such changes in order to provide continuous operational support to the organization's routine work with clients, providers, employees, and a variety of stakeholders that expect an adequate response from the company at all times.

An information system can be subject to varying degrees of flexibility. A generic example of flexibility would be one that is covered by the capability of the core information system. This type of flexibility should provide broad and generous leeway in response to changing business conditions; otherwise, the system could be suddenly interrupted if changes in the business environment produce a conflict with prescribed, in-program business rules or simply cause some unexpected form of information output or data overflow.

For example, when a sales management system includes a pricing scheme based on list price, a commercial discount, a financial discount, and a third possible discount based on special promotions, it is setting a limit by allowing the selection of only one type of discount, and not any multiple combinations of discounts. Therefore, customers can only benefit from using one form of discount for their orders. The commercial director, under pressure from the market, competitors, and customers, might decide to allow customers to combine up to two discounts for their orders. That will likely create a situation in which the information system will be unable to generate a satisfactory response, and system programming will have to be severely altered in order to implement the director's business decision. In this instance, the original flexibility is insufficient, and additional programming is needed to produce flexibility that will enable business benefits to be achieved.

Another type of flexibility is one that can be achieved through the use of a parametric function. In this case, business rules can be expressed in parts of the system that do not require programming skills to define and set those rules. Therefore, in anticipation of any changes in the business environment, an authorized individual can simply access the parametric function to define the necessary system changes, and the system will subsequently behave properly in response to the new business conditions, without requiring further action or attention.

An example of this type of flexibility is observed when defining the tax rate applicable to our business operations. The tax rate in this case is not established by hard coding or programming, rather, we define it through use of a parametric that allows a combination of rates for different types of taxes and effective dates to be considered depending on the type of product or service provided, the type of customer who becomes subject to the applicable tax, and any special taxation requirements relative to shipping or exporting of goods and services to various regions of the country, or to external territories and countries. Therefore, if it happened that a change is to be made in the Value Added Tax (VAT) rate on a certain date, it would suffice to access the parametric to enter the new tax rate and its effective date. As needed, the parametric would also allow the tax rate to be applied to the different types of business transactions that occur. This adjustment would also allow use of the current tax rate structure until the effective date of the new tax rate.

## Reliability

The reliability of an information system represents the probability that a system will maintain its operational capability within the parameters established in the system specifications, where these specifications set the expected system behavior, the operating conditions, and the period during which the system is required to maintain such performance. It should be noted that reliability does not necessarily mean that the system will do what it should do, but it means strictly that the systems will do what the specifications say it should do. For example, if the specifications for a system designed 10 years ago say it will support transactions that do not reach one million dollars and the system gives an error warning that such a limit has been reached, this rejection, however annoying, does not make the system unreliable. We cannot say that the system is failing, but we may want to consider a modification that resolves the issues of today's inflation and upward spiraling costs.

Therefore, we must consider any information system to be reliable when it performs according to specifications, as long as it does not produce results that are not properly controlled. In many cases, reliability is expressed in terms of percentage, where that percentage refers to the ratio of the number of cases that are not controlled, compared to all possible cases that are subject to control.

# Availability

The availability of an information system is a measure that indicates the proportion of time that the system is actually operating, compared to the time the system is supposed to be operating. System availability is usually expressed as a ratio in terms of percentage time available.

For example, consider an information system that is used to support customer operations and employees on a Wide Area Network (WAN) or directly on the Internet. Information is collected to show that the average daily time that the system is available for use is 22 h and 15 min, and this is in contrast to the 24 h required. Given the condition that the system should be available to customers who may require Internet connection at any time in a given 24 h period, we would say that the system has an availability of 92.70%. That means that the rest of the 24 h timeframe, 1 h and 45 min, is unavailable to customers and other users because software updates, information backups, and maintenance operations are being performed.

However, if that same information system is intended for users in corporate offices, its availability may only be required during normal business hours, and that could provide for 100% availability to that group of users. In this scenario, where users may require access to the system from 8 to 20 h per day, that will allow sufficient time to conduct maintenance tasks without interrupting the system, allowing the system to achieve full 100% availability.

# Capacity Required for System Operations

Information systems should provide the capacity required for proper functioning of business processes. However, this detail is sometimes taken for granted when the operational capacity is not specified in concrete terms. It is necessary to know or at least have a reasonable estimate of system capacity in advance of its design and implementation, and that results from planning the operational needs and requirements of the system, with anticipation of any capacity problems or issues that may arise.

The system stress tests are among the many tests that a system must pass before the system is made available to end users. The purpose of these tests is simply to verify that the system will maintain its performance in peak working conditions, and they should be performed in a diligent manner to validate operational use of the system. Information system capacity is critical, because if the information system does not have the required capacity, it will likely miss business transactions that produce revenue, and business profitability will ultimately suffer.

Consider, for example, a ticketing system for a tourist facility that is expected to respond at the pace at which customers arrive; otherwise customers will accumulate at the point of sale, forming lines of varying lengths. Eventually, each tourist receives tickets and is given access to the facility and invited to enjoy the visit. It is obvious that if the tourist arrives and the seller is busy with another customer, the tourist will usually wait his turn to purchase tickets. However, if the capacity of the ticketing system is reduced, longer customer lines will form, and some tourists may even give up and leave the ticketing queue to spend the day at another venue; these tourists may or may not return at another time. In any case, today's revenue has been lost.

These lost revenues should be considered a cost associated with the limited capacity of the system to service customer needs and interests. In most instances, this lost revenue can be calculated for comparison with the cost of implementing a system with greater capacity that would have prevented the situation. To that end, the system capacity must be considered as a viable means to achieve revenue and associated business benefits.

## Capacity to Increase Activities

Analogous to the discussion above related to capacity for system operations, when the business unit or organization anticipates significant business growth, this too can be addressed in terms of system capacity required to support that growth. To that end, the organization needs to plan for the additional system capacity that is anticipated to be needed to support business growth and the extra activities associated with that growth.

Having this additional capacity could be critical in cases where information systems scalability, extensibility, and flexibility are limited. Capacity will have less importance in cases where such features have been clearly established so that the system will be able to adequately respond to new and emerging business needs as they arise.

Either way, these additional requirements and the capabilities required to give satisfactory coverage should be estimated to assess whether the system can continue to respond, or to identify the point at which full capacity will be reached to cause rejection of the addition of new business activities. This possibility should be considered in assessing the potential consequences that might ensue for the business, along with estimating the cost of the measures that can be taken to ensure the system capacity is sufficient to give a satisfactory response to the increased activity.

## Compatibility

Information system compatibility is the ability of the system, technical architecture, or solution to interact effectively with other components of the overall system, whether these information system components reside within the same organization or in another location or different organization. In the latter case, when two information systems of different organizations are compatible to the point of working transparently as one system, we refer to that system as having integration or interoperability.

System compatibility can be achieved in several ways. The first and most basic mechanism for compatibility incorporates components known as emulators, which make a system behave as if it were another type of system. This makes it possible to integrate one system with another by virtue of emulated behavior, where one system component imitates the behavior of another type of component for the purposes of interoperability required by the first system.

The second mechanism of compatibility involves the preparation of specific interface components that are inserted between two systems to handle and facilitate effective communication between them. A current version of such a mechanism is found in Web services that invoke an external system to perform operations within an information system, regardless of the client system architecture, but with respect for the rules established within the client system.

The third mechanism of compatibility is seen when information systems are subjected to standards that are applied to ensure that systems are compatible with each other on an equity plane, where both systems use a common language defined by the stakeholder community or by an independent standards organization. Examples of this compatibility can be found in government and financial systems that have specified steps for transactions such as grant management, fund transfers, or tax payment reconciliation. We can also see this mechanism in use in the commercial sector in areas such as credit card transactions, where compatibility has been created for the exchange of business data related to customer orders, invoices, and bills. This mechanism can be used by virtually any player in the market as long as they respect the basic rules of proper label content, formats, and a few other basic requirements.

## Security and Privacy

In information systems, security and privacy is a subjective component that represents the means to create a secure system that protects privacy using a consistent effort to control the risk of invasion and the violation of the rights of users. These are matters that in recent years have been subject to regulation by many governments, especially in Europe. Abuses by unscrupulous companies and individuals have created a social response that has demanded the protection of public authorities through enforced laws and regulations, and through substantial penalties for offenders. This is seen as a means to control unauthorized use of information collected on individuals, particularly with regard to financial transfers and transactions of a personal nature.

Three types of data can be derived from information systems, warranting three different types of protection according to their sensitivity. First, a basic level of protection is given to data that identify the person but do not include specific information about that person. Next, the average level of protection is applied to protect the economic and financial data of the persons concerned. Finally, a high level of protection is applied to files that include data about sexual orientation, religious beliefs, union or political affiliation, health or disease, and any other information that could be used to establish a profile on any individual. Consequently, the use of safety devices and safeguards in information systems for data privacy are no longer an option but an obligation. These mechanisms should include an audit capability related to access and protection of information at those levels of protection, as required by law and with the conditions laid down in legislation in each geographic area.

The value of providing security and privacy protection should be quite evident. If we choose to ignore established laws and requirements, we can easily calculate the probability of an inspection, either automatically at the initiative of relevant government agencies, or when motivated by a complaint from a customer who feels their privacy is threatened. Considering the volume of data that we are using, its nature, and the impact of penalties, we can calculate the cost of neglecting these criteria in comparison to the cost of considering and implementing safeguards in a timely and rigorous manner. Furthermore, there is distinct business value in avoiding a tarnished business image that could result from complaints or conditions that reflect inadequate attention to security and privacy issues.

Most people will agree that it is important for any business to secure and protect the data in information systems relating to clients, providers, prices, and a whole universe of commercial and financial data.

# Chapter 24

# Operational Benefits

The project is always a temporary endeavor, the existence of which is clearly defined by a unique purpose and an end point that is determined at its onset. It provides a means to realize certain conditions and outcomes that provide benefits to the performing organization.

For this reason, when we encounter a project for which the main products are equipment, hardware, software, or tools, and the period for investment redemption is expected to be short-term in nature, we should look for potential benefits from various perspectives that will be different from those that produce returns in a long-term project payback period. Such short-term benefits should focus on improving the overall business performance of the organization, to include the containment of operating costs and the savings resulting from improved and efficient processes.

Several areas where we can achieve benefits associated with the support to operations and cost control are discussed in the subsections of this chapter.

## Standardization of the Platform

Any new project initiated to improve the level of standardization of the platform on which the system resides could focus efforts at the hardware and devices level, or it could focus efforts at the software level, associated with the operating system, the database management software, the Internet information server, or the application server. Each of these types of projects would clearly represent a potential opportunity to reduce costs.

Platform standardization presumes to simplify the working environment of the information system, and this means that we have an opportunity to reduce the total number of components that are to be integrated to form the total system. This

271

simplifies the work environment, leading to a reduction or simplification of the potential problems that could appear in the information systems environment. If we change the number of components needed for the system to work, the number of interfaces and relationships between them will also drastically reduce, providing added assurance that the information system will continue to run smoothly.

The components of the information system environment may grow or reduce in number, and with them the likelihood of errors, incidents, problems, and conflicts between them does the same in a geometric manner until do the information system unmanageable. Therefore, platform standardization is a way to reduce the number of incidents that we experience as a result of conflicts between the different integrated components of the information system. It also reduces the number of system stoppages, the number of difficulties that system users experience, the number of times we must perform system maintenance, the number of hours devoted to amending or correcting various aspects of the information system configuration, the number of hours lost due to unavailability of the information system for users, and the number of hours spent by different levels of the organization in trying to re-establish operation of the system after each modification or correction. In summary, a lot of problems are potentially reduced when we create a simpler technical environment.

Simplification of the information systems environment, characterized by a reduction in the number of components involved in the system, will also reduce costs. This occurs because the associated maintenance contracts with suppliers of these products will no longer be necessary, and can be discontinued when they are no longer required by the information system.

We can also opt to develop the necessary expertise and knowledge about system components internally. This will eliminate having an absolute dependency on suppliers and third-party companies to resolve any system-related difficulties that may arise. When we are able to achieve more reliance on internal skills and abilities, we will make cost savings in the information system environment.

## Standardization of the Supplier

In a normal information systems operating environment, there can be a wide variety of system components, hardware and software, which must work in a seamless and integrated manner to support global operations. When everything is working fine and smoothly, the complexity of the information system is hidden to users, who have only limited visibility via user interfaces. We might consider those user interfaces as the outer skin of the system, which can be used without having to worry or even know about the inner complexities of network components. Like the skin on the human body, the outer appearance is not necessarily representative of what is inside. However, when something goes wrong, the underlying network of component relationships and dependencies emerge to reveal the delicate balance between all the components, which must work together as a system to respond to the business needs and interests that they serve.

In a similar manner, there may be times when suppliers do not see or understand the total complexity of all system components beyond the component(s) they represent or service. There will probably be a number of occasions when system problems become obvious and indisputable to most technicians involved in the system. However, it seems that there are too many occasions when it becomes difficult to establish the ultimate source of a problem because of the different opinions of the cadre of suppliers who attempt to diagnose and resolve the problem. Often, the problem is shifted from one supplier to another, with each attributing the problem to defects in system components other than their own in order to evade responsibility for the problem.

For this reason, a standardization of suppliers is needed. This is a reduction in the number of suppliers who provide or maintain the various components of the information systems. Such supplier standardization will provide benefits in a number of ways:

- By reducing the number of systems contracts that we manage, maintain, and control, the administrative work required will be simplified, facilitating control of the remaining contracted services, warranties, and services. This offers particular advantages with regard to the personal computers used as workstations, or any other equipment that the organization owns in larger quantities. The organization must be able to effectively link equipment with the relevant contracts for the purposes of maintenance or repair. Otherwise, the organization may concede repair costs when there is uncertainty as to whether the equipment or system components are under warranty. The organization would do well to have fewer suppliers so as to more easily manage their involvement in system component and equipment inventory control for the purposes of maintenance and responsiveness to warranty conditions.
- Developing an improved negotiating position when renewing contracts will be beneficial in selecting service providers who understand the business needs and interests of the organization. Effective negotiations will lead to selecting only those service providers that demonstrate a level of commitment similar to ours. Perhaps only one qualified vendor should be selected, which should provide a lower overall cost, allowing us to obtain the benefits of economy of scale as a reduction in operational costs.
- Managing system maintenance and problem resolution can be simplified to create timely and quality responses. Our systems management effort is simplified when we no longer need to perform preliminary diagnoses to assign the appropriate provider to each incident or problem identified. When there are fewer vendors to be contacted, we can complete a more simple investigation and resolution of the problem. Presumably, having a single vendor will reduce this administrative aspect of systems management even further.

Moreover, the establishment of long-term relationships with suppliers can offer the opportunity to establish partnerships of high value for both parties, which may be turned into true alliances that can help them achieve success in their respective markets.

# Standardization of the Application

Standardization of the application refers to the preferences we specify relative to software application components that we are considering for integration into the system information environment. This usually includes consideration of standard applications available in the marketplace, and usually shies away from products that are less well known and without commercial support, such as open-source solutions or even commercial products that are still in a stage of development and about which little is known about features and functionality or whether there have been any successful implementations.

For the purposes of application standardization, choices are normally made in favor of solutions that have more implementations across industries, that have performance and operational results that are known to be reliable and secure, and that provide indisputable business advantages to the organization, based on results achieved by the many previous implementations. This approach is preferred for a couple of reasons.

First, the cost of maintaining a standard, commercially relevant solution will always be lower than the cost of maintenance required for a similar solution that is still in its evolution stage. Adverse and costly results are sometimes associated with noncommercial products that are developed internally or with emerging products that are poorly implemented.

If the product has modest visibility in the marketplace, has few implementations, and does not have adequate support for maintenance, when we need a time-constrained improvement we will have to assume responsibility for that work, either internally or through a specific work order to the provider. In this case, any approach to making improvements will incur additional costs and present new risks associated with the work.

Additionally, depending on how such a development effort is performed, a problem arises when, during the evolution stage, subsequent versions are developed that will differ from our "standard version", and updates might reside only on our system. We will not therefore be able to gain the benefits of subsequently improved versions issued by the provider.

Before going forward, and to respond to those who may already be wondering, we will put the question, "Does this mean that a standard product is always better than a customized development for any company or organization?" In answer, we will say "No, not at all, but rather the opposite."

In as much as every business has unique characteristics, so it is that every organization has different information systems and applications needs that have different importance and implications in terms of their business processes. There are mission-critical systems that are part and parcel of an organization's competitiveness in the marketplace. These systems will have some specific features that differentiate them from the systems of competitors, and these are used to create and maintain a sustainable business advantage over time. The special features that are used to create a business advantage cannot be obtained by purchasing a standard product that is, by definition, available to any competitor in the marketplace. Rather, the better solution will most likely be the development of a customized and organization-specific information system, which enables benefits to be achieved by the organization while keeping such benefits away from competitors.

In the same company, there may be many other applications that are not at the core of the business, perhaps with the function of facilitating certain business needs or compliance with external obligations. Such systems are usually aimed at managing economic and financial matters to meet the obligations associated with tax and transparency with partners, and to address personnel management relative to financial obligations with employees, financial institutions, and social welfare organizations. Many issues like these can be resolved through the use of standard tools without negatively affecting competitiveness. This is because there is no distinct differentiation provided by standard tools, and they do not provide any competitive benefits to the business. However, the acquisition and installation of standard solutions could have some internal business risk, and, of course, there will be additional costs associated with the purchase.

## Consolidation of the System

Consolidating the information system involves actions contributing to strengthening the foundations on which the information system is built. It also includes efforts to create or enhance the robustness of the system against risks and difficulties that may threaten its operation.

There are several ways in which system consolidation activities can contribute to improving information system operations. A few examples are presented below for consideration.

■ A contingency plan should be defined and implemented to identify any prominent risks that threaten the information systems and, consequently, the business. Appropriate response measures should be specified to ensure business continuity with minimal adverse impact should risk events materialize and affect information system operations.

■ The servers and hub of information processing might need to be moved from their current location to a more secure location to protect them against the most common and most likely risks. For example, if we are working in a region where floods occur frequently, the server room should not be in the basement, but rather in a floor high enough to ensure that the system will not be affected should flooding occur.

■ A secondary center of information processing should be established to serve as a backup, outside the main premises of the company, or at least far enough away to ensure that they will not simultaneously be exposed to the same risks. If the primary center catches fire, experiences a flood, suffers an earthquake, or any other disaster, the secondary center of information processing could continue to provide support to customers and the workforce, thereby avoiding business interruptions.

■ Duplicate servers should be created that are updated simultaneously and permanently as a means to facilitate the prevention of adverse effects on the business in the event that one of the servers has to be stopped for unexpected maintenance or repairs.

■ Lines of communication, storage disks protected under different checksum schemes, power supplies, and any items that in one way or another could cause an interruption in service if they fail, should be duplicated. This is particularly important when information systems are critical to business operations, as in organizations such as banks, airlines, and medical centers, where the loss of immediate access to critical information has significant business consequences.

Any effort to consolidate information systems will provide quantifiable and justifiable benefits. The benefits to be realized can be viewed in terms of costs saved as a result of business preparedness against adverse events. However, more often, benefits will be seen in terms of loss that has been avoided, and relative to information system operations, potential losses could be quite significant and very substantial.

## Cost Reduction

Each project will cause some change in an organization, with that change presumably leading to a more favorable condition for the organization. No-one in a position of responsibility would support the project if the investment produced a situation worse than the one replaced.

One of the most common objectives when projects are selected and performed is to achieve cost reductions that did not previously exist within the organization. There are a number of ways in which projects can facilitate cost reductions. A few of them of discussed below.

■ It may be that maintenance of the new information system and its components has a lower cost than the previous system. In the medium term, therefore, the new solution represents a saving resulting from reduced system maintenance costs for the new system.

- It may be that the new equipment is more energy-efficient and consumes less electricity to operate. This could reduce the information system's operating cost as a result of lower electricity consumption and a reduced need for air conditioning. A similar result can be achieved if a newly installed operating system makes more efficient use of system resources.

- In environments where there is extensive use of telephones, it can be profitable to have a system that filters outgoing calls and channels them according to the most appropriate means based on the type of call (i.e., national, international, landline, and mobile) according to the conditions of the phone service provider used by the company. Going a step further, it might be beneficial to consider the introduction of IP telephony systems, better known as VoIP, as a means to provide a telephone service with a significantly lower cost than traditional voice solutions.

- In areas of communications, it may be possible to obtain significant cost reductions through the digitization of content at the source to enable the electronic transmission of information in lieu of bags that carry massive collections of documents between the sales offices and headquarters and vice versa. Also, the digitization of documents may also facilitate more effective handling of information transferred between offices, and perhaps enable electronic incorporation into the database management system as a means to store and retrieve customer information.

All these activities provide quantifiable savings that can be integrated into a project business case in order to be considered in the analysis of project profitability. Of course, the business case will be monitored and further checks will be applied to ensure and verify that the promised benefits are being achieved.

## Increasing the Speed of Business

Computing speed may be a feature of little relevance by itself, but if we consider it as the technical feature that offers a measure of technical performance in equipment used in solving business problems, it acquires an importance and relevancy. Obviously, it would be very difficult to justify a project for the technological renovation of PCs in an institution, based solely on the increase in computing speed to be achieved by the new equipment. However, we are not talking just about computer speed; rather, we are referring to increasing the speed of business operations as a result of ensuing development and implementation projects, with the potential for significant benefits to the project customer.

A few years ago, a bank that had enjoyed recognition as the preference of customers in their region began to suffer the consequences of increasing competition from another financial company that was developing an ambitious business expansion plan in the region. The result of that company's effort was to attract many customers away from the first bank. However, there were also customers of both businesses. This caused concern for the first bank, but it had no action or answer to make in response.

As this situation was examined, it became clear that the actions of customers were occurring in a manner that can be likened to a well-known experiment involving a frog. The experiment is based on the premise that if you throw a frog into hot water, it jumps out quickly. However, this does not happen if you put the frog in cold water, then gradually increase the temperature of the water. In this case, the frog does not immediately jump out of the water.

The first bank saw its new competitor increasing its presence in the region, including opening new offices and entering into institutional and corporate relationships. The first bank, with a traditional business model, was not fully aware of the threat posed to its future. The situation gradually evolved until one day the people of a certain town, who had traditionally relied on the first bank for the collection of their taxes, now entrusted this function to the other new bank in the region. Suddenly, alarms were activated in the first bank, and it finally understood the extent to which the new bank was threatening its future. The first bank realized it must do something about the situation as it was losing a market.

The first bank began its recovery efforts by meeting with business leaders in the region to investigate how the situation had arisen. What they found was that the differentiating factor for the second bank was the speed it showed in its business operations, and this included a reduced time for performing financial transactions, as well as in granting loans to customers, cutting in half the time clients waited to receive approved funds.

The first bank made the decision to attack its competition by designing and building a new operating model and a new information system. Project evaluation time was expedited, and project resolution was reduced from more than 15 days to just 3 days.

The result of the project effort gave the first bank a renewed competitiveness, which allowed it to withstand competition from the second bank and to recover much lost ground in terms of customers. The benefits that this project represented to the bank were dramatic and involved a radical change in the evolution and trend of business processes that allowed it to regain the lead in the region. Among the other prominent business benefits achieved, the first bank was proud of the level of operational efficiency that was ultimately achieved.

## Productivity Improvement

Another key benefit to be provided by any project with the aim of implementing a new information system is to improve productivity. Productivity is defined as the measure of production capacity per unit of time that is achieved by any production unit, which can be an individual, a team of any size, a department or business unit, or the entire enterprise.

Productivity improvement may result from a single user improving personal performance, thereby performing more operations per unit of time. It may result from the implementation of a change project that simplifies the procedures performed by multiple participants in the production process. A further source of improvement might also be found in the simplification of processes. This could include the removal of process steps or actions that were previously required and are no longer needed, the designation of process steps as optional, or simply a reduction in the number of process steps and actions that need to be performed.

These types of productivity gains can be found in a variety of situations. For example, we can examine and update the process for the allocation of pre-approved credit limits in a manner that is personalized for customers. When the customer comes to the office to request a loan or to buy a new car, if the amount requested does not exceed the preset limits, the customer could receive immediate confirmation of loan approval without requiring the attention of management. This would allow the loan process to move directly to the transaction of issuing the previously approved funds without any undue administrative time needed to accomplish that end.

This practice allows the customer to eliminate uncertainty with regard to receiving desired financial services, which reduces the likelihood that he will do business with another financial institution. The customer knows that the current bank has clearly recognized the request, and, although there may be a waiting period of a few days, the customer has no uncertainty about receiving requested funds in a reasonable period of time. An efficient process like this can influence an ongoing customer relationship and increase customer loyalty.

An efficient process also improves the productivity of the employee actually handling the pre-approved loan request. The process allows the work to be accomplished in an expedient manner, without referrals to other managers or employees, and this enables the employee to complete more such loan actions every week. Therefore, an efficient process serves the business interests of both the customer and the organization.

## Integration and Standardization

The integration and standardization of business functionality that is applied across different business units is a source for business improvement within the organization. While we may focus on the integration and standardization of functionality or processes associated with information systems operations, the potential for business improvement can be found in other business practice areas. The following brief points are made to describe a few examples of how integration and standardization can influence information systems operations.

Integration eliminates the need for interim actions, as process transactions are completed across system components in a near synchronous way. This requires less attention from staff, and frees them up to perform other relevant duties associated with the process. As more information system integration is achieved, fewer interfaces are required for system operations and, therefore, there will be less risk associated with problems of information synchronization that cause process fulfillment problems.

However, the use of interfaces as mechanisms for integrating the different applications has always been a problem and a continuing source of concern for those responsible for information systems. The difficulties of maintaining the various information systems at the same level of change through synchronized interfaces have caused multiple maintenance interventions.

Moreover, the excessive integration between different information systems would be another difficulty, because in a monolithic environment we might find if we take this idea to the limit and build an absolutely integrated system, it would form a block where we cannot evolve or replace any part independently. This will prevent us from taking advantage of innovations in many of the components and will make our information system rigid and inflexible. This runs the risk of the information system becoming obsolete with the first changes occurring in the environment.

We must find a balance between integration of custom's developments and positioning about standardized components that are easily manageable and interchangeable with one another.

# Chapter 25

# Business Enhancement Benefits

When we are facing a project where the main products are programs, applications, and software components necessary for effective management of the business, we must pay special attention to certain factors that will be, in all likelihood, those that generate profits for the business. If we also take into account considerations that such projects are aimed at rapid recovery of the investment in a short period of time, the benefits that make the project profitable should be very obvious. Thus, for an investment project with a short-term return, we must pay special attention to how the interaction between information systems and users is resolved. The focus becomes the interface that people must use to work with the implemented solution and how this interface provides advantages and benefits that enhance business performance.

Many of the technical aspects of this type of project will be relegated to a second-place or background level. The more important project aspects will be those related to using the new system, and to the features and functionality that the new system provides to help users to become proficient in its use so that they can contribute to enhanced business performance.

The business benefits to be achieved from each project effort are the focus of this chapter. The following subsections present a consideration of the ways in which those business benefits can be achieved.

## Cost Reduction in Business Processes

There are a variety of ways by which to reduce the costs associated with business processes, and the effect is universal and well known: if we reduce our business process costs, competitiveness will grow along with profitability. The competitiveness achieved by optimizing our costs represents a durable advantage that will allow us to easily improve our position in the market, winning new business and new clients, and extending our relations with our existing clients to provide us with additional business benefits.

A significant approach to reducing the costs associated with business processes is by optimizing operations that can be done now rather than later. This is sometimes referred to as creating data at the source. For example, certain operations can be fulfilled through customer self-service mechanisms, leading to data that can be stored immediately on the system. Also, when certain data are entered into the system, it can be used immediately for any required calculations, making answers available as needed in the future. In turn, these actions can reduce the requirements for time and effort from employees responsible for given process steps.

Another approach considers cost reduction relative to the way the process is accomplished. Thus, when we are changing a business process, we should examine the prescribed steps to determine any opportunities for cost reduction that can be exploited in different ways.

Consider a typical process in any organization, such as opening a bank account, applying for a business loan, or buying property. In these instances, the individual representative of the organization must provide valid identification, such as an identification card or driving license that will be photocopied and attached to the application in order to show that the person's identity has been verified through specific documentation. This same process can be resolved, however, by scanning the required identification documents once, and storing them in a specialized database that is used to manage all similar digitalized identification documents. Individuals who subsequently require verification regarding their role in a relevant business process can then access this database to accomplish the required verification. This provides a higher level of service to the customer. It also offers very significant savings that can be quantified by calculating how many such operations are performed for each period of time, with consideration of the cost of paper and toner that would otherwise be consumed, along with the cost of maintaining the copier machine.

Another approach to achieving a cost reduction may lie in developing processes that are transferred from the organization to the customer, replacing work traditionally performed by employees. This is particularly apparent in utility companies such as those involved in water, electricity, and gas distribution.

Utility companies have provided services to communities and neighborhoods for some time, and the default approach to managing service distribution has been to install metering devices that monitor and sometimes control the consumption of individual customers. A company agent will visit each device location to access and read the current consumption values of each customer, without any interaction with the customer to record consumption. Often, this approach has been difficult or impossible; it has not been easy or cheap to carry out, and companies have assessed that the cost of obtaining an accurate reading in some circumstances is much more expensive than it should be. Accordingly, they have removed the agent in charge of meter reading with an agent who periodically distributes a sheet within communities for self-reading and recording by individual customers. Customers are given instructions that enable them to register and enter an authorized website where they can enter correct consumption readings based on the self-service check-list they have used. As a backup, the agent will then return to collect completed checklists, perhaps a week or so later. The costs associated with the process of read-ing that are saved with this system are enormous and, to prevent fraud, there is a verification program that randomly checks the readings of a sample of homes and businesses each period to test their veracity.

## Increased Speed of Business Processes

Our society is increasingly demanding higher speed in every aspect of our lives, and the business world barely thinks of anything else. Speed in our response to every challenge or encouragement that we face is essential, and business processes should provide an effective response to all customers and their needs in order for a com-mercial organization to survive and continue in the market. For this reason, it is important to have appropriate speed in the management of business processes to enable us to reduce the response time to a minimum.

Financial institutions have long been working in this direction, and have done everything possible to shorten the response times of their operations, particularly for operations related to loan and credit contracts. They have made efforts to stream-line the response time for evaluations of loan applications from weeks to days and to perform these loan pre-approval activities as a means to provide additional cus-tomer benefits.

In some cases, they do more by undertaking proactive campaigns to offer credit to "preferred customers" on very favorable financial terms. They do this by means of emails, postal mail, SMS transmissions, and phone calls, suggesting possible ways to invest the available capital. In the current battle to attract, retain, and enable loans for the best customers, the approach is to have customers perceive themselves as business partners. They will be given a better response to their needs and inquiries, leading them to believe that their financial institution knows them and their financial interests better than other businesses.

The improvement in the speed of our business processes represents our response to the demands of the marketplace. If the customer values speed in business, and in certain markets this is highly valued, this provides a decisive difference that can place us well ahead of any of our competitors that do not have such efficiencies. The more we listen to the demands of the marketplace, the more likely the customer will choose us first.

This is particularly true in the field of consumer goods, where the customer is typically an individual who is prone to act compulsively. For customers who do not have self-imposed discipline, or do not perform a comparative analysis to support each major purchase, visible signs of business efficiency will suffice as validation of their purchase decisions. Conversely, any signs of a delayed or uncertain response to customers could cause then to hesitate in making a purchase, and that, very simply, results in lost opportunities.

## Personal Productivity Improvement in Business Processes

The human factor is an inevitable component in any business process, because, despite automation, the process always requires some level of manual intervention. This intervention is normally performed by an agent or operator who must make certain decisions or carry out certain process steps that the system itself cannot perform. Although the long-term trend has been oriented toward increasing the automation of operations, taking full advantage of the possibilities that computers offer, the human factor is still necessary in every business process, and it represents one of the most important components of costs associated with performing the process.

Among the ways to improve the productivity of personnel involved in the business process, we can consider the delegation of responsibilities and decision making in business processes. To that end, we can develop a revised authorizations schema that enables individuals to make decisions regarding business process performance, and, in that regard, we can also reserve authority for critical business decisions for upper-level managers.

We may also increase staff productivity in business processes through automated pattern definitions, which allows automated decisions to be applied to cases that fit neatly into expected patterns. In turn, cases that do not fit into the expected patterns will be treated as exceptions, requiring separate evaluations and judgment by trained personnel. The impact of this type of improvement in staff productivity can be calculated as the difference between two potential scenarios, one without the new system in place, and the other with the new system in place. The difference between the two scenarios is the value contribution that is achieved by an increase in personal productivity. This difference should represent an offset in the costs of the project with subsequent verification of the benefits achieved.

## Functional Improvement

Functional improvement is an advantage that can be taken literally if we are in a project environment in which we can compare the information system being implemented with an earlier version of the information system that is already in operation. In such a comparison, it will be readily observable how improved business performance is achieved by the system with new features and functionality.

These improvements are represented by functionality such as the ability to check the status of our account at any time from our hotel room without having to go to the reception desk, the ability to use "shopping carts" on Internet retail sites, which can be saved for future access or use to establish repeat purchase patterns, and the ability to integrate fax directly with the information system so the system can send faxes, with content from relevant databases, to external partners, customers and suppliers for the purposes of additional management and further processing.

In any case, functional improvements represent the translation of improvements made in the business process for use in the information system. They may also represent progress made in the computerization of the operations that comprise the process. In either case, it will presume that the improvement of process performance can be evaluated and its value contribution properly quantified.

## Introducing Changes to Business Processes

Benefits to the business may also come directly from changes in the design of business processes, without implying a functional improvement of the information system that supports it. This situation may arise where the result of process re-engineering leads to the elimination of steps that were previously required and now have simply become obsolete or much simpler.

As always, a measure of the impact of these changes is needed relative to the cost before and after the new business process is introduced. The difference between the two costs is the value provided by the implemented change and, as such, may be included in the project business case to show that the new process and its impact are verifiable and profitable.

A special consideration of changing business processes is presented in the next section.

## Facilitating Adherence to Business or Legal Standards

The changes introduced by an organization may respond to different business conditions determined by the company to be applicable. Business process changes may be required as a result of external pressures that are not discretionary, but mandatory. This includes required responses to business and industry standards, government regulations and mandates, and the application of legal standards and practices.

The advantages to be gained from a project to improve business processes for which the core products are software components with a short-term payback period can be solved through support to business standards or regulatory rules. Usually, these projects have a bearing on adapting the information system to new or modified standards and regulations, as prompted by various industry sources and governmental agencies. This consideration will be particularly important in some industries, and may have less influence in other areas.

In information systems designed to withstand economic and financial impacts on the organization, the critical issues are compliance and liability. This includes taking account of existing legislation in the preparation of accounting information, income statements, balance sheets, the annual report, or routine and special tax information.

Similarly, information systems that support personnel management necessarily have to comply with legal constraints related to employee remuneration, salaries, and allowances, as well as the required deductions and contributions to social security and other competent authorities who are included in the process as a matter of regulation. In this area, an organization must ensure that it complies with the relevant mandates and financial obligations.

In general, there is really no business function of the company that is exempt from these considerations. There has been a growing awareness focused on scrutinizing how personal information is used. Advertising aimed at creating awareness of specific abuses has influenced many countries to develop very strict regulations for the protection of personal data. Noncompliance or failure to properly respond to regulations can lead to very significant penalties, including the potential for criminal liability in extreme situations such as the lack of regulation enforcement that has allowed the smuggling of information.

# Chapter 26

# Improved Management Benefits

For a project to be considered strategic, it should offer advantages that transform the way information systems are used in the organization. Any project that addresses the way in which users perform work represents an opportunity for the organization to adjust work methods and procedures, and to transform the way in which those methods and procedures are handled by the information system. In some instances, our processes may also influence a transformation in the way our customers relate to our company, and under extraordinary circumstances we might even drag the rest of the market to follow in the footsteps of the business transformations that we lead. However, added customer benefits and the advantage we gain over competitors would be a logical and favorable consequence of our management actions.

These changes may be of a varied nature and include offers such as a telephone service to handle customer questions and claims on a 24 h basis, the possibility of booking a holiday vacation online without limitations to a default package (but providing more personalized selections according to preferences for hotel, flights, and car rentals), services for acquiring theater tickets, theme park tickets, or access to any tourist facility, or even the ability to choose an airline seat and a menu for meals you wish to be served on board. All of these examples can be regarded today as more or less standard features available to consumers. They are benefits that a few years ago were unthinkable and unavailable.

Being able to imagine and dare to make them available to customers was the result of a strategic decision aimed at breaking the rules that existed at that point in time. Those prevailing rules provided the basis for someone to create a new market situation that was more favorable to the business interests of the organization. There is little doubt in these cases and others that the innovators had achieved the success they were looking for. However, until the point at which their innovations gained the acceptance of customers, there was a distinct need to manage the transformation to avoid losing customers during each period of change.

Projects that target the implementation of information systems can also produce benefits that will change the competitive balance between companies participating in any market. The following subsections examine several areas in which opportunities to achieve benefits from improved management can be used to generate business value within an organization.

## Superior Access to Information

Current information systems are very powerful tools in any organization, because they provide the support needed to effectively carry out the business functions of the organization. These systems enable all information concerning the business to be used at high levels of detail, in real time, and in a natural and almost imperceptible way. This information is produced in every business organization by each employee of the company on a routine basis as they register their operations, customers, suppliers, employees, and partners. Orders, sales, purchases, shipments to customers, suppliers, and providers occur as a result of business operations that provide the information system with its most valuable input: data.

However, difficulties can sometimes arise in extracting this information from the system in a form that can be used by managers, supervisors, and executives for purposes beyond the simple control of operations. These members of the organization need information that has commercial significance to enable decision making at the highest level. They need business-relevant information that has been collected and compiled for their use in planning and directing the strategic interests of the organization.

Thus, when access to information is improved, it is easier for data to be collected at different points in business operations in order to generate information in a transparent and immediate manner to users who are dependent on that information. Also, that information has to be handled in a way that manages risks associated with data transfer, which can include simple transcription errors, biased interpretations, and mistakes in the communication process. Information has to be viable and accurate in order to avoid producing a wrong decision that leads the company into a lower performance scenario. Of equal importance, the time needed to apply appropriate precautions to preserve the quality of the information should not introduce any significant delays between the need for information and the availability of information. In certain markets and economic sectors, delayed decisions based on delayed information availability could have impacts that reduce the organization's business advantage.

To have access to information is to find the information we need, when we need it, but it also means finding the appropriate information format and level of detail that can be examined, analyzed, and interpreted, as required, for use in making business-relevant decisions.

## Superior Reliability of Information

In today's complex business environment, having relevant information can be very important. It is, perhaps, more important to have reasonable assurance of the quality and accuracy of information. Having the assurance that we are basing our business decisions on information that is deemed reliable allows us to enjoy similar reasonable assurance about the quality of our decisions based on such information. If the information we use in our work is not reliable, all our work will be akin to a building constructed on quicksand and will not be sustainable. Information is the stuff of which decisions are made, and it is the basis of our strategic and operational business plans. We need to ensure the quality of our information as a means to bring coherence and a reasonable certainty to our plans for the future.

Poor information and lack of reliability can be a condition that is equal to or worse than a total lack of information. Such unreliable information only introduces an additional source of uncertainty to the business processes we use and in the decision environment we face.

If an information system can improve the reliability of the information that is handled and managed, this will subsequently improve the quality of business decisions, and, in turn, that will improve the confidence of executives and managers using the information system. An information system can achieve information reliability in several ways. One important way to improve reliability is to maintain a direct and permanent relationship between the aggregated data of the business and its components. This facilitates the verification and traceability of data, and it allows all users to learn and know where or how each data value is formed.

Another way to improve the reliability of information is through the unification of multiple databases that store the same information. For example, the same sales data may be stored in both the trading system and in the auxiliary system of customer accounts. Both systems can provide instant responses to data inquiries, but each system could potentially have different information for the same data element as a result of independent access and manipulations of each database. Database unification can be used to prevent these discrepancies, because nothing undermines the confidence of information system users more than getting two different results from a single data point of information.

# Increased Speed to Access Information

Speed is pervasive in virtually every aspect of our lives, and perhaps more so in aspects of our work, especially work that is related to business decision making and customer responsiveness. Customers, suppliers, business partners and anyone who has an interest in our organization wants answers to their questions, concerns, or needs, and they all want it immediately.

Although information system users want to access the information they require for their work in the most appropriate form and with reliable accuracy, it is also true that they want immediate access. To that end, any information system that is based on a hierarchical menu system where the user must follow a path of choices requiring more than three clicks to find a required report will lack the immediacy expected by the user.

This trend for speed, which has always in some way been motivated by the needs of executives and decision makers, who are under extraordinary pressure to produce decisions in a short period of time, is now exacerbated by the influence of the Internet and generational change. The once available opportunities for reflection and applying the foundations of decision making have been replaced by the immediacy of response. Having speed in the process of accessing business information has become essential in making decisions based on reasoning and reliable information. Despite the speed of business, managers must avoid producing answers based on impulse, instinct, and improvisation, which have a more uncertain outcome.

# Improved Capacity of Synthesis and Navigation

An information system cannot be considered strategic if it does not offer a range of functions and features that facilitate the management of the company by providing the necessary tools for making top-quality decisions. The information system should provide information to its users and it must be true, accurate, adequate, and it must be in the format and with a level of aggregation or detail that is most appropriate for the analysis of conditions and the decisions that are being considered.

In many cases, isolated data provide limited utility because, when taken alone, they cannot provide sufficient context for business use. For this reason, it is important that the information system can offer users synthesis and navigation capabilities that allow them to change the focus on the information. This would include, for example, the capability to examine the profitability of a particular customer against all customers in a given region, market segment, or an entire company. It may also provide the capability to analyze customer relationships by the types of products purchased, or according to alignment with sales staff and sales offices.

It is equally important to have navigation capability in every way possible, up, down, and laterally through database records. This allows for better and alternate views of synthesized information as a means to improve decision-making considerations. Navigation capability helps put the data in a proper context, which completes its meaning and facilitates interpretation.

## Enhanced Capacity for Collaboration and Information Sharing

The work of leaders and management in modern organizations is increasingly a task that takes place in the construct of teams. The concept of partnership in the workplace has advanced from being a good choice to becoming the only acceptable choice for effective work performance. There are no excuses for a lack of participation by isolated individuals; in today's business world and in today's highly technical teams, it is necessary for all team members to be engaged in collaboration and information sharing to support the work effort.

Strategic information systems must facilitate this collaboration by allowing information sharing among different users. Information-sharing practices should provide all team members with the ability to view the same information presentation, with the same composition, structure, and data. It should also provide the ability to share notes and personal observations about that information with others, to highlight, explain, or focus attention on those aspects of the information bearing on the work effort or that might otherwise arouse work-related interest.

These capabilities should provide a valuable benefit, particularly when supporting collaboration among users as a means to resolve problems and address unusual situations in a flexible and secure manner. System-based collaboration can also influence a reduction in the need for elaborate interactions that require formal written requests and responses instead of the simple exchange of information. It also reduces the need to run from one person to another in search of the individual who has the necessary information.

When the information system provides this capability, an advantage is achieved through a reduction in the time and effort required to find relevant information. An advantage is also achieved through consequential and substantial savings of costs related to the information-sharing process, taking into account the high-cost profiles often involved in that process within the organization. It should be noted here that we are talking about the generally higher, executive-level profiles of upper management.

## Improved Ability to Refine and Customize Information

Among the benefits that improved information management provides are those related to improving the capacity to shape, refine, and customize information. This capability can be realized in ways such as the ability to export the information to common office tools like those used for presentations, spreadsheets, and word processing. Data can also be exported to other more specific applications such as statistical analysis software packages.

The system can also be set up to provide information as alphanumeric or numeric data in different formats, such as bar graphs, pie graphs, or any other format that may be appropriate. This provides the ability to view the data as a snapshot, as a variation, or as an historical trend of values recorded. In short, it provides the possibility of obtaining the information in a format that is most useful and appropriate to the purpose that each user requires.

If we consider a system's ability to remember the presentation and the format that each user requires or prefers, then a default pattern of presentations can be created and accessed whenever the user enters a similar query. When the system retains information in the preferred format, that facilitates ease of access by users, but it also represents saving a significant effort to arrange the information in the appropriate format each time it is needed by a user.

## Improved Ability to Automatically Recommend and Solve Information Needs

An information system designed to support decision making can provide business value that differentiates it from other common and competitive information systems if it has the capability to recommend actions based on an automated assessment of the information it maintains. This ability is representative of the business intelligence that the system contains and offers to users. It may be the result of several initiatives aimed at enriching information system functionality.

The first and simplest option for achieving this capability is the inclusion of business rules within the program used. This is an aspiration that has existed since the beginning of computer use for business purposes, and those rules have been introduced since forever in information systems.

For example, these rules are often found in the automated generation of purchase orders to suppliers when a product reaches a certain threshold. When that threshold is reached, it triggers the system to automatically generate an order to replenish the product and thereby prevents the situation where products are unavailable when needed. In a similar manner, automated business rules can be established to manage and apply risk controls that block the service of orders to customers when the customer has an unpaid, outstanding balance. This automated action can include the generation of an internal report to a sales agent who can ascertain if back payments have been made by the customer but have not yet been entered into the system. The agent can also consider the customer's history and authorize the purchase by overriding the business rules.

We can also find examples of more sophisticated business intelligence systems that are capable of learning from users by identifying repeated patterns of behavior. This allows the system to deduce parameters that must be taken into account, given that certain circumstances will always apply the same decision, which can be derived from a certain level of repetition as an unwritten rule. Therefore, the system can infer a rule and apply it automatically with varying degrees of firmness that can range from absolute to calling on the user to make a final determination of the recommended action. To that end, you can always construct an automated recommendation or decision-making process, but still give the user the ability to accept or reject the automated outcome.

# Index

Milton Keynes UK
Ingram Content Group UK Ltd.
UKHW031144141024
449569UK00024B/1089